TALKING SHAKESPEARE

RELATED TITLES FROM PALGRAVE

Shakespeare and the Loss of Eden
   Catherine Belsey
Shakespeare 1609: Cymbeline and the Sonnets
   Richard Danson Brown and David Johnson
A Shakespeare Reader: Sources and Criticism
   edited by Richard Danson Brown and David Johnson
Shakespeare: The Tragedies
   John Russell Brown
Interpreting Shakespeare on Screen
   Deborah Cartmell
Shakespeare Feminism and Gender (New Casebook series)
   edited by Kate Chedgzoy
Shakespeare: The Comedies (Analysing Texts series)
   R. P. Draper
An Introduction to Shakespeare
   Peter Hyland
Shakespeare: The Tragedies (Analysing Texts series)
   Nicholas Marsh
Shakespeare: Texts and Contexts
   edited by Kiernan Ryan
Shakespeare: The Histories
   Graham Holderness
Shakespeare on Film (New Casebook series)
   edited by Robert Shaughnessy
Shakespeare in Performance (New Casebook series)
   edited by Robert Shaughnessy

Talking Shakespeare

Shakespeare into the Millennium

Edited by

DEBORAH CARTMELL and MICHAEL SCOTT

palgrave

First published 2001 by
PALGRAVE
Houndmills, Basingstoke, Hampshire RG21 6XS and
175 Fifth Avenue, New York, N. Y. 10010
Companies and representatives throughout the world

PALGRAVE is the new global academic imprint of St. Martin's Press LLC
Scholarly and Reference Division and Palgrave Publishers Ltd (formerly Macmillan Press Ltd).

ISBN 0–333–77791–3 hardback
ISBN 0–333–77773–5 paperback

This book is printed on paper suitable for recycling and made from fully managed and sustained forest sources.

A catalogue record for this book is available from the British Library.

Library of Congress Cataloging-in-Publication Data

Talking Shakespeare: Shakespeare into the millennium / edited by Deborah Cartmell and Michael Scott.
        p. cm.
     Includes bibliographical references and index.
     ISBN 0–333–77791–3 (hardcover)
     1. Shakespeare, William, 1564-1616—Criticism and interpretation.
  I. Cartmell, Deborah. II. Scott, Michael, 1949.

PR2976 .T25 2001
822.3′3—dc21

                                                        00-053053

10   9   8   7   6   5   4   3   2   1
10   09   08   07   06   05   04   03   02   01

Printed in China

To Peter and Sheila Davison

Contents

Acknowledgements   ix

   Introduction   1
     DEBORAH CARTMELL AND MICHAEL SCOTT

I **Shakespeare, Theory and Contexts**   7

1 Talking Shakespeare   9
    MICHAEL SCOTT

2 How Does *Hamlet* End?   24
    NIGEL WOOD

3 Shakespeare and the Elizabethan Stage: Touring
    Practice in Shakespeare's Day   39
    PETER DAVISON

4 Studying Shakespeare and His Contemporaries   55
    EMMA SMITH

5 Shakespeare and History   70
    DERMOT CAVANAGH

II **Shakespeare and National Identity**   83

6 'Home, Sweet Home': Stratford-upon-Avon and the
    Making of the Royal Shakespeare Company as
    a National Institution   85
    COLIN CHAMBERS

III **Shakespeare, Performance, Sexuality
     and Race**   103

7 *Twelfth Night*: 'One face, one voice, one habit, and
    two persons!'   105
    JANICE WARDLE

8   Shakespeare and the Homoerotic   123
    MILES THOMPSON AND IMELDA WHELEHAN

9   Shakespeare and Race: *Othello* I.iii   138
    DEBORAH CARTMELL

IV   Shakespeare, Film and the Future   **149**

10 The Unkindest Cuts: Flashcut Excess in Kenneth
    Branagh's *Hamlet*   151
    BERNICE W. KLIMAN

11 Showing Versus Telling: Shakespeare's *Ekphraseis*,
    Visual Absences, and the Cinema   168
    GABRIEL EGAN

12 Shakespeare and the Future   187
    KIERNAN RYAN

13 Why We Talk Shakespeare   201
    MICHAEL J. COLLINS

Appendix: Bibliography of Shakespeare and
Electronic Sources   213
    JOSEPHINE WEBB

Notes and References   221

Notes on Contributors   246

Index   248

Acknowledgements

Thanks are due to De Montfort University for supporting the project and to Palgrave for patience and understanding. We wish to thank our families for their support throughout.

Introduction

DEBORAH CARTMELL AND MICHAEL SCOTT

Talking Shakespeare, as its title implies, focuses on the reciprocal relationship between past and present, the way Shakespeare talks to us, the ways in which we talk about Shakespeare, and the way in which Shakespeare, ultimately, is 'all talk'. Indeed, the approach employed throughout the book is a consideration of the ways in which the past informs the present, as well as how the present informs the past.

Shakespeare has become, among other things, a great screen-writer, one who can be 'updated' and made relevant to today's youth (witness Baz Luhrmann's *William Shakespeare's Romeo + Juliet*, 1996, or Gil Junger's *Ten Things I Hate About You*, 1999). In the latter film, a rewriting of *The Taming of the Shrew* in the genre of teen-pic, the black English teacher who scorns feminist and white male writing as elitist makes an exception when it comes to Shakespeare: his texts are regarded as truly universal. Indeed, contact with Shakespeare transforms the lives of the teenagers in the film, or to quote from *Henry V*, their brush with Shakespeare has 'gentle[d]' their 'condition'.

This Arnoldian assumption that, no matter how diluted, Shakespeare is good for us, is interrogated throughout the book through an exploration of dominant issues and approaches in Shakespeare studies, ranging from Shakespeare and *his* contemporaries to Shakespeare and *our* contemporaries. The chapters in this volume approach the plays from a variety of perspectives: editing and theory (Nigel Wood), theatrical practices (Peter Davison), Shakespeare and his contemporaries (Emma Smith), Shakespeare and history (Dermot Cavanagh), Shakespeare and nationalism (Colin Chambers), twentieth-century performances (Janice Wardle), Shakespeare and the homoerotic (Miles Thompson and Imelda Whelehan), Shakespeare and race (Deborah Cartmell), Shakespeare and film (Bernice Kliman and Gabriel Egan, respectively) and Shakespeare and the future (Kiernan Ryan). The book is framed by a discussion of how and why we 'talk Shakespeare' (Michael Scott and Michael J. Collins, respectively). Lastly, in an appendix, Josephine Webb surveys material available on Shakespeare in the electronic or 'virtual' library. There seems to be a growing rift between Shakespeare in popular culture and the ways in which Shakespeare is approached by academics today; and this Introduction, by referring to *Henry V*, examines how many of the chapters in this volume address this division.

In the first chapter, 'Talking Shakespeare', Shakespeare's texts are read in terms of the ways in which they announce themselves, to quote from *Hamlet*, as 'words, words, words', that is, literary constructions which call attention to the ways in which society constructs itself. Michael Scott considers how, when appropriated for different ideological reasons, Shakespeare's words are doing the very thing they argue against. A game is taken for the real thing. Importantly, *Henry V*'s Chorus, like Chaucer's narrator, relinquishes the author from blame ('And eek men shal nought maken ernest of game')[1] by immediately informing the audience that the play is an artificial construct. Indeed, Henry's protean character, the fact that it refuses to be pinned down as a 'real person', has perplexed critics of the twentieth and twenty-first centuries in their desire for him to be someone they can love or hate; at any rate, 'identify with'.[2]

The following chapters look at both old texts in new contexts as well as new texts in old contexts. Nigel Wood, through a close reading of the different endings of *Hamlet* (Q1, Q2 and F), considers the similarities between editing and interpreting and the differences between the play as written text and the play as performance. For Wood, an understanding of the variety of texts 'opens up the text' as 'a set of precise alternatives' 'with infinite shades of emphasis and address'.[3]

Peter Davison's 'Shakespeare and the Elizabethan Stage: Touring Practice in Shakespeare's Day' reconstructs touring practices at the time of Shakespeare, partially from what is known about more recent theatrical practices. In this case, although aware that it is only conjectural, an argument can be made that some features of touring practices remain relatively unchanged over 450 years.

Emma Smith, in 'Studying Shakespeare and His Contemporaries', looks at Shakespeare's plays within the current vogue for league tables, and notes that in his own time, he was quite far down. Smith considers Shakespeare's own 'anxiety of influence', reflecting on his allusions to his predecessors (*Woodstock* and Thomas Kyd's *The Spanish Tragedy*) and his followers' responses to his own plays (John Fletcher's *The Woman's Prize, or the Tamer Tam'd*).

While Smith stresses the value of considering Shakespeare in his time, Dermot Cavanagh reflects on how Shakespeare's texts are read insofar as they produce 'a context for' the present, meaning *our* time. With special reference to the 'garden scene' in *Richard II*, Cavanagh looks at ways in which the plays inquire into the political premises upon which the narrative is founded. The Gardener in *Richard II*, like Williams in *Henry V*, blurs distinctions between the high and the low, calling into question the rightful governance of the elite. Shakespeare's history plays, argues Cavanagh, 'may be one example of works which show the consequences of political and social values in the *process* of their becoming and also the contradictions and dialectical relationships by which they are defined'.[4]

These contradictions are often forgotten due to the persistence of 'benchmark' productions, such as Olivier's wartime film adaptation of *Henry V* (1945), which, in spite of its excision of lines and episodes which place a question mark over the rightfulness of Henry's cause (including the treatment of the traitors, the threats of rape and pillage before the gates of Harfleur, Henry's exchange of gloves with Williams, his acknowledgement of his father's guilt in the usurpation of Richard, the hanging of Bardolph, the order to kill the French prisoners, the lewd remarks to Burgundy and the Chorus's reminder that Henry's victory was short-lived), ironically resulted in critics hailing it as 'authentic Shakespeare'.[5] Certainly, Olivier's *Henry V*, produced at a time in which literary critics and theatrical practices were in unison, became a benchmark for both the play as well as for future film adaptations of Shakespeare.

Janice Wardle surveys theatrical productions of *Twelfth Night* and reveals how John Barton's 1969 production has become a benchmark upon which all others are judged, as it was uniquely produced at a moment when academic analysis and theatrical practice were in step with each other. The persistent dominance of such benchmark productions in people's minds is considered in chapter 6 by Colin Chambers, in his analysis of the shaping of

the Royal Shakespeare Company and the consequent nationali-
zation of Shakespeare. Under the artistic direction of Peter Hall –
especially his attention to verse speaking – Chambers demonstrates how a notion of Shakespeare's essential 'Englishness'
emerged.

Undoubtedly, Shakespeare is shaped by a belief in both his
quintessential 'Englishness' and his essential goodness and, as
such, has been appropriated by the Conservative Party, who see
in Shakespeare the embodiment of the right-wing values which
they aim to perpetuate. Former Prime Minister, John Major,
sums up the British Conservative attitude to Shakespeare in a
speech made to the Tory Women's Conference in June 1993:
'People say there is too much jargon in education – so let me
give you some of my own: Knowledge. Discipline. Tables. Sums.
Dates. Shakespeare.'[6] This is a Shakespeare who represents the
embodiment of wholesome values and who, clearly, has nothing
to say about matters such as homosexuality. Writing in the *Observer* on a remark made by a schoolteacher accusing Shakespeare
of blatant heterosexuality, Barry Hugill epitomizes the popular
belief that 'of course', 'Shakespeare had not much to say about
homosexuality, but the only sensible response to that is "so
what?"'[7] This is far from the view of Miles Thompson and
Imelda Whelehan who, in the next chapter, survey critical responses to Shakespeare's homoeroticism, concentrating on attitudes towards cross-dressing. Once again, we see a split between
popular and 'academic' readings of Shakespeare. Thompson and
Whelehan observe how the paranoia of the early modern period
has been replaced with the homophobia of the nineteenth,
twentieth and twenty-first centuries, where even today the subject is prudishly ignored in the teaching of Shakespeare in the
English national curriculum.

Shakespeare research at the beginning of the twenty-first century is fighting against such popular misconceptions. Unlike the
mid-twentieth century, literary responses are very much at odds
with popular perceptions of Shakespeare. For instance, the
representation of homosexuality and race (increasingly of interest to literary critics) tends to be ignored by dominant forms of
communication, such as cinema. In the next chapter, what happens to Othello when he is really black (rather than a representation of a black man) is discussed in view of the two mainstream

films of the play: that of Orson Welles (1952) and Oliver Parker (1995). It is argued that a black man in the part endorses what is arguably a stereotype, in the same way that Leo Africanus, a black man who wrote an account of Africa in the sixteenth century, endorsed cultural and racial stereotypes by his own blackness. Certainly, cinema poses a unique problem in the portrayal of racial stereotypes – for instance, in Branagh's *Henry V* (1989), Fluellen (played by Ian Holm) is made less ridiculous through the excision of the episode with the leeks, a gesture towards 'political correctness' in a possible effort not to offend the Welsh.

Branagh's 1996 film of *Hamlet*, with its multicultural cast and mixture of American and British actors, is discussed by Bernice W. Kliman in the following chapter. Kliman considers Branagh's cut version of the original four-hour play and his use of flashcuts which, she argues, often produce problematic results – that is, they yield less rather than more. Kliman considers the confusion surrounding the representation of Ophelia; for example, the inclusion of flashcuts of a sexual relationship between Hamlet and Ophelia make her a victimizer as well as victim, insofar as she betrays father, brother, and lover alike. Gabriel Egan, however, in the next chapter, argues that in the case of Branagh these flash-cuts need not infer more is less in their translation of Shake-speare's 'hard words' into seemingly unequivocal and 'easier' visualizations. Egan suggests that the flashcuts of the sexual rela-tionship, for instance, need not necessarily be translated as real, but, rather, should be regarded as characters' mental images. Egan argues that Shakespeare's long descriptions, normally shown rather than told on screen, often distort the play text. The subject of seeing and telling is often distorted in screen adaptations – for example, Egan notes that the Chorus in *Henry V demands* an audience imagine rather than see, alerting us to the notion that mental images are as manipulable as stage pictures. Films of Shakespeare that prioritize showing over telling, accord-ing to Egan, are problematic and should alert us to the need to return to 'talking Shakespeare'.

In the context of current readings which either see the plays as anticipatory of modern times or consign them unremittingly to the past, Kiernan Ryan considers what Shakespeare has to say about the future and how the plays consistently and peculiarly conceive of reality in the future perfect tense. Ryan reflects on

Shakespeare's representation of what he calls 'the slipperiness of the future', what Macbeth means by feeling 'the future in the instant' (I.v.54–6). Ryan demonstrates how Shakepeare's writing consistently conceives the historicity of the performance, while alerting us to the impermanence of Shakespeare's own time. Indeed, Shakespeare's interest in prophesy has encouraged readings of his works as 'prophetic' of our own time, rather than as reflections on the concept of the future.

In the final chapter, Michael J. Collins discusses Shakespeare in the realm of popular culture and recent performances and asks why we treasure Shakespeare to the extent that we do. Collins suggests that value is achieved not just from what we learn from Shakespeare but from the pleasure (almost a forbidden word in English studies) that we derive from the plays. Taking the game too seriously has led to much name-calling of Shakespeare: among them, racist, sexist and homophobic. The tendency in literary studies is either to throw sticks or to canonize, as Harold Bloom has done in his best-seller, *Shakespeare: The Invention of the Human* (1999). Ironically, while Bloom despises both academic and popular approaches to Shakespeare (as one reviewer noted, the book's motto might be 'neither Foucault nor Miramax'[8]), he has much in common with the latter insofar as he replaces critical investigation with worship. This volume aims to interrogate the game as a game and not, like football manager Bill Shankly (and many critics, both defenders and attackers of Shakespeare), argue that Shakespeare's dramas are not just a matter of life and death, but are indeed much more important.

I Shakespeare, Theory and Contexts

1. Talking Shakespeare

MICHAEL SCOTT

Does Shakespeare, through his plays, talk to us, or do we, through reading and performing Shakespeare, merely talk to ourselves? In 1993 a Conservative Chancellor of the Exchequer, Nigel Lawson, proclaimed Shakespeare to be a Tory.[1] Nearly thirty years earlier the distinguished Labour Party Minister, Richard Crossman, had regarded the dramatist as a mentor for modern political history and perceptive sensibility.[2] Critical schools of every spectrum of Western belief have seemingly acquired him for themselves since the 1960s. He has been pro-Semitic and anti-Semitic, pro-feminist and anti-feminist, racist and anti-racist, Catholic and Protestant, believer and agnostic. The question of interpretation, as Terry Hawkes in particular has demonstrated, depends more on the interpreter than the interpreted.[3]

Extending this view into the study of the plays in performance, James Bulman notes:

> In any criticism of performance, it must be recognized, we are bound by the perspectives of our own time and place. Indeed, as theorists are quick to point out, traditional assumptions about universality and continuity in the performance history of Shakespeare's plays are themselves cultural constructs.[4]

It was ever the case. In the eighteenth century Nahum Tate responded to then current sensitivities which, with Dr Johnson, could not endure the ending of *King Lear*. Tate rewrote it with a happy ending and his stage version remained that most frequently performed for 150 years. In the latter part of the twentieth century demands were made for changes to plays such as *The Merchant of Venice* and *The Taming of the Shrew*, while *Othello* has received relatively few major productions because of a paucity of appropriate or available black actors to take the lead role.[5] It has become almost politically incorrect for a white actor to

9

black up for the part. So offended was the contemporary dramatist Arnold Wesker with *The Merchant of Venice* that he wrote the
play afresh from a Jewish perspective in 1976.[6] Similarly, directors from the 1970s onwards have attempted a variety of means to
mitigate the apparent female subjugation to the male in *The
Taming of the Shrew*, turning it into a discourse on battered
wives, possessive husbands, or crafty male/female financial part-
nerships acquiring money from dullards.

In all this rewriting or manipulation of texts, it appears that
what occurs is an attempt to impose solutions on to Shakespeare.
If society imposes its own dominant or fashionable ideologies on
to Shakespeare, the dramatist still prompts our interpretations by
raising questions through the plays. In *The Taming of the Shrew*, for
example, Shakespeare raises issues about levels of perception.
What is a social reality? What is a natural reality? Is there a
connection between the two? He does so by staging the questions
as part of the play. At the simplest, although brutal, level, Petruchio questions whether the brightness in the sky is the sun or the
moon; whether a person arbitrarily met on a journey is a beautiful young lady or a withered old man. How, the play asks, do
you communicate any reality except through a social dominance
of language? A relationship is created between words and
perception. The dominant ideology – which, in the case of *The
Taming of the Shrew*, is that of the dominant sexual partner – sets
the meaning by defining the language. In *Romeo and Juliet* the
question is posed as to whether individuals have the ability to
change an essence of being by altering language itself. The words
'Capulet' and 'Montague' are names but, as such, are syn-
onymous with attitudes, even ideologies, permanently in conflict,
one with another. They are the equivalent to the terms 'Protestant' and 'Catholic' in modern-day Northern Ireland. The
name, the title, the description, imply a social reality which
might be divorced totally from individual desire or experience.
Social reality, however, dominates. Naively, Juliet says of
Romeo:

> O, be some other name!
> What's in a name? That which we call a rose
> By any other word would smell as sweet
> *Romeo and Juliet*, II.i.84–6[7]

Language is power and power, like language, begins with the relationship of the word or name to its referent. In insurrection, in the reversal of one political ideology by another, names themselves are obliterated. As the Serbs in 1999 forced the Kosovo Albanians out of their homeland, they took away all records, even of the people's names. In *Richard II*, when Northumberland unwittingly calls the deposed King 'my Lord', Richard immediately turns on him:

> No Lord of thine, thou haught insulting man,
> Nor no man's lord. I have no name, no title,
> No, not that name was given me at the font,
> But 'tis usurped. Alack the heavy day,
> That I have worn so many winters out
> And know not now what name to call myself!
> *Richard II*, IV.i.244–9

A usurped people, a usurped king, are nameless. They lose the totality of their identities in the ethnic cleansing of war, revolution and barbarity. The oppressor then seeks to impose his or her own language on to the oppressed people, attempting to eradicate the native tongue. Although the Normans were unsuccessful in their attempted suppression of the Anglo-Saxons, the English over centuries became adept at oppressing languages in the British Isles – Welsh, Scots and Irish Gaelic – and, subsequently, in the Americas with the native Indian tongues. But the issue does not have to be as overtly extreme as this implies. In *King Lear* Edmund questions the subjugation of the individual by the moral attitudes dominating language and thereby social and hierarchical structures. The words 'bastard' or 'illegitimate' have a significance far beyond the description of 'born out of wedlock'. What is the relationship between these words and the naturalness of the sexual act leading to conception? They represent a fabrication based on a socially constructed vocabulary:

> Wherefore should I
> Stand in the plague of custom and permit
> The curiosity of nations to deprive me
> For that I am some twelve or fourteen moonshines
> Lag of a brother? Why 'bastard'? Wherefore 'base',

When my dimensions are as well compact,
My mind as generous, and my shape as true
As honest madam's issue?
Why brand they us with 'base, base bastardy',...
                    The History of King Lear, I.ii.7–10

In the narrative, Edmund turns such linguistic discrimination to his own perverted use in deceiving father and brother and, later, Goneril and Regan, but the issues of language hold attention throughout the play. The honesty of Cordelia is expressed at first not in words but in silence, since words have already been debased. Her final statement of fidelity is also found in the silence of her death. There is no breath as the distraught Lear studies her face and lips for a sign of life. In *Hamlet*, similarly, peace for the troubled protagonist comes not from his soliloquies, musings or deliberations. It comes from 'the rest' in 'silence', which is his death. In death there is no more language, no more constructed fabrication of natural reality. Falstaff in *Henry IV Part I* ruminates on the word 'honour' as justifying courageous but ultimately ridiculous actions in war:

... honour pricks me on. Yea, but how if honour prick me off when I come on? How then? Can honour set-to a leg? No. Or an arm? No. Or take away the grief of a wound? No. Honour hath no skill in surgery, then? No. What is honour? A word. What is in that word 'honour'? What is that 'honour'? Air. A trim reckoning! Who hath it? He that died o' Wednesday. Does he feel it. No. Doth he hear it? No. 'Tis insensible then? Yea, to the dead. But will it not live with the living? No. Why? Detraction will not suffer it. Therefore I'll none of it. Honour is a mere scutcheon. And so ends my catechism.
                    I Henry IV, V.i.129–40

Shakespeare seemingly prompts us to reject Falstaff's attitude but simultaneously ambiguously tempts us to accept it. The dramatist neither sides with Falstaff nor with those who follow 'honour' as a means for their constructed forms of existence: the elements of power, authority and glory. In *Othello* this goes beyond the name to the relationship between what a man does and what he is. When Cassio is dismissed as Othello's lieutenant after his drunken brawl, he speaks to Iago of the anguish that, in losing his office, he has lost also his reputation which is an essential part of himself: 'Reputation, reputation, reputation – O, I ha' lost my reputation, I ha' lost the immortal part of myself, and what remains is bestial. My reputation, Iago, my reputation' (*Othello*, II.ii.256–9).

Shakespeare uses words to foreground the relationship between language and perception. He uses them also to question the relationship between the play, the playwright and the audience. In *Twelfth Night* Fabian comments on the ridiculous affectations of the beguiled Malvolio: 'If this were played upon a stage, now, I could condemn it as an impossible fiction' (III.iv.125–6).

Edward Bond, in his play on Shakespeare, *Bingo*, portrays the Elizabethan at the end of his life reflecting:

They stand under a gallows and ask if it rains. Terrible. Terrible. What is the right question? I said be still. I quietened the storms inside me. But the storm breaks outside. To have usurped the place of god, and lied.[8]

Bond's historical construct has usurped his talent, authority and responsibility. Thus Shakespeare is portrayed as the dramatist of language in the mood of self-reproach. It is another imposed interpretation. Throughout his plays Shakespeare reveals that language can be power and can be used to gain it, keep it or lose it. Michel Foucault has pointed out the relativity and thereby changing relationships of words:

The affirmation that the earth is round or that species evolve does not constitute the same statement before and after Copernicus, before and after Darwin; it is not, for such simple formulations, that the meaning of the words has changed; what changed was the relation of these affirmations to other propositions, their conditions of use and re-investment, the field of experience, of possible verifications, of problems to be resolved, to which they can be referred.[9]

If this is the case, then a complex relationship is created in drama between characters such as Edmund or Iago, who change the referents for meaning and other characters in the play, but this extends beyond, into the audience, where further changing referents are found. An early twenty-first-century audience with a grasp of feminist issues will understand *The Taming of the Shrew* in a different way from a sixteenth-century audience or, for that matter, a twentieth-century one.

The complexity of meanings, however, goes beyond the text, since language in drama is not circumscribed by words. Shakespeare's language goes beyond his poetry and prose to the communication of the actions of the play, the semiotics of the drama and its narrative.

A useful experiment in rehearsing Shakespearean drama is to take the protagonist out of the action for a period in order to question elements of the play. If Lear, for example, is removed for a time, certain issues begin to clarify. To the other characters, he is a difficult old man. Regan and Goneril do not know how to deal with him because he wants everything on his own terms, even if they contradict each other. Looking at the play without Lear present, Goneril and Regan's attitudes can be seen to follow an understandable logic. Lear, for these female constructs, appears to want authority without responsibility, love on demand, and instant attention for himself and his expensive retinue. Why should he have a hundred knights who will cause disruption in their households? Why should he employ any retainers? Restore the king to the centrality of the action and the questions become subsumed by imperatives surrounding his character. His point of view dominates through his perspective and his language.

Yet, if we analyse the play further, we find even greater anomalies in the narrative. Lear, on his arrival at Regan's castle, does not even have the hundred knights about which the argument rages. Kent asks the Fool why the king 'comes with so small a train' (vii. 230). The Fool replies:

> All that follows their noses are led by their eyes but blind men, and there's not a nose among a hundred but can smell him that's stinking. Let go thy hold when a great wheel runs down a hill, lest it break thy neck with following it; but the great one that goes up the hill, let him draw thee after.
>
> *The History of King Lear*, vii.235–41

The Knights are emblematic of the king's loss of power and authority. They do not exist. The argument, in a narrative sense, is fallacious.

Similarly, if we consider the first scene where Lear constructs the competition through which the one who 'doth love us most' will receive 'our largest bounty', the greatest proportion of land, we find another narrative anomaly. Lear, as is implied by Shakespeare through Burgundy's later speech in the same scene, has, outside the play, already decided the proportion of land going to each daughter. Burgundy protests:

> Royal majesty
> I crave no more than what your highness offered;
> Nor will you tender less
> *The History of King Lear*, i.183–5

He is asking Lear to reconsider his punishment of Cordelia in line with what had been previously promised as dowry. In constructing the impression that there is a dominant language which exudes power, Shakespeare simultaneously provides indicators which deconstruct the language of authority itself. His language both demonstrates power and undermines it in a complex interweaving of words which are remote from the realities that the characters experience. The play distrusts talking. It rather resorts to the elements: the blind man at Dover or the naked man on the heath. During the storm it is that madman, Poor Tom, who complains of the cold and it is the Fool who describes exactly what he sees, as Gloucester appears with a torch: 'Look, here comes a walking fire' (xii.103). Words rarely have the truth of such simplicity.

In *Hamlet* words exude from the protagonist in probably the most famous speeches in all literature. Yet, in rehearsal, if we temporarily remove Hamlet from Claudius's court, a different set of perspectives from those conjured by the prince's words is found. There is another narrative hinted at by Shakespeare, but one subservient to the story he has selected to tell. Claudius, on the death of the king, has acted quickly to ensure the safety of the state at a time when the Norwegians, under Fortinbras, are likely to invade. He has ensured stability by marrying the dead king's queen and proclaiming her son as his heir. Further, he acts quickly and decisively to end Fortinbras's proposed invasion. His message to the old Norwegian king secures peace without bloodshed. Denmark, after the sudden death of King Hamlet, can feast and rejoice at the wedding and can feel secure in the social policies enacted by King Claudius. Without Hamlet's perspective all would appear well. Place him back in the play and chaos ensues, because moral imperatives demand questions, even at a time of stability. The play oscillates between a variety of perspectives presented through character personas. The critical difficulty arises when the narrative of the play is taken solely as a story, or the figures in the play are considered as life-equivalents. Shakespeare, however, through words, action and narrative, creates patterns which sometimes harmonize, but more often play against one another in the dramatic moving pictures which are presented.

The dramas operate on contradictory and complementary levels, leading us to become involved in meanings not necessarily related to the questions superficially being asked. As an audience we may empathize or not with the character of Hamlet, as the play helps to dictate or our own ideologies determine. Rather than to search for or impose meanings on the story, or on the nature of the characters, an alternative critical viewpoint can be found. This is not to consider *Hamlet* in narratological terms at all, but rather as an element of language in a communication system that we call a play. Hamlet, Lear, Macbeth, Othello, Claudius, Cordelia, Banquo, Iago, are constructs. They are elements of language in a communicative sign system we call a play. They thereby extend words into action. They do not live but, rather in the context of their respective plays, they communicate and signify in a pattern of expression which is not necessarily dependent on the conclusions of the plots.

When a Shakespearean play was first performed, the actors would have been given their own parts, not a copy of the whole play. They performed their parts and listened for their cues. They were thus being used by Shakespeare, almost as words in a complex language system which he was dictating. They were part of a constructed pattern. This pattern is held up to scrutiny, just as words are scrutinized in the discourse of any communication process. The difference is that a modern audience or reader demands the pattern to communicate with the present, even though it was first constructed for a communication process four hundred years ago. Edward Bond considers Shakespeare as a man of his time, not for all ages, as Ben Jonson held. Certainly, in joining in the communication process at the opening of a new millennium we have to take into consideration aspects of Shakespeare's contemporary intellectual ambience which gave rise to the patterns themselves. Stephen Greenblatt writes of renaissance literary texts:

> Social actions are themselves always embedded in systems of public signification, always grasped, even by their makers, in acts of interpretation, while the words that constitute the works of literature . . . are by their very nature the manifest assurance of a similar embeddedness. Language, like other sign systems, is a collective construction: our interpretive task must be to grasp more sensitively the consequences of this fact by investigating both the social presence to the world of the literary text and the social presence of the world in the literary text.[10]

If this is the case with literary texts, it is equally so with the complexity of a dramatic score operating not only on levels of linguistic but of semiotic communication. We must, in researching a play for production, begin, in however rudimentary a way, with the intellectual concerns of the time.

Shakespeare created his communicative systems when a dominant philosophy was concerned with *homo universalis* – many-sided, universal man. The universe, in no longer being seen as earth-centred, ironically made man appear to philosophers as more important, rather than less. It was the many-sided individual who fashioned himself into what, in giving a history of Hamlet, the construct Ophelia states he once was:

> O what a noble mind is here o'er thrown!
> The courtier's, soldier's, scholars, eye, tongue, sword,
> Th' expectancy and rose of the fair state,
> The glass of fashion and the mould of form,
> Th' observ'd of all observers
> > *Hamlet*, III.i.153–7

Renaissance, ego-centred humanism, in producing books and pamphlets on the ability to become a perfect prince and accomplished courtier, as exemplified by Castiglione's *The Book of the Courtier* (1528), was concentrating on the epitome of man. The individual theoretically could be self-fashioned into perfection. The courtly manuals demonstrated a new reality. George Bull writes of Castiglione:

> The truth was that the self-interested endeavour of Castiglione's contemporaries at the small Courts of Italy to justify the profession of the courtier – to synthesise the idea of the warrior and the scholar, the Christian believer and the classical hero, the self-contained man of *virtù* and the dutiful servant of the prince – provided an opportune answer, gracefully and fully expressed, to a need felt urgently in the north of Europe as medieval values dissolved.[11]

A movement, thereby, of self-construction into a particular image was started from small elitist communities and spread rapidly through the intellectual cities and courts of renaissance Europe. It appears in Shakespeare that time and again he deconstructs such images of the ideal courtier holding them up for critical scrutiny. *Hamlet, Measure for Measure* and *King Lear*, for example, examine the dissected pieces of the corporate courtly ideal as found not only in protagonists but reflected across many characters. In *Othello* Shakespeare takes the inspection to probably its most startling stage image in relation to the semiotics of the drama. The colour of the protagonist interacts with the conceptions of the ideal and the expectations of the audience. It is a play on which to dwell, not only to see the questions raised by the issues of the play itself but by the fact of the conscious theatricality of drama. It is also one of the plays, as we have noted, which causes modern theatre to reflect on issues of social and racial efficacy before productions are even staged.

The reasons for such concern may be that modern society wants to contemporize Shakespeare too much. It wants him to conform, in other words, to what it expects to hear from him. Yet, if we approach the plays by temporarily freezing our own prejudices and attempting to locate the organization of the dramatic constructs in their historical moment, it may be possible to find a talking Shakespeare, a mode of discourse through drama.

Greenblatt's thesis on self-fashioning in the Renaissance is informative in seeing a reaction to such constructions in Shakespeare's plays. *Othello* can thereby be appreciated in the context of a deconstruction of a dominant social ideology and the expression that ideology allows. Shakespeare, in this play, as vividly as anywhere, demonstrates that self-fashioning is dependent on social fashioning, and that this social construction of the self ensures its position in a hierarchy of values. He does this by concentrating on the nature of power and its interaction with language, highlighting the whole by the central visual images of the black man assuming authority in a white society.

Michel Foucault suggests that power operates through the desires it produces rather than those it forbids. The notion of forbiddance as found in the central doctrines of Christianity – the forbidden fruit in the Garden of Eden, the negatives of the Ten Commandments – has a certain attraction or utility. This is held in an uneasy and creative tension with the desires constructed through operational power, whether that power be religious, or secular, or both. Renaissance dramatists from Shakespeare to Ford experimented with this tension in developing the action of their plays. It is one of the means by which they can still talk to a contemporary world. It is not an issue of universal human values but of a recognition of the way in which society constructs itself through forms of authority which naturally repress and yet, simultaneously, attract individuals. This can find a reflection in drama.

The forbidden incestuous lust of brother and sister in Ford's *'Tis Pity She's a Whore* and the psychological attraction of Beatrice–Joanna to the pock-marked servant De Flores in Middleton's *The Changeling* are set within frameworks where power over individuals is unleashed by desires demanding satisfaction, through deliberate rebelliousness against social norms or constructed values. The rebelliousness of the sexuality is ironically a permitted desire within the social construct of the dominant ideology. It is allowed by being forbidden. In Charles Marowitz's rewriting of *Othello* for the twentieth-century stage, the contemporary dramatist challenges bourgeois middle-class women in the audience in an offensive, yet simultaneously attractive way. His Desdemona confronts them with the possibility of hidden desires for intimacy with the blackness of Othello's body, for the fulfilment of sexual fantasy:

> Wouldn't you have, if you'd had the chance? Not just big, and not just black, but holy and black, strong and black, elegant and black.... Wouldn't you have, if you'd had the chance? If his arms had lifted you, like a baby into a waiting cradle, and his mouth had eaten away the hunger of a thousand poached summers; days filled with dry flirtations and rough-and-love-less goodnight kisses. Wouldn't you have? If one night, the dream had sprinted out from under your sheets and stood rock-solid by the foot of the bed saying: Let's! And the hell with everything else! Wouldn't you have? Wouldn't you?[12]

Marowitz's communication process is in line with the confronta-tionary nature of Shakespeare's plays, a form of challenge which may have been diluted by time and sanitized by modern conven-tion. Shakespeare's Othello as a black man is the outsider who attracts and yet repulses the society which consumes him.

In Webster's *The Duchess of Malfi*, the Duchess being perse-cuted by Bosola famously cries out, 'I am the Duchess of Malfi still' (IV.ii.139).[13] Some contemporary scholars consider this a statement of feminine individuality, or an existentialist reaffirma-tion of the self in the context of social rebellion. It may be regarded as both or either in modern productions, since both are issues of contemporary sensitivity which critics and audiences can impose on the text and read from it. Similarly, however, it is equally legitimate to see it not as an expression of rebellion but an acquiescence to the norm of society. The Duchess's affair with one who is inferior to her has been conducted from a dominant position in a socially constructed hierarchy of power. Her family is the political coterie enforcing the dominant ideology in the society represented by the play. The Duchess's sexual desire, Webster shows, is unleashed actually by her authority and that of her brothers, not against it. That she dies because of it is an irrelevance to the social structuring itself.

Whatever the time gap, however significant the changes in human values through history, people are both individuals and common elements within the societies they construct. If power operates in society through the desires it produces, the powerful in *Othello* are not Othello, or Desdemona, or Iago, but rather those figures in the shade, the implied Venetian hierarchy, almost totally outside the play. They are brought into the light fleetingly by Brabantio, but more particularly by the Turkish invasion. In contemporary parlance, they are the equivalent of 'the men in grey suits' manipulating power in Whitehall.

Othello as a character desires Desdemona. For the society which Shakespeare depicts it is an offensive desire, even though one that can be tolerated in the context of more weighty matters. Iago articulates the social revulsion with tabloid glee: 'thick lips'; 'the black ram tupping the white ewe'; the 'daughter covered with a Barbary horse'; Desdemona and the Moor 'making the beast with two backs'. When Brabantio challenges Iago in the affrontery of such images, 'Thou art a villain', Iago replies 'You are a Senator.' It is the reminder of the social status being undermined by not only the coarseness of the language but the significance of the image created. It is not Desdemona who is being abused, not even Brabantio, but Venetian society itself. The black man is an offence to the society in the very actions and the qualities which attract the Venetians to him. There is an oscillation of repulsion and fascination which is exemplified by Desdemona's love but which goes beyond that to the heart of the Venetian state.

Desdemona desires a controlled rebellion against socially constructed moral codes. Before the Senate, Shakespeare provides her with an eloquence equal to Othello's in the defence of the love she has and her desire to be with the black man. Power is operating through the desires society is producing. Desdemona wants Othello, Venice wants Othello, but he himself is an irrelevance to them as a character, a person or an individual. He is rather a desire. Desdemona, in her death, is the daughter of Brabantio still. Similarly, Othello's narrative and death has no effect on the power of Venice. The desire has been expunged like an act of cheap sexuality, as expressed in Sonnet 129:

> Th' expense of spirit in a waste of shame
> Is lust in action; and till action, lust
> Is perjured, murd'rous, bloody, full of blame,
> Savage, extreme, rude, cruel, not to trust,
> Enjoyed no sooner but despisèd straight,

Past reason hunted, and no sooner had
Past reason hated....

This is a characteristic, not only of black or white sexuality, but of
social intercourse which is dominated by any form of power or
self-gratification. As soon as the Venetians know that the Turks
are defeated, they recall Othello from Cyprus. He would be
inappropriate as a Governor. He is an 'expense of spirit'.

In *The Tempest*, Prospero instructs Ferdinand and Miranda that
'we are such stuff as dreams are made on, and our little life/Is
rounded with a sleep'. In *As You Like It* the metaphor is different:
'All the world's a stage'. Whichever, Shakespeare's playworld is a
construction in imitation of states of existence. Those states,
however, are, in themselves, a form of constructed experience.
Literary criticism, theatrical production, personal and social
ideologies can impose interpretations on to Shakespeare and do
so. They use Shakespeare to talk with one another and to all who
wish to listen. They use his plays as a vocabulary of their own.
The plays themselves are resilient to such employment because
as constructs they constantly draw attention to themselves. They
are artefacts, malleable within even the narrative boundaries that
appear to define them. In this, they are more than their endings,
more than their narratives. They are as words are, reflective
signifiers in a communicative process. They operate as language
does, but the language is more complex than sounds. It involves
visual and spatial relationships, narrative consistencies and
inconsistencies, ambiguities and contradictions and the conjura-
tion of seemingly real people, enacted by living people in an
overtly constructed environment, the theatre. The plays are historical in composition and yet contemporary in performance or
even in reading. In all this they demonstrate a stability of the
artefact and its natural instability. Just as the defeated Cleopatra
warns her followers that Octavius 'words' her, so, generally,
words cannot be fully trusted by anyone. The same is true of
Shakespearean plays and their interpretation. They are as
ephemeral as 'dreams', as 'acting', and, in being so, as transient
as the constructed lifestyles they reflect. Othello and Desdemona
are as words. They are spoken, performed and are gone. When
politicians, critics, directors or ideologues claim Shakespeare for
themselves, they are merely being drawn into the constructs he

created. They are doing what Chaucer ironically instructed his readers not to do. They are taking in earnest what is meant for game. They have fallen into the poet's trap. In *Talking Shakespeare*, significances do, of course, abound but they do not necessarily manifest a universality. They rather communicate reflections of those who act, watch or read the plays. In some ways, the drama thereby reveals that we may merely be talking to ourselves. But perhaps also we are being made to listen to what we are saying: to hear ourselves and to consider the construction of the societies in which we live. It is in this regard that *Talking Shakespeare*'s power and attraction is found.

2. How does *Hamlet* end?

NIGEL WOOD

Polonius has dabbled in the dramatic arts, and his commendation to Hamlet of the approaching Players not only notes their generic scope but also their professional competence, as the 'only men' both 'for the law of writ, and the liberty' (II.ii.397–8). This contrast, between literal adherence and ad hoc freedoms, is one that Hamlet apparently understands only too well. His advice to the First Player combines a great suspicion of actorly brio with the hope that a performance will not be 'too tame', the adjudication lying with one's 'discretion', where the 'action' is suited to the 'word', and, less predictably, vice versa (III.ii.16–18). For all the 'modesty of nature' (III.ii.19) that might be the guiding principle, the 'word' may still be suited to the 'action'. On the one hand, one needs to temper the egoistic display of those 'clowns' that tamper with what 'is set down for them' (III.ii.39), while, on the other, one needs to perform. The text of *The Murder of Gonzago* can only exist for the on-stage courtly audience as a pretext for Hamlet's precise design, realized in one of its hearer's specific reactions to a carefully calculated theatrical statement. In this instance, the 'law of writ' is interpreted precisely.

Leaving Shakespeare's calculations aside for the moment, what did Hamlet indicate by the contrast between written precedent and the 'liberty' of performance?[1] If the aim of criticism is to open the text up to knowledge of its meanings, both past and present, actual and potential, then Hamlet's advice to the Players can be taken to be at least an indication of how 'written' Elizabethan performance could be – on a par with sudden metatheatrical comment such as Rosencrantz's jibe, from the Folio version, at the 'little eyases' (II.ii. 337). Yet the plentiful evidence theatre historians have gathered about just what that enabling critical fiction, the Globe audience, is likely to have been like surely questions the universal validity of a criticism that takes textual notation on trust. In terms that Stanley Fish has made famous, what 'interpretive communities' did Shakespeare think

24

he was addressing? Or, more pertinently, even if in more direct
reference to readers rather than spectators, 'Is the reader or the
text the source of meaning?'[2] Without the capacity to assess
the *theatrical* language available to both writer and audience, the
dimension of physical and scenic gestures and sudden localized
drama is all but invisible, relegated to the supplementary and
supererogatory, the material of anecdotage and unreliable memory rather than analytics. One might rephrase the pertinent Fish
enquiry thus: 'Is it relevant to treat an early modern playtext as if
it were the final phase in the process of composition?' If not, then
what process of recovery *is* germane to such drama?

When reviewing the textual situation confronting the editor of
Hamlet, there should come a moment when the text's theatricality
is taken more or less seriously. In the phrase used by Wells and
Taylor, in their Oxford *Complete Works*,[3] a 'theatrical' text might
omit some lines actually written by Shakespeare because it represents the closest we can get to 'the "final" version of the play', and
this might indicate the result of pruning rather than of simple
accumulation.[4] The term is suggestive on two counts: first, it
encourages an analysis of the dramatic action that identifies its
generic language more precisely – as *sui generis* rather than *littera* ·
scripta – and thus incorporates acts of implication as much as
statement, and second, it faces the fact that certain plays exist in
multiple forms less because they are staging posts towards the
final destination than because assumptions about expected audiences encouraged clear differences in any one text's 'unity' or
underlying logic. Whatever we term *Hamlet* is seldom taken to
indicate this variety of possible texts. On the contrary, it gestures
to an abstract entity standing clear of any one performance or,
more crucially for this chapter, one text. Where hermeneutics
relies on notions of a stable or authoritative text, it claims authority in return from an author, not as the ghost within textual
traces, but as a unity of biographical witness. Yet the three
major texts that compose our modern reading editions of *Hamlet*,
the first two Quartos of 1603 and then 1604/5 and Folio text of
1623, testify to how little Shakespeare or the Lord Chamberlain's
Men saw fit to standardize the text. If not a thousand flowers left
to bloom, then there are at least three hardy plants all exhibiting
commendable durability, but the later hybrid has often been
chosen for display. As Philip Edwards, in his Cambridge edition

of 1985, has it, 'the study of the early texts of *Hamlet* is the study of a play in motion', and far from there being some settled unitary purpose, there is only an array of possibilities: 'the important decisions about the text of *Hamlet* are in the end literary decisions: not a matter of technical demonstration but of literary and linguistic judgement'.[5] Thus, after all the available theories about transmission have been rehearsed and set to work, the texts as we have them do not lead back to a single point of origin. For G. R. Hibbard (Oxford edition, 1987), this is a significant fact and should not be overlooked in our search for better and yet more authoritative evidence.[6]

In a sense, one could say that the choice of *Hamlet* by which to explore the consequences of a 'theatrical' text is simply kicking at an open door. I hope not; an empty coffer is not the same thing as an embarrassment of riches, and compositions exist, even if the search for master-texts involves a certain blindness to a variety of potentially contradictory forms. This search for the playhouse *Hamlet* can affect the critical process radically. In his *Re-Editing Shakespeare for the Modern Reader* (1984), Stanley Wells identified several editorial challenges in the recognition that the printed text exists just as notation. Thus, while there is ample evidence to suggest that the 1603 'bad' Quarto was superseded by later versions, it might actually be nearer a performance text. It provides pictures of the Ghost appearing 'in his night gowne' in the closet scene, and the deranged Ophelia entering, 'playing on a lute, and her haire downe singing'. Do we incorporate this information, or, if we regard it as part of the legacy of a corrupt (presumably non-authoritative) source, ignore it, along with other accidentals? The easiest answer is to provide a 'diplomatic' edition, one that 'makes only minimal corrections of errors and anomalies in the text as originally printed'.[7] '*Hamlet*' is thus free-range, and, as long as the reading public will wear it, all ensuing productions will carry the byline, 1603, 1604/5, 1623. Wells makes the point that this is to carry rationalization to an antiquarian fault, for a printed text should point to performance, and this requires lucidity and decisions. Directors, throughout Shakespearean theatrical history, have been accountable for their choices, and any student of performance history knows the difference between a rendition that is a transcription – worthy and not to be faulted in its good faith – and the significant re-visioning that recognizes that plays communicate in significantly different ways from other literary forms. This might involve the production of dramatic symbols that survive the place of their origin *because* of their figurative excess, not despite it.

One of the casualties of this approach is the pervasive belief that *Hamlet* is a failed attempt to incorporate irreconcilable material, from Saxo-Grammaticus, and Belleforest, to parody the Senecan excesses of Kyd in his *Spanish Tragedy*, and perhaps also to write a Protestant antidote to Mediterranean Revenge Tragedy (not for nothing is Hamlet's university Wittenberg). For Brecht in his seminal essay, 'The Popular and the Realistic' (*c.*1937), the limit factors for successful theatre do not recognize matters of historical veracity alone. 'Sensuous' theatre is not 'realistic' theatre. Indeed, realism and the sensuous are often irreconcilable.[8] How, then, to look at the close of *Hamlet* for its symbolic, 'sensuous' patterning rather than through the lens of simpler plotting? Conceivably, if one were put to the description of the plot, one's account would have to come to a full stop: 'Go, bid the soldiers shoot' (V.ii.356); or the Folio's stage direction, '*Exeunt marching; after the which, a Peale of Ordenance are shot off* '; or the simple '*Exeunt*' of Q2, or none at all for Q1. Here, using G. R. Hibbard's editorial choices as a base-text, are two significant closing passages, noting the most significant variants:

Hamlet:	If thou didst ever hold me in thy heart,
	Absent thee from felicity awhile,
	And in this harsh world draw thy breath in pain,
	To tell my story.
	A march afar off, and shot within
	[*March afarre off, and shout within* – F;
	A marche a farre off – Q2]
	What warlike noise is this?
	Enter Osric
Osric:	Young Fortinbras, with conquest come from Poland,
	To th'ambassadors of England gives
	This warlike volley.
Hamlet:	O, I die, Horatio.

The potent poison quite o'ercrows my spirit.
I cannot live to hear the news from England,
But I do prophesy th'election lights
On Fortinbras. He has my dying voice,
So tell him, with the occurrents, more and less,
Which have solicited – the rest is silence.

He gives a long sigh and dies
[*O, o, o, o. Dyes* – F; *Ham dies* – Q1; not in Q2]

Horatio: Now cracks a noble heart. Good night, sweet prince,
And flights of angels sing thee to thy rest.
Why does the drum come thither?

*Enter Fortinbras, with the English Ambassadors,
and Soldiers with drum and colours*
[*Enter Fortinbras and English Ambassador, with
Drumme, Colours, and Attendants* – F;
*Enter Voltemar and the Ambassadors from England.
enter Fortenbrasse with his traine* – Q1]

Fortinbras: Where is this sight?

Horatio: What is it you would see?
If aught of woe or wonder, cease your search....
                                        (V.ii.299–316)

Fortinbras: ... For me, with sorrow I embrace my fortune.
I have some rights [Q2, Q1; Rites – F] of memory in
this kingdom,
Which now to claim my vantage doth invite me.

Horatio: Of that I shall have also cause to speak,
And from his mouth whose voice will draw on more.
But let this same be presently performed,
Even while men's minds are wild, lest more mis-
chance
On plots and errors happen.

Fortinbras: Let four captains

Bear Hamlet like a soldier to the stage;
For he was likely, had he been put on,
To have proved most royally; and for his passage,
The soldiers' music and the rites [F; right – Q2] of
   war
Speak loudly for him.
Take up the bodies. Such a sight as this
Becomes the field, but here shows much amiss.
Go, bid the soldiers shoot.
   [*A dead march. Exeunt, bearing off the bodies, after the
   which a peal of ordnance is shot off
   Exeunt marching: after the which, a Peale of Ordenance
   are shot off* – F; *Exeunt* – Q2; Not in Q1]
                                                (V.ii.341–56)

Hamlet, here, is given the soldier's burial at which the preceding action rarely hints. The still and moving dialogue between
Horatio and Hamlet can be rudely interrupted by the 'warlike
noise' of Fortinbras's approach (V.ii.302). He may have Hamlet's
'dying voice' (V.ii.309), yet this verbal sanction cannot erase the
visual and stylistic shock Fortinbras's incursion marks. Horatio
hopes of 'flights of angels' to 'sing' Hamlet 'to [his] rest', and so
he may well enquire: 'Why does the drum come hither?'
(V.ii.3.13–14). Yet what the audience actually sees is Hamlet
accommodated to a warrior's image, where 'The soldier's
music and the rites of war' end up speaking 'loudly for him'
(V.ii.352–3). In this bald and hardly exhaustive account I could
have opted for an arrangement of these particulars that suggested some unified intention fulfilled inexorably in the fruition
of the closing scene, a trip for Hamlet through purgatorial madness to a mature recognition that there is 'a special providence
[even] in the fall of a sparrow' (V.ii.166–7). Certainly, one might
agree with Brian Vickers in his *Appropriating Shakespeare*
(1993) that Shakespeare transformed source narrative materials
to lend them dramatic focus, according to some shared aesthetic
principles. I see no abiding problem about the solving, for example, of the theatrical problem provided by a range of sources. Vickers celebrates such a creative authority in expansive
terms:

In *Hamlet* and *King Lear* Shakespeare reshaped his source
material to give a tragic ending, and in both cases he did so
by a remarkable demonstration of an author's shaping power,
which Current Literary Theory would be wholly unable to
describe.[9]

It is a central concern of any interpreter of Shakespeare's work,
whether in production or in the study, to wonder *which* author
is doing the 'shaping'. In A. D. Nuttall's *Why Does Tragedy Give
Pleasure?* the claim of final closure is repeated, whereby tragic
drama 'of all the literary genres' places 'the heaviest emphasis on
ending, and the ending is a mimesis of a death'.[10] Even a theatre
critic as liberal in interests as John Russell Brown takes short cuts
in his *Shakespeare's Plays in Performance* when identifying some
coherence out of this last scene. When dwelling on the final
'closed' composition of the charnel-house court in V.ii, Brown
notes that the sound of drums heard in the distance *succeeds* the
intimacies of 'the stillness and quietness of death'. The closing
scene is one where the clash between the interior horror of
introspection derived from the prison that is Elsinore is breached
perhaps in redemption by Fortinbras: 'This entry from the world
outside effects a last formality so that in procession the bodies of
Hamlet, the King, the Queen and Laertes are taken out of sight,
borne aloft to be placed "high on a stage" in view of the "yet
unknowing world".'[11] Performance study should have something to say about the distance that must exist between plot and
the precise symbolic patterns derived from it; in short, how plot is
a pretext. Brown's scene-painting of the mass removal of bodies
from the stage is in accord only with Q2, that has Fortinbras
order his men to take up the 'bodies'. It is singular in both Q1
and F. Hibbard, for good measure, adopts Q2 here and provides
a new stage-direction accordingly, incorporating 'A dead march.
Exeunt, bearing off the bodies, after the which a peal of ordnance
is shot off.' Edwards adopts 'bodies'. Both ignore the testimony of
Q2 for 'right' at its line corresponding to V.ii.352 of the extract,
and the significant distinction in interpretation between hearing
the phoneme as 'right' (freedom, that to which you are entitled)
and 'rites' (formulaic ceremony) is thus effaced. Conversely, both
Edwards and Hibbard elect for 'rights' from both Q1 and Q2
at V.ii.342–3 ('I have some rights of memory in this kingdom, /

Which now to claim my vantage doth invite me'), and ignore the testimony of the Folio's 'Rites', which would provide a much weaker statement. Without secure evidence one way or another, we may lose the possibility that Hamlet is actually a trophy of war at his conclusion, the martial music of drum and gunshot in jarring contest with the promised 'flights of angels'. What we can conclude is that the rest is surely not silence, and that Bradleyan considerations of Hamlet the *dramatis persona* do not exhaust the possibilities of *Hamlet* the more holistic dramatic experience.

It is not that Hibbard's text is untheatrical in its way; it is rather that he, as inevitably with many editorial decisions where the text of *Hamlet* is concerned, has chosen to portray Shakespeare's intentions pre-emptively. Hamlet may have died with a 'long sigh' on his lips more often than not on the Elizabethan stage, but we cannot be at all sure. Indeed, the fourfold repetition of 'O' could link more violently with the 'crack' of 'a noble heart' recorded by Horatio. Hibbard has supplied an extra English ambassador to top even the Folio's suddenly populous stage (s.d. V.ii.314), and brought 'Soldiers' into the scene, where either Fortinbras's 'traine' (Q1) or 'Attendants' (F) would seem the most definitely indicated. If soldiers are already on stage, then they presumably are the ones that ultimately carry off Hamlet's corpse – leaving a blank space before the final burst of ordnance. Or do courtiers clear the stage, with soldiers as some sort of ceremonial guard? Again, it may be probable to have the last sounds those of a funeral march before that last sudden percussion, but 'a dead march' is nowhere expressly indicated. When does the 'soldier's music' commence? Although valuable as the possible re-creation of *a* performance, Andrew Gurr and Mariko Ichikawa's narrative of the early staging of *Hamlet* follows the 'best-guess principle that led to the finished design of the Globe', and, as such, is a record of 'optimal performance', and yet its editorial choices (often from the Folio, yet its '*Exeunt marching*' does not quite underpin a 'funeral procession' described as the closing dramatic gesture) illustrate the drive towards a single set of favoured circumstances rather than a dispersed array of possiblities that the texts might produce.[12] These are not perverse deconstructions of a once patterned text. On the contrary, such lack of direct testimony surely calls forth those 'literary judgements' upon which Edwards eventually rests.

But these considerations are not directly the result of 'theatricalizing' our appreciation of text. That truism of Drama 101 courses, that 'showing' is always prone to overpower 'telling', might carry us so far, but it is a most preliminary perception. What Wells and Taylor's editorial principles help us explore is the open-ended nature of theatrical meaning – not simply some hermeneutic adventure playground, but rather the radical ambiguities of theatrical effect, especially a possibility of the theatre of the early modern period, and, I would argue, more muted though still possible thereafter once drama becomes a more ritualized activity. It is here that Vickers's and Nuttall's firm belief in aesthetic closure needs significant qualification. It is one thing to find in a playtext the certainties of armchair contemplation, the possibilities of well-wrought artefacts, but *Hamlet* can hardly be said to conclude just with the imitation of a death. Tragedy may conclude in a death, if a broad-brush summary of the plot is required, yet even that apparent truism is no universal. Oedipus, although blinded, lives on. *Macbeth*, too, draws to a close with the triumph of Malcolm's invocation of 'measure, time, and place' (V.vii.103), a prelude to his own coronation, where the tragic hero is present only as a head impaled on Macduff's staff. *Antony and Cleopatra* ends with an elegy from Octavius Caesar that is fulsome only on first reading:

> No grave upon the earth shall clip in it
> A pair so famous. High events as these
> Strike those that make them; and their story is
> No less in pity than his glory which
> Brought them to be lamented. Our army shall
> In solemn show attend this funeral –
> And then to Rome. Come, Dolabella, see
> High order in this great solemnity.
> (V.ii.357–64)

The pair are merely 'famous' (notorious?), and just who *has* made the 'high events' in which they have figured? Our pity should be in due proportion to our admiration for the 'glory' of their puppet-master, Octavius Caesar. For all Cleopatra's determination 'To fool [the Romans'] preparation' and 'conquer / Their most absurd intents' (V.ii.225–6), she and Antony will still shore

up 'high order' and 'great solemnity' in the closing tableau.
Octavius appropriates as he apparently celebrates, and there
was nothing new in this. Consider the split commemoration of
Brutus in *Julius Caesar*: Antony remembers 'the noblest Roman of
them all', stressing his example in promoting a 'general honest
thought / And common good to all', but Octavius caps this altru-
ism with the egoistic desire to have the bones lie as a trophy in his
tent before the provision of a *soldier's* funeral, 'ordered honour-
ably'. We might read back the comment that the victorious army
should 'use' him 'According to his virtue' (V.v.68–79), as profoundly ambiguous, for when has this official Roman ideology
had room for Brutus's conception of *virtus*? Four lines are spared
for the dead, and Octavius is 'away / To part the glories of this
happy day' (V.v.80–1).

Even given the practical consideration that it would be a resonant end to the theatrical action to conclude it with a sonorous set-
piece, one might wonder whether such a martial afflatus is in
keeping with the Alexandrian or Republican sentiments that
supply the significant 'other' to Roman imperialism – nor is this
an isolated example. When Coriolanus is borne off the stage he is
left to the mercies of those who remember that he 'hath widowed
and unchilded many a one, / Which to this hour bewail the injury'
(V.vi.152–3). Just as four captains bear Hamlet off the stage, four
are provided for Coriolanus, but as R. B. Parker points out in his
Oxford edition,[13] these pallbearers are likely to be the very conspirators who have just done him down. Coriolanus may die and
the tragic action be completed, yet the irony at the provisional
success handed to the Volscians at that moment was known widely
to be but a prelude to four and a half centuries of Roman
hegemony, Aufidius's death and their extirpation. For all
Caesar's magnanimity, a basic instruction in Roman history
would have corroborated Plutarch's verdict, that 'it was predes-
tined that the government of the world should fall into Octavius
Caesar's handes'.[14] He is a figure of undeniable worldly power at
the same time as he is the elegist.

The prevalence of the critical judgement that *Hamlet* proves an
artistic failure can, from this perspective, simply gesture to the
very reasons as to why it might prove a theatrical success. Johnson characterized it with a praise of its variety, where, at the same
time, the 'scenes [were] busy and various' and yet the 'process of

the action' possessed sufficient 'probability' for a tragedy, while
T. S. Eliot in 1919 could rue its lack of 'artistic "inevitability"', the
'complete adequacy of the external to the emotion' which only
helps us identify how Hamlet's emotion is thrillingly 'in *excess*
of the facts as they appear'.[15] Alastair Fowler's 1995 British
Academy lecture, on Shakespeare's 'Renaissance Realism', has
stressed the play's constant uncovering only of facets and perspectives – of *a* reality, *some* characteristics, or at most, a tentative
division between the denotative and the figurative – in some
coruscating hall of mirrors. Most tellingly, the *Times Literary
Supplement* entitled the abbreviated version of Fowler's piece
'The Case Against *Hamlet*'.[16]

Performance study is more than just a history of theatrical
precedent. In a significant sense, plays do not end as neatly as
that final exeunt would seem to suggest. Let us face the choice
awaiting the editor at V.ii.297–8; 'O God, Horatio, what a
wounded name, / Things standing thus unknown, shall I leave
behind me!' The closing tableau before the final cannon is heard
surely gathers meaning from a prior decision about whether
Hamlet thinks he is entrusting his memory and the value of his
mission just to Horatio or also to God. Similarly, how *is* the stage
populated at the play's end? Hibbard adds extra ambassadors to
the sudden pageant when Fortinbras enters, yet there is no
sanction for a plural here *plus* 'Soldiers with drum and colours'.
The Folio has one ambassador plus 'Drumme, Colours, amd
Attendants'; Q2 provides only 'Fortenbrasse, with the Embassa-
dors', and Q1 has presumably 'Voltemar and the Ambassadors
from England' entering separately from 'Fortenbrasse with his
traine'. The military ethos has been rendered a property of the
text constructed by Hibbard, yet the available versions only suggest it by the earlier mood music of the drum and Fortinbras's
direction to 'bear Hamlet like a soldier to the stage' (V.ii.349).
The command to 'Go, bid the soldiers shoot' (V.ii.356) would
seem to be superfluous if the pallbearers could just as well have
done the job themselves. Hibbard favours 'A dead march', yet,
however appropriate this would appear, it flies in the face of the
Folio's 'exeunt Marching'. There are yet more performance
aspects of this conclusion. T. J. B. Spencer, in his Penguin edition
(1980),[17] notes that the sounds of gunshot are ironically more
associated with Claudius: his celebration of Hamlet's 'loving and

a fair reply' will involve 'the great cannon to the clouds' (I.ii.121, 126); 'ordnance' is shot off at s.d. I.iv.6 to mark Claudius's drunken 'wassail' (I.iv.9), and he again marks his toast that commences the duel with Laertes with a trumpet signal to the cannoneer (V.ii.270–1). If Hamlet is indeed placed on a 'stage' in full view of the audience, then it is likely to have been that same stage area, the gallery, where his father in 'warlike form', in full armour, had appeared in the very first scene. Does Hamlet become in death the warrior his father was, or is his end a final closing of a process that exceeds a purely individual focus?

What Wells and Taylor recognize is that the desire of the public to have *a* reading edition effaces the full provenance of each individual text that helps the editor construct one. From the perspective of the literary historian performance precedes text, and, although its traces are diffuse and thus knowable principally through the labours of the editor, the multiplicity of versions is still hard evidence and the probability that there were coexistent texts without an authoritative source (that is, several 'Shakespeares', if you like) is an unshunnable fact about many works. Thus, although Q1 is shoddily constructed and even an inconsistent text in matters of orthography and stage direction, this might at the same time point to a proximity to actual performing conditions, a transcription (even if unauthorized) that you could not claim with as much confidence of either Q2 or the Folio. The notion of the 'theatrical' text that Wells and Taylor advocate carries with it an alternative logic or encoding to that of the uncorrupt edition – or even to that of the demonstrably 'best' version according to one's poetic tastes. Theatre language is not quite like that of other specialized idioms that we bring to mind when deciphering works whose centre of being can be contained in the book. Indeed, the demand for a more or less consistent textual existence for what we call *Hamlet* needs a later imposition of form and narrative that, however much it may now be found indispensable, is also eventually non-theatrical (if not antitheatrical) in both the early modern and modern senses of that word.

To return to whatever we may now call *Hamlet* is to recognize that there are basic areas of its dramatic form that are remarkably unfixed. When Leah S. Marcus examines the wide variations evident in the versions of 1603 to 1623, she traces a certain 'gentrification' in the later form. Even if we claim that Q2 might actually have preceded Q1, there is still a gathering process of formal patterning that hives off the Folio changes from the Quarto texts, be it judicious pruning or the inclusion of 'better' poetry.[18] If a purist were to isolate the Folio text as the preferable version – to the exclusion of all other witness – then it is likely that we would be left without many other traces of a fastidious aversion to the bodily that breaks forth so powerfully in the 'closet' scene of III.iv. We would have no denunciation of the 'heavy-handed revel', which, in a passage that Q2 includes immediately after I.iv.16, forms a symptom for Hamlet of the 'vicious mole of nature' that is apt to '[break] down the pales and forts of reason'. Within III.iv itself, we would miss Hamlet's anxiety that a choice of Claudius above the elder Hamlet would manifest 'a sense / [that] is "apoplexed" and translated "to ecstasy"' (Q2, after III.iv.72). This same decline and dislocation of humane 'sense' that is figured in 'Eyes without feeling, feeling without sight, / Ears without hands or eyes, smelling sans all' (Q2, after III.iv.73) produces a climax after III.iv.156, where he hopes that, for Gertrude, the 'monster custom' might profitably 'eat' the 'sense ... of habits vile', and 'use' oppose 'the stamp of nature' (after III.iv.159). Most tellingly, Q2 provides a much longer IV.iv, where, after F's line 8, Hamlet parleys with the Norwegian Captain before launching into his comparison between Man's infinite capacity for bestial ignorance and his aspirations towards 'godlike reason'. It is not that there are no hints of this in the Folio version, of course; the point is in the repetition and fixation that Q2 discloses.

For G. R. Hibbard, these cuts are evidence of Shakespeare's mature grasp of economical dramatic form. The lines that show such distaste at Danish 'revel' (after I.iv.16) simply mark time: 'The obvious reason for their disappearance is that they slow the action down.' Hibbard's very next sentence, however, points to the very reason that it might be included in one's ideal *Hamlet*: 'Eagerly awaiting a meeting between the Ghost and his son, the audience is tantalized with a repetition of one of the stock "complaints" of the Elizabethan satirist'[19] – which might very well be proverbial in content, but far less so as a dramatic *geste*. The slimming down of III.iv appears to have been carried out 'for good aesthetic reasons', as the 'excess' of the superfluous form 'smack[s] of self-indulgence on the part of the hero', and maybe of the author. Hamlet's reverie on Fortinbras's alacrity to revenge his father in IV.iv '[does] not advance the action', although it extends 'the speculative scope of the tragedy'. Crucially, the lines fail to 'reveal anything new' about him, as 'he is still very much where he was' at II.ii.291–308, confronting 'this quintessence of dust' (II.ii.306).[20] It must be stressed that this chapter does not set out to find Hibbard's editorial choices either incorrect or inconsistent. On the contrary, he shows commendable boldness in taking the decisions he does; it is rather that the editor must operate, at crucial points, as if s/he were a mere transcriber of fact, and that this is really an enabling fiction. *Hamlet* inevitably provides ample space for disagreement in textual editing as in literary interpretation, and Hibbard opts (as many others have done) for a text that equates economy of form with dramatic power. In Eliot's gnomic formulation, the 'external' should be 'adequate' to the 'emotion' released in some 'objective correlative'. The fact that *Hamlet* does not provide quite such a clinical experience is 'an artistic problem' in that Hamlet, the character, cannot 'objectify' his disgust – a thrilling search but, alas, without an artistic destination: 'more people have thought *Hamlet* a work of art because they have found it interesting, than have found it interesting because it is a work of art'.[21] Did Eliot, here, intend to describe drama?

For the theatre and a director interested in how *Shakespeare's* plotting works, how *Hamlet* ends, Fortinbras and all, is precisely, if complexly, plotted. No matter that generations of theatregoers have seen the play shorn of its more political dimensions, from Davenant's 1676 Players' Quarto down to Zeffirelli's 1990 film, where the rest is indeed silenced as Hamlet dies cradled in the loyal Horatio's arms. The distancing offered by the closing coda to the play is a consistent element of each *Hamlet* and it points to different, if still potent, dramatic conventions. The difficulties of knowing just what we are viewing when we encounter a Shakespearean playtext are not solved by omitting the apparently atypical or discordant.

To return to Fish's notion of an act of meaning: the unfolding of a design so that meaning is only ever gradually manifest is rarely a totally repeatable experience. Different audiences, or 'interpretive communities', not only receive different commu-

nications, but they may pre-empt a writer's or director's decisions: that sense of the 'audience-in-the-head', the destination of
the rhetoric, may involve a myriad of self-censorships – or create
other possibilities out of the practicalities of actual performance.
It is not a case of my promoting the ending of *Hamlet* that I most
prefer; it is rather that abstract preferences such as this, in lifting
a playtext out of its immediate moments of reception, encourages
a certain blindness to theatrical possibilities now and the structuring (and even creative) limits to Shakespeare's intentions then.

   This is similar, I believe, to what Stephen Greenblatt indicates
when he favours a reading of early modern theatre as a succes-
sion of communal exchanges, of 'social energies' shared between
auteur and audience. The project of establishing the 'best' or just
a 'reading' text of *Hamlet* cannot deliver that utopian goal: 'the
perfect, unsubstitutable, freestanding container of all of its meanings'. To borrow W. K. Wimsatt's term, this 'concrete universal'
promises an escape from 'shared contingency', and yet it does so,
doomed to failure, as there is no such flight from both ourselves
(and our often hidden projects when we write or direct) and
theatrical realities, composed of the adventitious and the prag-
matic as well as the conceptual.[22] This is a revisionary project,
and yet also a particularly modern one. It opens up the text,
however, not as some non-logocentric *plenum*, but as a set of
precise alternatives with infinite shades of emphasis and address.
In Alan C. Dessen's recent work on Shakespeare's theatrical
vocabulary, we can see at work something of this comprehension
of a 'language barrier', the over-reliance on the authoritative
word as the main semantic freight of any theatrical communication.[23] It is only then that the full excitement of any act of
translation and adaptation may be relished, and Shakespeare's
work in the theatre may be fully appreciated.

3. Shakespeare and the Elizabethan Stage: Touring Practice in Shakespeare's Day

PETER DAVISON

Although we know a considerable amount about touring drama in Shakespeare's time, working out precisely what were touring practices and what were the economics of touring are not easy. This is not surprising. Imagine leaping forward to the year 2400 and then looking back to our time with the benefit of partial newspaper and documentary evidence, and perhaps an old video of *The House* (the series of programmes about the Royal Opera), and attempting to construct a rational account of opera in our day. How would the researcher reconcile the fact that in order to tour, the Royal Opera needed vast additional grants, whereas Welsh National Opera, because it toured most of the year, was deemed to need much less money to do so? Or imagine coming across complaints by Welsh and Scottish Opera that, despite their also visiting very small towns without theatres – for example, Cwmbran, Harlech, and in the Rhondda Valley – their grants were kept below the increase in inflation, whereas the Royal Opera House received a 39 per cent increase over two years, even though for nearly half that time it would not be performing a single opera or giving a single concert. It is difficult enough to understand the 'logic' of such economics today with all the evidence before us; how much more difficult looking back from the year 2400.

Now think back to the theatrical conditions of Shakespeare's time, four hundred years ago. We have a substantial body of information about one theatre company, even details of its takings at the door; we know places companies toured to – though we cannot be sure whether they always performed; we know companies went bust on tour; we know companies performed illegally and got into trouble with the law and some actors ended up in jail – in Banbury, for example, in 1633. And we have all sorts of stories that may be apocryphal, but survive from Shakespeare's time in print, recounting the activities and mishaps of actors on tour. Even specific documentary evidence can be confusing. Thus, an actor called Distley (or was he Dishley or Diskly?) appears from the records to have been a member of two different companies at the same time.[1] Can we relate such diverse, partial and conflicting evidence to build up an overall picture of touring in Shakespeare's day? In addition to a mass of information about tour management in our own day, we have much detailed information for the centuries between Shakespeare's time and ours to show how touring was practised. For example, Tate Wilkinson, a very successful Yorkshire theatrical entrepreneur, left a considerable body of information about the touring company he ran in the eighteenth century, and we even have some details of what Wilkinson called 'little runabout scouring troops . . . [which] vaunt, look big, and promise . . . But tap 'em and the devil a drop comes out.'[2] I have several large volumes of newspaper cuttings and other miscellanea, including telegrams, letters, photographs and even cuttings of dresses worn on stage, recounting in very great detail how the actor and actress I grew up with toured between 1877 and 1922.[3] The records from the past 250 years show a remarkable consistency of practice. Thus Tate Wilkinson reckoned that if he had to make serious changes to his cast, or even to change the play, provided he knew by 2 p.m., he could 'paper the town' to give that advice in time for that evening's performance; today, the 'cut-off time' for Welsh National Opera (even with the advantages of telephones, faxes and rapid travel) is 1.30 p.m. But can one rely on that practice being in force a further 150 years ago? I think that is likely, but being likely is not the same as being certain. What is certain is that, as Philip V. Thomas put it, in addition to many vagabond and unlicensed entertainers, there were 'under aristocratic, civil and ecclesiastical patronage, hundreds of actors and players travell[ing] the length and breadth of England by the end of the sixteenth century, despite growing pressures against their doing so'.[4] What is also certain is that, despite official opposition, the hazards of the road, pitiful financial rewards and even imprisonment, men (and later women) were driven by a delight in performing to travel the roads before the roads were even worthy of that name, and the excitement of performance did attract audiences.

What I seek to do here is to draw on many kinds of information from Shakespeare's time and from later periods in order to give some indication of touring practice in Shakespeare's day, making special reference to the company Shakespeare acted with, the Lord Chamberlain's Men, in a specific year, 1597, in order to focus this account. My reference to the difficulty of producing a rational explanation for our own day should indicate how uncertain such a reconstruction must be and how conjectural are any conclusions I suggest.

The first London theatre, called appropriately, the Theater, was built by James Burbage in 1576 and was followed the next year by the adjacent Curtain (though the name had nothing to do with theatrical curtains, and its origin is not known). These two theatres, between Finsbury and Spitalfields, were sited close to what is now Shoreditch High Street. Shakespeare's company played at both between 1594 and 1599 and then moved south of the river to the Globe theatre in Southwark. To the west of the Globe, and built a little earlier, were the Rose and the Swan (the subject of de Witt's famous drawing). All these theatres were outside the walls of the City of London, but in 1609, Shakespeare's company, now the King's Men, also performed in an indoor (or private) theatre, the Blackfriars. Shakespeare's company and the rival companies managed by Philip Henslowe at the Rose and Swan were, in effect, 'the London duopoly' which offered London dramatic performances in the 1590s.[5] Performance in London was strictly regulated; no performances were allowed on Sundays and Holy Days, nor in Lent, nor when plague deaths rose above about thirty in a week. Despite what seem pretty firm restrictions, there are uncertainties. Thus, as Leeds Barroll has shown, restrictions to playing in Lent were not always strictly observed.[6] Barroll gives the plague deaths from 1603 (30,360 – about 15 per cent of London's population) to 1609[7] and is able to calculate when the London theatres were closed down. Understandably, with such dreadful figures in what Dekker called in a pamphlet of that name, 'The Wonderful Year', the theatres were closed for most of 1603, also for the last half of 1607, much of 1608, all 1609, and several months of 1610.[8] Plague was bad in London in the 1590s; in 1593 there were some 15,000 deaths. Companies, especially Shakespeare's, also performed at Court before Queen Elizabeth and King James. One seemingly obvious recourse London companies might have if their playing were restricted in London was to tour the provinces, but this was not quite so simple as it might seem. First, touring for a London-based company presented logistical problems, something evident to this day. Secondly, restrictions against playing in Lent and on Sundays applied generally. Thirdly, plague did not confine itself to London's boundaries, and provincial authorities were concerned that travellers might bring plague with them. Thus, when Shakespeare's company visited Marlborough in 1608 – a plague year in London – there are many payments in the town's records for the alleviation of sickness, presumably the plague. In 1610, when Queen Anne's Players visited the town, Marlborough again made many payments to alleviate sickness. There were also payments to whip away wandering men and women, and to such an extent that a penny was spent on the provision of new whipcords.[9] Nevertheless, from 1594 until Shakespeare's death, the Chamberlain's/King's Men seem to have visited on average about two places a year. They only visited three or more places in 1597 (6), 1603 (6, plus a court performance at Wilton for which they were paid a special and generous fee),[10] 1605 (3), 1606 (5), 1607 (3), 1610 (5) and 1613 (5).[11]

Because so much of the drama that has come down to us, especially that which we still perform, read and study, has its origins in the London 'duopoly' (all Shakespeare's plays, for example), it must seem (as it still does for some people today) that theatrical activity was centred on London, especially as London, with a population of, perhaps, 200,000 in 1603, was so much bigger than anywhere else in England. The next biggest cities were Norwich, with populations of 15,000; Bristol with 10,000; York with 11,000; Exeter with 9,000 and Salisbury with 7,000. Marlborough, to which I shall refer later, and which, paradoxically, was visited by more companies of players between 1594 and 1622 than Bristol, probably only had a population of about 1,500.[12] The wages in the provinces were much less than those in London. Thus, wages in Wiltshire in 1655, after high inflation and a civil war, had still not reached what was paid in London in 1589.[13] Yet, despite the small populations of the towns they could visit, and the impoverished nature of many of those living there, there was considerable dramatic activity. Not only did the London-based companies visit from time to time (just as today the Royal Shakespeare Company might occasionally visit Newcastle upon Tyne), but there was a host of other licensed dramatic companies crisscrossing the country, as well as individual entertainers such as rope-dancers and musicians, not to mention unlicensed vagrant performers. The distinction between licensed and unlicensed troupes or individuals is important. To be legal, companies had to have a powerful patron, such as the monarch, or the Lord Chamberlain, or the Earl of Pembroke, at whose estate at Wilton in Wiltshire Shakespeare's company performed before James I in 1603. Many of these provincial companies never played in London. A good example, partly because I shall refer specifically to dramatic activity in Marlborough later, is the the Earl of Hertford's Men (or Players). Hertford (Sir Edward Seymour) had estates in and around Marlborough (as did Pembroke) and in Hampshire. The company bearing his name seems to have come into being in the spring of 1582, performing at Canterbury. Performances in some dozen other locations up to 1606 have been noted, three in Marlborough, and they may have taken part in a great festivity for Queen Elizabeth at Seymour's Hampshire estate, Elvetham, in 1591. That led to their appearance at Court on 6 January (Twelfth Night) 1592. They never performed at a London theatre. However, they may have a particular distinction to fame. It has been rather charmingly suggested that Bottom's 'rude mechanicals' may have been modelled on Hertford's provincial players, although this is nowadays rarely supported.[14]

The size of touring companies is a matter of dispute. David Bradley argues persuasively for rather large touring companies challenging what he describes as 'probably an unshakeable myth of theatrical history' that company size was reduced for touring.[15] John Wasson has shown that the average size of companies visiting the Clifford household was eleven, varying from five in 1596 to nineteen in 1609. He also shows that the size of companies for which no patron was recorded grew on average over the years from six in 1594 to a dozen in 1627, with thirteen in 1620 and 1626.[16] G. E. Bentley lists touring companies of fourteen in 1611 and 1612; fifteen in 1619 and 1635; sixteen in 1612; and twenty in 1619 and 1624.[17] Looking back a little, we know that in 1591–92, the Admiral's and Strange's combined company (which included five of those who would become sharers in the Lord Chamberlain's company) petitioned to return from tour early because they found the cost of touring intolerable.[18] In 1593, Pembroke's Men were 'feign' to sell their apparel because they could not meet the cost of their tour.[19] The size of a company was of some economic significance, especially in the 1590s.

Touring has always been hard and often unprofitable. It is hard for us, used to fast transport and full of complaints when trains and planes are held up and motorways jammed, to appreciate just how hard was travel even in the early days of the railways. My great-grandfather, Frederick Hobley, had to travel from Thame in Oxfordshire to Narbeth in South Wales for his first teaching appointment in January 1852. He writes in his reminiscences that he travelled from Thame to Oxford by carrier's wagon, stayed overnight there with a friend, then continued by Great Western train to Bristol. Here he took a ship to Tenby and then another carrier's wagon to Narbeth. It took him three days. On his return, the railway had been opened to Swansea, so he again took a wagon to Tenby; then a stagecoach for the 51 miles to Swansea. That was pulled by four horses and these were changed no less than eight times – so it took 32 horses to pull them that short distance. When they arrived at Didcot, it was 2 a.m. and there was nowhere to stay, so he and a friend walked through the night for six hours to get home for breakfast. How much more difficult was it for touring actors in Shakespeare's day? Ben Jonson said that they 'walked with their shoes full of gravel ... after a blind jade and a hamper' to 'stalk upon boards and barrel heads'.[20] At the end of their journey they might find they had no audience, no money, nothing to eat, and not even a candle by which to learn their lines for the play they had to perform the next day, as this account of the actor Munden suggests when he began his career in the 1780s:

On the night of his arrival at Leatherhead, Mr. Munden expected to perform; but, visiting the theatre, or rather the barn, how great was his surprise to find not a scene raised, nor a bench formed.... The following night was appointed for a performance. The rehearsal over, and the barn-yard cleared, planks were laid and saw-dust strewed for expected company; but in vain was the night appointed; in vain the rehearsal; in vain the barn-yard cleared, and the sawdust was strewed, to preserve the tender feet of red-cloked damsels, and rustic swains. No swain, no damsels came; all was solitary, and manager and mate went comfortless to bed.... The two following nights were equally unsuccessful. A play was at length bespoke, by a gentleman of the neighbourhood, for the Saturday night, which, being a night of fashion, an audience assembled, and the profits of the evening, allowed to each performer, amounted to six shillings, and two small pieces of candle! This was the first money our hero ever gained by acting.[21]

Munden went on to play at the Theatre Royal, Covent Garden, but his early experience, though two hundred years later than Shakespeare's, was undoubtedly that of the minor, 'runabout scouring troops' of Shakespeare's time which Tate Wilkinson described. One such was an unlicensed company run by Richard Hudson of Hutton Buscel and Edward Lister of Allerton, both properly weavers (as was Bottom), not actors, who with three other men and four children played in thirty-two farms and yeomen's houses on the Yorkshire Moors between 29 December 1615 and 18 February 1616. At a trial at Thirsk, Hudson was sentenced to be whipped and all those who had patronized them and supplied food were each fined ten shillings. What was remarkable about this tour was that this little company trudged some 150 miles across the North Yorkshire Moors in the depths of winter. Another small Yorkshire company, also unlicensed, under Christopher Simpson, performed Roman Catholic plays to yeoman and gentry of that faith.[22] They were eventually charged under the vagrancy laws and each fined ten shillings. Further south, a company of six run by Richard Bradshaw ended in Banbury jail in 1633. They had a false commission which purported to allow them to act and they had got away with this at Leicester, Market Bosworth, Stanton, Solihull, Meriden, and at Sir Thomas Lucy's house at Stratford-upon-Avon.[23] The Lucy estate was where, by tradition, Shakespeare was caught poaching.

It will be apparent from these accounts that the mode of travel was walking. Indeed, the word 'stroller' is first recorded in the *Oxford English Dictionary* in Dekker's *Lanthorne and Candle-light* (1608), meaning 'a proper name given to Country-players, that . . . trot from town to town on the hard hoof'. A little earlier, in his *Newes from Hell* (1606), Dekker writes of a 'Companie of country players, being nine in number, one sharer & the rest Iorneymen that with strowling were brought to deaths door.'[24] This vividly reveals the harshness of a strolling actor's life, but also is one of a number of indications of company size. Even a company as small as Bradshaw's would need a horse and wagon to transport props and costumes. That Bradshaw was so equipped is indicated by the evidence of one of his company, a lad called Drewe Turner. He said he had been with the company for twelve months but, anxious to limit his part in this illegal action, maintained he did 'nothing but drive the horse and beat the drum'.[25] Queen Elizabeth's favourite clown, Richard Tarlton, has accredited to him a book of jests. These are probably apocryphal, but like the realistic backing to a fictional film, the setting may well be more reliable than the stories themselves. Tarlton tells of the Queen's Players arriving at a gentleman's house and of their wagon being unloaded of the apparel it was carrying.[26] The richer actors might be able to afford a horse. We know that Edward Alleyn, son-in-law to Philip Henslowe, the proprietor of the Rose and Swan Theatres, did travel by horse. He sent it back from Bristol for Henslowe to sell at Smithfield in 1593.[27] However, as the Marlborough and Bath records show, it cost 9d to hire a horse for a journey of ten miles (return) and 1s for a day; and horses had also to be fed.[28] This was more than an actor was paid in a week. Henslowe's *Diary* shows that on 17 July 1597 he agreed to pay Thomas Hearne 5s a week for his first year and 6s 8d a week for his second. On 8 December, William Kendall was hired for two years at 10s a week in London and 5s a week in the country 'euerie week of his playing'; that suggests he was only paid when he acted and that in the country he may have been fed as an addition to his lesser pay (a common practice for tradespeople).[29]

The company with which Shakespeare acted was as superior in the realm of theatre as Bradshaw's and the North Yorkshire companies were inferior. Nevertheless, they faced similar problems. They needed a licence to perform – and that they had; they needed venues in which to play if they were on tour; they had to get from place to place; they needed audiences; and probably they needed additional financial support, either from the town authorities where they played – a 'reward' as it was often called – or from a wealthy individual. I should like in the concluding part of this chapter to consider how the Lord Chamberlain's men may have managed their tour of 1597, a tour necessitated by the forced closing of the London theatres from 28 July 1597 because of a scandal evoked by a performance of a play by Thomas Nashe, performed by a rival company at the Swan, called *The Isle of Dogs*. What precisely was the seditious and slanderous matter it contained we do not know and the play has not survived, but, quite unexpectedly, the Lord Chamberlain's Men found they no longer were allowed to perform in London. Three means of earning money were open to them: they could sell props and costumes as Pembroke's Men were 'feign' to do in 1593 because they could not meet the costs of touring;[30] they could sell their playbooks, and the Chamberlain's Men sold *Richard II* to the printer, Andrew Wise (entered by him in the Register of the Stationers' Company on 29 August 1597); or they could tour.

We know from town records that the Chamberlain's Men visited Faversham, Rye, Dover, Bristol, Bath and Marlborough in 1597 and we know the amounts they were paid as 'rewards', sums totalling £5 3s for playing to the leading citizens. What we do not know exactly is the order in which these towns were visited nor precisely how they got from place to place, nor what plays they presented, nor what they earned from further performances; and we do not know how many actors and supporting theatre people (for example, the bookkeeper, stage-hands, 'gatherers' and musicians) went with them. The Chamberlain's Men, when performing at the Globe and Blackfriars, probably had at least as many supporting staff and musicians as adult actors (boys were apprentices, and not paid by the company but by the actor to whom they were apprenticed).[31] A tour might economize on actors (by increased doubling of parts) and on supporting staff (by having actors help out). What follows attempts to answers these questions with reference to this particular tour. It cannot be stressed too strongly that it is conjectural and only outlines the issues.[32] It is important to note that this evidence is from takings at the Rose Theatre, a rival house to that where Shakespeare's company (which was organized on a sharing basis) performed. The London theatres were closed down on 28 July 1597. The Rye records show that the Chamberlain's Men played there before 27 August and they presumably played at Faversham on the way to Rye. They had also played at Faversham in 1596 and some printed accounts confuse these two visits.[33] They seem to have been in Dover on about 3 September and in Bristol between 11 and 17 September. When they visited Bath and Marlborough is not recorded. Pembroke's Men played at Bristol a week or so before the Chamberlain's Men and were back in London playing *The Spanish Tragedy* at the Rose on 11 October.[34] The Chamberlain's Men must have been back about this time because they sold *Richard III* to Andrew Wise and he entered it in the Stationers' Register as his 'copyright' on 20 October. It would seem, therefore, that the Lord Chamberlain's Men were out of London for about eleven weeks. In that time they would have had to walk some 350–475 miles, depending on their route, and give enough performances to sustain themselves.

One problem with town records is that they are usually fair copies made at the end of the year for audit, and we cannot be certain that what is recorded is in chronological order. The following extracts from the Marlborough records for 1597 will indicate the nature of the evidence to which I shall refer later. There were 37 payments in 1597 totalling £59 3s 11d. The entries have been modernized and expanded and the number of the entry is given first.

1.	Schoolmaster [of free grammar school, founded 1550]	£13	6s 8d
2.	for the Almsfolk	£1	4s 0d
14.	wine for the Lord Chief Justice [probably a gallon]		3s 4d
15.	wine for the Justices in Whitsun week		3s 8d
16.	for the setting forth of soldiers	£3	4s 7d
19.	Lord Chamberlain's Men		6s 4d
20.	Diet for Lord Chief Justice [Sir John Popham], Michaelmas Sessions	£6	7s 9d

22.	for the gibbet	10s 7d
27.	for sugar loaf for my Lord of Hertford	16s 0d
28.	for sugar loaf for my Lord of Hertford and others	£1 16s 5d

It will be obvious that the amount allowed for the Chamberlain's Men, which would scarcely pay one actor for a week, was in sharp contrast to the amounts allowed for the Lord Chief Justice or for sugar (literally 'a sweetener') for the local lord, who lived at Tottenham Lodge in the Savernake Forest, about two miles east of Marlborough. Although the entry for the players is next to that for the Michaelmas Sessions (Michaelmas Day is 26 September), it cannot be certain that the company was present at the time of the Sessions, at which at least one of the accused was sentenced to be hanged. However, that time fits conveniently later than the visit to Bristol between 11 and 17 September. It is not beyond belief that the company actually played before the Lord Chief Justice and the Earl of Hertford, but of that more later. It will also be apparent that the sum paid the schoolmaster is about half what a master carpenter could earn *in London* (if he worked throughout the year), but the schoolmaster almost certainly lived at the school, costs were lower in Wiltshire, and he may have had other privileges. His pay is given as a single annual amount and placed first in the accounts. He might have been paid for the year when it started in the autumn of 1596 (the year ran from Michaelmas to Michaelmas), or his pay might have been staggered, even though the total was given as a lump sum. We simply, as with so much, do not know.

What is puzzling is why so many companies visited Marlborough, for they were not generously treated and the town council was Puritan-inclined. The 6s 4d of 1597 was more than their 2s 8d in 1594, the lowest sum paid to any company of actors by Marlborough. For that reward they would be expected to give a special performance for the mayor (or bailiff) and the counsellors and would then be allowed to give performances for the general public. The Earl of Hertford's Men received 15s in 1592, but they were the local lord's company. From 1598 rather larger sums were often paid, the most being 23s 4d for the King's Players (as Shakespeare's company had been renamed) in 1606. Compared to other towns, Marlborough was frankly stingy, yet

between 1590 and 1622, 43 companies of actors visited Marlborough; 41 visited Bath (not then a large city) between 1592 and
1617, and the same number visited Bristol between 1593 and
1634. It was often thought that companies visited these three
towns because they were on the main road west, but this is not
so. Only Shakespeare's company in 1597 and the Queen's Players
in 1598 visited all three towns. Only seven companies visited both
Bath and Bristol, a mere eleven miles apart, in the same year, and
only twice were Marlborough and Bristol visited in the same
years, 1613 and 1621, by the Lady Elizabeth's Players.[35]

From Henslowe's accounts it is possible to glean some idea of
what Henslowe's company at the Rose earned. For example, for
25 performances given in the seven weeks from 26 January to 14
March 1597, £155 0s 11d (£22 3s a week) was taken; of this, £122
2s 11d would go to the players, or £17 9s a week, and the balance
to Henslowe, the theatre owner. By counting the pennies taken at
the door (which Henslowe enters separately), we can tell that
audiences averaged 870.[36] The size of that company has been
calculated by David Bradley as comprising 16 adult actors;[37] to
these would be added boys (who would not be a drain on the
receipts) and support staff. It will be apparent that, roughly
speaking, a little over £1 per week per adult actor would be
necessary to sustain a company (though the actor might get
only half or even less than that) and, as the theatre and company
continued in existence, they must have been profitable. This
tallies with what William Ingram has calculated that a company
of six required to survive on tour: 10–14s per day.[38] The amount
per actor was about the top rate allowed by the Proclamation of
1589 for a master carpenter: 9s a week. Watermen, comically
featured in *Shakespeare in Love* (1998), received only 3s a week,
or 1s if they were fed. If these figures could be applied to the rival
Chamberlain's company, they would receive all the takings –
£155 0s 11d or £22 3s a week – plus the £5 3s in rewards received
from the towns visited, but they would have to pay all the
expenses that Henslowe paid for his companies at the Rose out
of his share of the takings. Touring was (and is) expensive, so it
might be appropriate to calculate on the portion Henslowe took
as roughly equivalent to touring costs, and work on the basis of
the London average audience of 870 for 25 performances in
seven weeks producing £122 2s 11d for the company. Over an

11-week period that would require taking £192 and giving 39 performances with average audiences of 870, and that assumes London prices could be demanded in the provinces. There are various implications of these conjectural calculations. The first is the impossibility of drawing audiences of that size in places like Rye and Marlborough; the second is the impracticability of walking some 350–475 miles at up to 20 miles a day and giving so many performances, bearing in mind that on Sundays performances were not permitted. The first likelihood is that a smaller company toured, despite David Bradley's contention that it is a myth of theatrical history that company size was reduced for touring. In fact, in the twentieth century, company size is often reduced for touring.[39] If the Chamberlain's Men reduced for touring to a ten-cast company, they would need to take £120, not £192, over the 11 weeks. This would reduce the number of performances they would have to give or, alternatively, reduce the average sizes of the audiences required. We do not know what plays the company took on tour, but I believe, from an examination of the 1597 text of *Richard III*, and the fact that it was sold to Andrew Wise immediately on the company's return to London, that that was one of the plays. Further, I have argued – and it can be no more than an argument – that that text of the play has been modified for performance by ten men and two boys.[40] This tallies fairly well with David George's findings that 'There is much evidence that 10 is about the right number' for companies visiting Gawthorpe Manor (see below).[41]

It is now time to return to the puzzle why so many companies visited Marlborough for such little recompense. Did they perform at private houses as well as in towns? Considerable work has been done on visits to private houses by acting companies. Evidence for this at the bottom end of the scale has been given earlier. In 1959 Lawrence Stone produced evidence from household accounts of actors entertained by the Earl of Cumberland and Lord Clifford; in the 1850s the house and farm accounts of the Shuttleworth family in Lancashire revealed details of such visits. As well as minor local companies, better-known companies – Derby's, Dudley's, Mounteagle's, Stafford's, and the Queen's Players – performed for the Shuttleworths at Gawthorpe Manor between 1608 and 1619 for fairly small sums of money and their keep. These companies were probably associated at this time, directly or indirectly, with Sir William Stanley, sixth Earl of Derby, and his estates at Knowsley and Lathom House, some thirty miles from Gawthorpe Manor.[42] We know that the Chamberlain's Men played *Titus Andronicus* before Sir John Harington (Queen Elizabeth's godson and the inventor of the water-closet) at Burley-on-the-Hill in Rutland in 1596.[43] Thus, the record of visits to provincial towns in this period (which is fairly readily recoverable) tells only part of the story. Close by Marlborough lay the estate of the Earl of Hertford and at Wilton, 30 miles to the south, the Pembrokes had, and still have, their estate. As mentioned earlier, both gave their patronage to acting companies. We know that Shakespeare's company visited Wilton in 1603 to perform before King James I. Is it not likely that one of the reasons for visits to Marlborough was the possibility of playing (and being entertained) by Hertford and the Pembrokes? Unfortunately the household accounts of these families no longer exist for this period, so it is not possible to provide evidence for what must be a guess. The gifts of sugar loaves to Hertford suggest he was in the vicinity at that time, though one cannot be dogmatic about that. What may provide indirect support to this supposition, however, is the date when acting companies ceased to visit Marlborough: 1622. In the preceding year, both the Countess of Pembroke, a great patron of the arts and especially of drama (she translated from the French Robert Garnier's *The Tragedie of Antonie*, 1595), and the Earl of Hertford died. Marlborough's Puritan predilictions could then freely come to the fore and those frowned on actors and drama. In the Civil War the town was staunchly for Parliament and was twice sacked; in reprisal, Parliamentary forces destroyed Hertford's house. When the town burnt down in 1653, to mark its support, Cromwell raised the money for its rebuilding.

Another conjecture might be advanced on the basis of the Marlborough records. It certainly looks as if Lord Chief Justice Popham, who lived ten miles from Marlborough at Littlecote (the house still stands), was conducting the Sessions at the time of Shakespeare's company's visit. At about this time Shakespeare was writing the second part of *Henry IV*. This features a Lord Chief Justice. Did Popham's character play a part in this? John Aubrey was not a wholly reliable gossip, but in his *Brief Lives* he says that, like Prince Hal, Popham led a wild youth, enjoyed 'profligate company, and was wont to take a purse with them'. He, like Hal, underwent a sudden conversion.[44] Might not the better-informed members of the audience of *Henry IV Part II* appreciate this allusion?

As more work is being done on provincial drama by individual scholars, and especially by the magnificent series, the Records of Early English Drama (REED), published by the University of Toronto, the richness, the variety and the uncertainties of the actors' struggle to make a living around four hundred years ago is gradually being revealed. What is certain is that, as today, there were hierarchies of companies. There were those like the RSC – Shakespeare's company and that in which Edward Alleyn performed for Henslowe; there are those today as excited by drama and as short of funds as Bradshaw's and Hudson and Lester's little companies, such as Third Party Productions, which brilliantly realized *Richard III* in 1994 with just six dedicated actors. Although it is dangerous to extrapolate from the present to explain the past, as I have been guilty of doing, one can argue that the history of touring drama has a continuous seam.

SOURCES

The endnotes will direct readers to a number of articles from which valuable information can be gleaned about touring in the Elizabethan period. The most substantial corpus of information is to be found in the Records of Early English Drama (REED) published by the University of Toronto Press. So far these have covered six cities (York, Chester, Coventry, Newcastle upon Tyne, Norwich and Cambridge), and nine counties (Cumberland with Westmorland, Gloucestershire, Devon, Herefordshire with Worcestershire, Lancashire, Shropshire, and Somerset with Bath). It is important to appreciate that they are devoted to drama, and so what is not at first sight anything to do with drama – such as the visit of the Lord Chief Justice to Marlborough and the gifts of sugar loaves to the Earl of Hertford in the little extract printed above – are inevitably excluded. Another useful volume of this kind, published by the University of Toronto Press and Cambridge University Press is Ian Lancashire's *Dramatic Texts and Records of Britain: A Chronological Topography to 1558* (1984). Earlier volumes of records are useful but not always reliable. These include J. T. Murray, *English Dramatic Companies* 1558–1642, 2 vols (London, Constable, 1910) and E. K. Chambers, *William Shakespeare: A Study of Facts and Problems*, 2 vols (Oxford, Clarendon Press, 1930). These both incorrectly record details of the Chamberlain's 1597 tour. For example, Chambers records the reward for the Chamberlain's Men as 6s 8d, not 6s 4d, and he and Murray conflate the 1596 and 1597 visits to Faversham. Chambers also takes the Bath accounting year to end at Midsummer, not Michaelmas. However, used circumspectly they contain useful information, for example, on the fate of Bradshaw's touring company at Banbury. Tate Wilkinson's *The Wandering Patentee* (see n. 2) is a mine of information (and often very amusing).

Two books by Andrew Gurr are specially helpful: *Playgoing in Shakespeare's London* (2nd edn, Cambridge, Cambridge University Press, 1996), and *Playing Companies* (Oxford, Oxford University Press, 1995), especially chapter 3, 'Travelling Companies'. A general account, with interesting suggestions for Shakespeare's links with Marlborough, can be found in Michael Justin Davis, *The Landscape of William Shakespeare* (Exeter, Webb & Bower, 1987). Of many other books that could be mentioned, three will be found very useful: Ann Jennalie Cook, *The Privileged Playgoers of Shakespeare's London*, 1576–1642 (Princeton, Princeton University Press, 1981); G. E. Bentley, *The Profession of Player in Shakespeare's Time*, 1590–1642 (Princeton, Princeton University Press, 1984); and Leeds Barroll, *Politics, Plague, and Shakespeare's Theater: The Later Stuart Years* (Ithaca, Cornell University Press, 1991).

4. Studying Shakespeare and his Contemporaries

EMMA SMITH

The work of the Polish theatre director Jan Kott has been influential in Shakespeare studies, not least for the title of his collected essays, *Shakespeare our Contemporary*. For Kott, Shakespeare was a fellow-traveller of the mid-twentieth century, a writer who understood the political and emotional life of the modern period. Echoing Ben Jonson's famous judgement on Shakespeare as 'not of an age, but for all time', Kott identified Shakespeare's 'modern relevance' as his most enduring quality.[1] Kott's is a Shakespeare untrammeled by the specifics of his own period, an eternally relevant cultural property in which each successive generation can find its own resonances. We are all, according to this interpretation, Shakespeare's contemporaries.

Against this lavish, expansive sense of communion with Shakespeare through the ages, it may seem to diminish his aesthetic stature to argue for a more precise sense of temporal context. Putting Shakespeare back into the social, cultural and theatrical milieu of early modern London arguably imprisons him in the equivalent of doublet and hose – an antique, unfamiliar and restrictive mental and spatial costume. Shakespeare our contemporary may seem a much more approachable figure than Shakespeare the Elizabethan or Jacobean. This chapter, however, will suggest some of the often unexpected ways in which reading Shakespeare among his own contemporaries, the other playwrights of the early modern theatre, can illuminate and animate his plays. Most school and university syllabi and many scholarly studies sever Shakespeare from the literary culture of the period, or invoke comparisons only to flatter Shakespeare by contrast to the drab mediocrity of his fellows. Shakespeare's imagination tends to operate as the elusive philosopher's stone, the material credited with the powers to transmute base metal into gold, whereas the drama of his contemporaries remains, with a very few minor exceptions, resolutely leaden.

It is interesting to note, though, that the earliest commentators on Shakespeare's art do not identify him as the towering genius that posterity has constructed. Robert Greene's famous denunciation of the young playwright as 'an upstart crow, beautified with our feathers'[2] suggests he is a plagiarist, over-dependent on others' material rather than transcendent of it. For other writers better disposed to him, Shakespeare was just one playwright among a roll-call of literary notables. For example, Francis Meres's references to Shakespeare in *Palladis Tamia* are often quoted as an early, perhaps the earliest, identification of the playwright's genius, but this is true only from a highly selective reading. To be sure, Meres does describe Shakespeare as among the best writers of comedy and tragedy, but he actually lists Shakespeare some way down a list of dramatic worthies, many of whom are now unknown. Meres's catalogue of 'our best for Tragedie' reads:

the Lorde *Buckhurst*, Doctor *Leg* of Cambridge, Doctor *Edes* of Oxforde, maister *Edward Ferris*, the Author of the *Mirrour for Magistrates*, *Marlow*, *Peele*, *Watson*, *Kid*, *Shakespeare*, *Drayton*, *Chapman*, *Decker*, and *Benjamen Johnson*.

His list of comedians is similarly extensive:

So the best for Comedy amongst us bee, *Edward* Earle of Oxford, Doctor *Gager* of Oxforde, Maister *Rowley* once a rare Scholler of learned Pembrooke Hall in Cambridge, Maister *Edwardes* one of her Majesties Chappell, eloquent and wittie *John Lilly*, *Lodge*, *Gascoyne*, *Greene*, *Shakespeare*, *Thomas Nash*, *Thomas Heywood*, *Anthony Mundy* our best plotter, *Chapman*, *Porter*, *Wilson*, *Hathway*, and *Henry Chettle*.[3]

Putting Shakespeare back among these other writers, rather than conscripting him to the service of literary timelessness, can highlight what is distinctive, as well as what is generic or derivative, about his work.

It's worth remembering that playgoers of the period probably neither knew nor cared about the identity of the author of the play they were about to see. The few contemporary references to

Shakespeare's plays in performance, such as the description of the fire at the Globe theatre at a performance of *All is True* (*Henry VIII*), or John Manningham's account of seeing 'twelve Night or what you will', do not refer to their author by name, and the same is true for many early quartos of Shakespeare's plays.[4] 'Talking Shakespeare' is a kind of anachronism for the consumers of the early modern theatre. Perhaps authorship itself is an anachronistic category for the study of early modern drama,[5] where other axes of interpretation and categorization such as the playing company or theatre, topical currents, lead actor or genre seem likely to have predominated for those first audiences of sixteenth- and seventeenth-century plays. Looking at, say, Shakespeare's tragedies alongside those of Marlowe, Webster, or Marston, or at his comedies alongside those by Dekker, Greene, or Jonson, or any of the scores of plays unattributed to any, or a single, author, will give a different sense of the repertoire of playgoing experiences available in early modern London. Alternatively, smaller-scale comparisons between a Shakespeare play and a thematically, generically or structurally similar play by another author can produce a sharper sense of each.

This chapter will consider three pairs of plays – *Richard II* and the anonymous *Woodstock, The Taming of the Shrew* and John Fletcher's *The Woman's Prize, or The Tamer Tam'd* and *Hamlet* and Thomas Kyd's *The Spanish Tragedy*[6] – in order to identify a Shakespeare in dialogue with other theatrical writers on an equal basis, assuming audience knowledge of previous plays, struggling with the burden of dramatic tradition, borrowing snippets or topics, or himself providing the basis for other drama. The aim is to suggest areas for investigation rather than to develop an overarching framework. Shakespeare emerges as a man of the theatre of his own time: the theatre which sustained and stimulated his own writing career.

RICHARD II AND WOODSTOCK

Richard II begins with dissension. Bolingbroke, son of John of Gaunt, has been summoned before the king to 'make good the boist'rous late appeal' (I.i.4)[7] he has alleged against Thomas Mowbray, Duke of Norfolk. The two adversaries meet to exchange accusations of 'high treason' (27), bandying the term 'traitor' and its cognates, until Richard intervenes to establish the grounds for this dispute: 'What doth our cousin lay to Mowbray's charge?' (83). Henry Bolingbroke then fleshes out his insinuations: 'he did plot the Duke of Gloucester's death' (100), a deed for which 'blood, like sacrificing Abel's, cries / Even from the tongueless caverns of the earth / To me for justice' (104–6). Mowbray answers the charge of murder in a notable circumlocution: 'For Gloucester's death, / I slew him not, but to my own disgrace / Neglected my sworn duty in that case' (132–4). It is not clear what Mowbray is admitting, but the phrase 'sworn duty', referring to the obligations of a subject to his sovereign, may point obliquely to Richard's involvement in the death of Gloucester. Much goes unsaid in this scene, but the murder of Gloucester before the play began reverberates through *Richard II*. In Act IV, questions are still being asked at the parliament called to investigate. Bolingbroke demands of Bagot: 'What thou dost know of noble Gloucester's death, / Who wrought it with the King, and who performed / The bloody office of his timeless end' (IV.i.2–4). Later in the scene, York enters to announce Richard's agreement to abdicate in favour of Bolingbroke, so that the unresolved matter of Gloucester's murder is intertwined with the play's movement to dethrone Richard and crown Bolingbroke in his stead.

The murder of Gloucester is, then, an occluded and irretrievable event which is not part of the play but which cannot be separated from it, rather like the murder of the old king in *Hamlet*. But in its insistent stress on Richard's past conduct, the play shows itself heavily dependent on a contemporary play of unknown authorship, *Woodstock*: a play in which the murder of Gloucester takes centre stage. It seems clear both that Shakespeare knew this play, and that he expected his audience to know it, and by reanimating this dialogue with a now largely forgotten play, *Richard II* gains a further dimension.

In the second scene of Shakespeare's play as it was printed in quarto form in 1597 and 1608, John of Gaunt laments 'the part I had in Woodstocks bloud'.[8] The alternative title for the Duke of Gloucester, Woodstock, reminds audiences of the earlier play of the same name. (By the time the Folio text of the play is printed in 1623, the word Woodstock is replaced by 'Glouster', perhaps suggesting that the play of *Woodstock* is no longer remembered.) *Woodstock* was written some time between 1591 and 1594,[9] and has been described as 'the boldest and most subversive of all Elizabethan historical plays'.[10] It focuses on the early part of Richard II's reign, and events range from the period immediately preceding his first marriage in 1382 until around 1397, the date of Woodstock's death. In *Woodstock*, the king is presented as a weak and greedy ruler, swayed by his favourites into policies damaging to the populace, including increased taxation. Richard dismisses his old advisers in favour of his new court parasites, and rides roughshod over the views of Parliament. The opposition to this action is located in the figure of Thomas of Woodstock, Duke of Gloucester. Even the plays' titling is indicative: for the author of *Woodstock*, Richard's failings effectively decentre him in his own reign, whereas Shakespeare's play denotes a certain sympathy for its king by making him its titular subject, even its tragic hero.

Woodstock's eponymous hero is a man of principle who 'remains loyal to the orthodox doctrine that a tyrant must be endured as a divine visitation',[11] and his murder robs the state of self-restraint. After his death, the nobles revolt against a king who has done nothing to earn our sympathy, and against whose downfall the play seems to propose no counter-argument. Gloucester is insistently characterized as a plain-speaking, plain-dealing, plain-dressing man, introduced as 'Plain Thomas, for by th'rood so all men call him / For his plain dealing, and his simple clothing: / Let others jet in silk and gold, says he / A coat of English frieze, best pleaseth me' (I.i.99–102). The word 'plain' and its cognates reverberate through the play, as the conflict between royal folly and noble rectitude is symbolized through the moral index of dress and appearance. This has its comic apogee in a scene in which a courtier arrives at Plashey House, Woodstock's country seat, 'attired very fantastically' (II.ii.125), and mistakes its plainly-dressed master for a servant, tipping him a coin for stabling his horse. Woodstock wonders that 'this fellow that's made of all fashions should be an Englishman' (III.ii.155–6), and the play clearly identifies the quality of Englishness not with the king and his court but with the country, both as geographical and demographic locale.[12]

Although *Woodstock* might be seen to draw the sting of its criticism of Richard through its deployment of a nobleman, rather than a commoner, as its conduit, the play is radical in its representation of the people. Political discourse in *Richard II* is entirely confined to the nobility, and even the Gardener and his servant interlocutor who appear in III.iv are co-opted to this social rank through their non-naturalistic use of blank verse. *Richard II* presents a *coup d'état*, not a revolution, as two noblemen, both kinsmen of Edward III, swap positions. Apart from the news of the reception of Bolingbroke and Richard on their entry into London, when 'rude misgoverned hands from windows' tops / Threw dust and rubbish on King Richard's head' (V.ii.5–6), the play is unconcerned with the role of the commons in its representation of political turmoil. By contrast, *Woodstock* gives a voice to the iniquities suffered by the people. John of Gaunt's depiction of a debased England 'leased out...Like to a tenement or pelting farm' (*Richard II*, II.i.59–60) is presented by the author of *Woodstock* not as a rhetorical climax to a speech of royal indictment, but in terms of its effects on the people themselves. In III.iii, a Grazier, a Farmer and a Butcher, men defined by their trades and representative of their fellows, discuss the 'blank charters'. 'I smell something', notes the Grazier (III.iii.83), but they are powerless, in the climate of repression and fear, to protest. Whistling a satirical ballad, naming Tresilian (rhyming with 'villain'), Green and Bagot as the authors of the discontent, is grounds for arrest for treason. The play thus daringly incorporates and stages the absurdity of political censorship, in contrast to the silent excision of the deposition scene from the early quartos of *Richard II*. Whereas censorship is apparently acted upon Shakespeare's passive text, *Woodstock* actively presents and critiques censorship as the consequence of tyrannical rule.

As Woodstock sleeps in prison in Act V while his murderers wait in the wings, he is visited by two ghosts. The first, the ghost of the Black Prince, Woodstock's brother, urges him to escape his assassins and thus save himself and Richard: 'for pity wake! prevent thy doom! / Thy blood upon my son will surely come: / For which, dear brother Woodstock, haste and fly, / Prevent his ruin and thy tragedy' (V.i.73–6). *Woodstock* thus explicitly states what *Richard II* implies: that it is the murder of Woodstock which is the key to Richard's downfall. This is echoed by Bolingbroke in the first scene of *Richard II*, when he vows vengeance on Mowbray for Gloucester's death when it should be, and ultimately is,

Richard on whom revenge is taken. In this light, then, the plays could be seen as two halves of a dramatic diptych, a theatrical interplay of cause and effect in which the consequence of the events of *Woodstock* is displayed in *Richard II*. It is a familiar tactic to read, even to perform, history plays by Shakespeare sequentially, so that the civil wars of the *Henry IV* plays, for example, are seen as the fulfilment of the Bishop of Carlisle's grim prophecy in IV.i of *Richard II*; here it is necessary to read across the usual restraints of authorship in order to re-establish *Richard II*'s contemporary sequentiality. *Woodstock* is not merely background or source material for Shakespeare's play, but a companion piece which articulates some of the silences and absences of *Richard II*. Geoffrey Bullough, in his work on the sources of the play, includes *Woodstock* and allows it a particular prominence in the creation of *Richard II*: 'almost it seems as if [Shakespeare] were trying to avoid covering the same ground; as if, knowing *Woodstock* . . . he were assuming a similar knowledge in his audience'.[13] Bullough almost admits that the play is not integral and comprehensive, not self-identical and closed, but that it exists in a dialogue with *Woodstock*, the play inseparable from its composition and initial reception. Without *Woodstock*, *Richard II*, as it was written by the Elizabethan Shakespeare and experienced by its early audiences, is incomplete.[14]

THE TAMING OF THE SHREW AND THE WOMAN'S PRIZE, OR THE TAMER TAM'D

Perhaps the same attribute of incompleteness could be applied to *The Taming of the Shrew*: why otherwise would John Fletcher have written a sequel? Fletcher was a playwright with the King's Men who collaborated with Shakespeare on *The Two Noble Kinsmen* and *Henry VIII*, and his mock sequel to Shakespeare's early play can be seen as a further, more distant kind of collaboration. *The Woman's Prize, or the Tamer Tam'd* was written in 1611. As Ann Thompson points out, Fletcher's sequel to Shakespeare's play puts *The Taming of the Shrew* 'into its traditional context of the war between the sexes, a context in which normally, as in the stories of Boccaccio and Chaucer, a story about a husband outwitting or triumphing over his wife is capped or balanced by one in which a wife outwits her husband'.[15] The conventional dialectic of these gender arguments is recapitulated by the double structure of the two plays. At the end of *The Woman's Prize*, the epilogue proposes a truce: both sexes should be taught 'due equality; / And as they stand bound, to love mutually' (7–8):[16] between them, the two plays suggest a mean of gender relations.

That Fletcher's play is written as a self-conscious riposte *to The Taming of the Shrew* is clear. The prologue tells 'Ladies' that *The Woman's Prize* is a play where '[t]he victory's yours, though got with much ado' (4), and Shakespeare's Petruchio, now a widower, returns as Fletcher's major protagonist. The play begins with the wedding guests discussing Petruchio's second marriage and reminding the audience of his first. Tranio reveals that 'yet the bare remembrance of his first wife...Will make him start in's sleep, and very often / Cry out for Cudgels, Colstaves, any thing; / Hiding his Breeches, out of feare her Ghost / Should walk, and weare 'em yet' (I.i.30–5). This time, Petruchio's friends assert, he will be in sole charge of breeches-wearing, as his new wife, Maria, 'must do nothing of her selfe; not eate, / Drinke, say sir how do ye, make her ready, pisse, / Unlesse he bid her' (44–6). But Petruchio is in for a shock. His seemingly compliant bride has her own agenda, as she swears that 'till I have made him easie as a child, / And tame as feare; he shall not win a smile, / Or a pleased look' (I.ii.113–14). To this end, she locks Petruchio out of her chamber on their wedding night, lays in supplies for a siege and fortifies it against his invasion. Her cousin 'Colonell *Byancha*' is the 'Engineir' (I.iii.63–4) of the fortifications. 'The chamber's nothing but a meere *Ostend*,' reports Sophocles, 'in every window Pewter cannons mounted...and all the lower works lin'd sure with small shot' (I.iii.89–92).

Much critical interest in Shakespeare's *The Taming of the Shrew* has been focused around Kate's final speech in Act V, and on whether this represents capitulation, accommodation, resignation or defiance. Directors and actors have struggled to define the tone of the speech: for Sinead Cusack, who played Kate for the Royal Shakespeare Company in 1982 under the direction of Michael Bogdanov, 'there's a privately shared joke in the speech. And irony'; another RSC Kate, Fiona Shaw, directed by Jonathan Miller in 1987, interpreted it as an acceptance that '"I acknowledge the system. I don't think we can change this" – which is a terrible indictment of... patriarchy'; Charles Marowitz ended his production of the play with 'a pale and beaten Kate, now successfully brainwashed'.[17] Fletcher's interpretation of the gender politics of Shakespeare's play suggests that the ambiguity so variously interpreted by recent theatre practitioners is not only a modern critical preoccupation with textual indeterminacy, nor a reflection of twentieth-century feminism. In his recollection of *The Taming of the Shrew*, Fletcher hedges the issue about whether Kate is tamed into submission to her husband by the end of the play, thus identifying this uncertainty as a thoroughly contemporary view. Petruchio's friends remember Kate as 'a Rebel' and 'Tempest' (I.i.19–21), and the threat of her return still haunts Petruchio's sleep, suggesting that her fiery independence was not quelled by her husband and that her speech of apparent submission was only provisional. On the other hand, Maria, parleying with her new husband from her 'baracadoed' (I.iii.58) bedchamber, salutes him:

> You have been famous for a woman tamer,
> And beare the fear'd name of brave wife-breaker:
> A woman now shall take those honours off,
> And tame you;
> Nay, never look so bigge, she shall, beleeve me,
> And I am she: what thinke ye.
>
> (I.iii.268–73)

Petruchio's renown as a 'wife-breaker' suggests that he is remembered for taming Kate, although the comment on his ongoing nightmares suggest that his hold over her was not as complete as Maria supposes. In tackling Petruchio's reputation, Maria can be seen as a figure for Fletcher himself, tackling the reputation of *The Taming of the Shrew*, and of his predecessor with the King's Men, Shakespeare.

Fletcher's response to *The Taming of the Shrew* shows that there are other possibilities for gender relations in and outside marriage than those in Shakespeare's play. His character Byancha may pick up Shakespeare's Bianca, Kate's more orthodox sister whose disobedience to her husband Lucentio serves as the foil to Kate's suprising compliance: 'The more fool you for laying [money] on my duty' (V.ii.129). But Fletcher's Byancha goes far beyond this matrimonial niggle in her self-assertion. The *dramatis personae* describe her as 'Commander in chief' to her cousins, themselves dubbed 'the two masculine daughters of Petronius'. She is an active and sardonic participant in the negotiations between Maria and Petruchio, and in place of marriage she proposes an extraordinary vision of a women's utopia, couched in the idiom of classical, masculine heroism, thus reappropriating the gendered rhetoric of the Trojan wars to her own separatist purposes:

> go good Sister
> Goe home, and tell the merry Greekes that sent you,
> *Ilium* shall burn, and I, as did *Æneas*,
> Will on my back, spite of the Myrmidons,
> Carry this warlike Lady, and through Seas
> Unknown, and unbeleev'd, seek out a Land,
> Where like a race of noble *Amazons*,
> We'le root our selves, and to our endlesse glory
> Live, and despise base men.
>
> (II.ii.31–8)

Maria's behaviour to Petruchio has the immediate object of teaching him a lesson within the same terms he has operated, substituting her own dominance for his. Byancha's is a more far-reaching challenge to the ultimate circumscription of women in and by marriage, however much they might try to rearrange its inherent hierarchy. Maria is a Fletcherian heroine like Shakespeare's Beatrice in *Much Ado About Nothing*: a witty woman whose impulses are directed towards marriage and conventional comic closure. At the end of *The Woman's Prize*, Petruchio's feigned death brings the couple together (there are elements in *The Woman's Prize* of Shakespeare's *The Winter's Tale* which would also repay comparison), and their reunion is flanked by the marriage of Livia, Maria's sister, to Rowland. *The Taming of the Shrew* ends with three married couples, suggesting that there is no alternative for women but to be married. *The Woman's Prize*, however, allows for a different conclusion. It might be anticipated that Byancha's expressions of a radical gender ideology and her resistance to normative patterns of femininity and

its fulfilment in marriage would be punished by the play's conclusion, which would force her into marriage with some leftover
male in order to tidy up the ending. But no such enclosure is
proposed for Byancha, who remains outside the institution of
marriage even at the end of the play. It seems that, in his development of Shakespeare's Bianca into his own Byancha, Fletcher
has allowed for more possibilities for women than could be
incorporated in Shakespeare's play.

The gender politics of *The Taming of the Shrew* are its most
enduring interest and, rightly, the focus of critical and theatrical
attention. Fletcher's play is a vital indication of how Shakespeare's play might have looked to contemporaries, and how
the early modern stage imagined its own alternative ending to
the story of Petruchio and his wife.

HAMLET AND THE SPANISH TRAGEDY

Implicit in studies of Shakespeare alongside his contemporaries
is the question of value. Nowhere is this more obvious than in
accounts of *Hamlet* in relation to its parent genre, revenge tragedy, and in particular to the play which established the pattern,
Thomas Kyd's *The Spanish Tragedy*. Most discussions of the two
plays turn on the apparently self-evident fact 'that *Hamlet* is a
better play than *The Spanish Tragedy*': as the theatre critic Benedict
Nightingale advised, after seeing the Royal Shakespeare Company's production of *The Spanish Tragedy* in 1997, 'all contemporary directors of *Hamlet* itself should be forced to spend an
evening reading Kyd. The experience would doubtless remind
them of how much subtlety Shakespeare brought to revenge
drama'.[18] But *Hamlet* is, without doubt, a revenge play, and a
play with a complicated relationship to its dramatic predecessors.
Entered on the Stationers' Register in 1602 as 'The Revenge of
Hamlet Prince [of] Denmark',[19] the play's plot prompted A. C.
Bradley's famous faux-naïve comment:

> Suppose you were to describe the plot of *Hamlet* to a person
> quite ignorant of the play, and suppose you were careful to tell
> your hearer nothing about Hamlet's character, what impres-
> sion would your sketch make on him? Would he not exclaim:

'What a sensational story! Why, here are some eight violent deaths, not to speak of adultery, a ghost, a mad woman, and a fight in a grave! If I did not know that the play was Shakespeare's, I should have thought it must have been one of those early tragedies of blood and horror from which he is said to have redeemed the stage'?[20]

Bradley unerringly points out that *Hamlet's* plot borrows freely from a repertoire of sensational revenge tragedy tropes, and also indicates that only two elements, the characterization of Hamlet, and the knowledge that the play is by Shakespeare, lift it from this genre. The dramatic legacy of revenge tragedy, however, makes its presence felt in *Hamlet*, and not simply as the crude Grand Guignol from which Shakespeare effortlessly soars.

In Kyd's play, revenges multiply. The original revenge, for the death of Andrea, whose ghost appears at the opening of the play, is superseded and entwined with Hieronimo's revenge for his murdered son Horatio, which has its echo in the other grieving fathers Castile, the Viceroy of Portugal, and the Painter. So too for Shakespeare: Hamlet's revenging of his father is reflected and refracted through the revenges of Laertes and Fortinbras of theirs, and Hamlet is at once the subject and object of revenge. The shift of the focus from sons in Kyd to fathers in Shakespeare is distinctive. Kyd's play, at the beginning of the revenge tragedy genre, is a play which looks forward. Its momentum is towards revenge and conclusion, its concerns are for the thwarted future represented by the death of the son. Shakespeare's play, on the other hand, is staged at a point when revenge tragedy is looking a bit outdated, and is crucially characterized by retrospection: by the search for the truth about old Hamlet's death, nostalgia for the forfeited past of his reign and for the lost certainties of a previous age. The play's present is overshadowed, literally haunted, by a past which is both irretrievable and unquiet. *Hamlet's* – and Hamlet's – progress is impeded by irresolution and complication. The play's inscription of revenge is nostalgic for the ethics and aesthetics established by Kyd, and this dramatic relationship is symbolized by the inset entertainment 'The Murder of Gonzago'.

'The Murder of Gonzago' represents a fossilized, remembered dramatic past which Hamlet seeks to bring into meaningful con-

junction with his own present: 'the play's the thing, / Wherein I'll
catch the conscience of the King' (II.ii.605–6). Hamlet's deployment of the play-within-the-play immediately recalls Hieronimo's
in *The Spanish Tragedy*. In Kyd's play, Hieronimo enacts his
revenge for the murder of Horatio via a tragedy he has written,
'Soliman and Perseda', which the court is persuaded to perform
as a celebratory entertainment to mark the nuptials of Bel-
Imperia and Balthazar. Like 'The Murder of Gonzago', 'Soliman
and Perseda' strikes some as an inappropriate genre for the
occasion: 'me thinks', ventures Balthazar the bridegroom, 'a
comedy were better' (IV.i.155).[21] Through the performance of
his play, Hieronimo is able to make his enemies kill each other, in
a highly ritualized spectacle of poetic, and dramatic, justice. At
the end of the carnage, Hieronimo addresses the bewildered
court:

> Haply you think, but booteless are your thoughts:
> That this is fabulously counterfeit
> And that we do as all tragedians doe,
> To die today for fashioning our scene,
> The death of Ajax, or some Roman peer,
> And in a minute starting up again,
> Revive to please tomorrow's audience.
>
> (IV.iv.76–82)

Hieronimo gloats over his audience, in a macabre tribute to the
power of drama which plays on the frisson that acted deaths
might be real ones. As James Shapiro has written, there is 'something particularly disturbing about theatrical representations of
violence: neither the actor to be executed nor the spectators who
witness the execution can be entirely sure that the violence is not
real'.[22] Hieronimo does not merely play-act revenge, he enacts it
through his play, in a dazzling reflection on the power of a drama
still stretching its limbs out into the newly discovered physical
and imaginative space of the London playhouses. Hieronimo's
play asserts drama's potency, as 'Soliman and Perseda' forms the
self-reflexive climax of *The Spanish Tragedy*: the play ends, and has
its theatrical and effective consummation, in a play. If we compare this with Hamlet's use of the play-within-the-play, we can
see how the theatre has been derogated, debased, wrested from

the active mode into the reflective. It is no longer a medium for doing, but for representing. It is impotent. It occurs halfway through the play rather than as its conclusive climax, as in *The Spanish Tragedy*. Hamlet stage-manages 'The Murder of Gonzago' not to get revenge, but to find out whether he has the grounds to revenge. The inset play doesn't achieve anything other than to confirm something Hamlet already believed, and, in prompting Claudius to his guilty prayers, it actually inhibits Hamlet's taking of revenge, rather than furthering it.

Hieronimo loves theatre; Hamlet fears it. His speech on the player's acted passions betrays a real mistrust of theatrical insincerity:

> Is it not monstrous that this player here,
> But in a fiction, in a dream of passion,
> Could force his soul so to his own conceit
> That from her working all his visage wanned,
> Tears in his eyes, distraction in's aspect,
> A broken voice, and his whole function suiting
> With forms to his conceit? And all for nothing.
>
> (II.ii.552–8)

Hamlet is threatened by theatrical power; Hieronimo uses it triumphantly to get his revenge. Hamlet finds himself in a revenge tragedy plot with which he, like everyone else in the early modern theatre, is entirely familiar, but in which he cannot act. His soliloquy immediately after the aborted performance of 'The Murder of Gonzago' is his unconvincing attempt to inhabit the genre his play demands:

> 'Tis now the very witching time of night,
> When churchyards yawn, and hell itself breathes out
> Contagion to this world. Now could I drink hot blood,
> And do such bitter business as the day
> Would quake to look on.
>
> (III.ii.378–81)

Harold Bloom has investigated what he described as 'the anxiety of influence': the haunting sense of artistic predecessors against whom writers must differentiate themselves as a psychological imperative of imaginative writing.[23] The poet is thus 'locked in Oedipal rivalry with his castrating precursor'.[24] We could figure an anxiety of influence in the drama of this period, not as a feature of writers but a feature of texts. It isn't the case that Shakespeare was overshadowed or haunted by Kyd, but it could be seen that *Hamlet* is haunted and overshadowed by *The Spanish Tragedy*. Perhaps this makes a different sense of *Hamlet*'s anxious inscription of paternity: instead of the commonplace reading of the Oedipal psychology of the play's representation of Hamlet, his parents and his stepfather/uncle, we could read an Oedipal textuality, in its representation of *Hamlet* in relation to its parent genre, revenge, and in particular, that old man of the theatre, *The Spanish Tragedy*, which, like Hamlet's own father, is dead but won't lie down.[25]

Shakespeare's contemporaries shaped his work and its early modern theatrical context in ways which our reverence for the distinct, distinctive genius of Shakespeare has elided. If, as Kott stated, Shakespeare is our contemporary, we have to acknowledge that they were there first.

5. Shakespeare and History

DERMOT CAVANAGH

Colonization of American Indians, vagrancy, the Elizabethan conquest of Ireland, witchcraft, topography, same-sex desire: what has contemporary criticism done to traditional conceptions of Shakespeare's historical concerns? Any consensus over the substance of and rationale for his imaginative engagement with history has long dissipated. Of course, Shakespeare has always been considered a writer *of* history, but, increasingly, his works have been seen as always historical in representing cultural practices far beyond the primary sources included in modern editions. Even if limited to the 'history plays', any casual survey of recent monographs and articles would find these texts depicted as addressing a range of political and social topics apparently remote from their immediate concerns. The 'return to history' in critical thinking has increased both the amount of material to be considered as providing Shakespeare with sources, and also extended its range, promoting an understanding of 'history itself as the commonplace book of Renaissance drama'.[1]

There is a deeper and more substantial issue here in distinguishing 'traditional' from 'new' analyses of historical context. Perceiving Shakespeare's poetry and plays 'as part of a culture and as expressing that culture in the way that a historical document reveals forms of life'[2] is not a new way of deciphering their implications. Earlier interpretations of Shakespeare's works often acknowledged how rooted his texts are in both general and specific contexts of ideas and events and how they articulated the political norms and moral values of early modern society (as well as more universal concerns). As Douglas Bruster has argued, the proclamation of a 'new historicism' has obscured 'the long tradition of topical and occasionalist readings of Renaissance plays...a conviction about the importance of the real to the drama of the early modern era'.[3] Yet, since the 1980s, Shakespeare's writing has been perceived as not only concerned with history or conditioned by it, but as a contribution to its *making*: it is this understanding that explains the diversity and significance of the cultural processes that are now felt to be coterminous with his work. In this chapter, the new significance attributed to context as a factor in the interpretation of Shakespeare's works will be analysed, especially in relation to the history plays. To evaluate this, a scene from *Richard II* will be discussed to examine just how far such approaches have succeeded in identifying the political implications of these texts.

This new emphasis upon the reciprocal relationship between Shakespeare's texts and history has led contemporary critics to stress how early modern writing and drama worked to *produce* the culture in which they originated, a view arising from the premise that

> Literature is *part* of history, the literary text as much a context for other aspects of cultural and material life as they are for it. Rather than erasing the problem of textuality, one must enlarge it in order to see that *both* social and literary texts are opaque, self-divided, and porous, that is, open to the mutual intertextual influences of one another. This move means according literature real power. Rather than passively reflecting an external reality, literature is an agent in constructing a culture's sense of reality.[4]

Thus, Shakespeare's works help constitute, rather than simply express, conceptions of sexual, national and racial difference; they grant (or deny) legitimacy to forms of political or religious authority and establish norms of justice and injustice. Moreover, critical interpretation of Shakespeare is perceived as equally subject to material social conditions and, therefore, as equally value-laden. Recent historicist approaches are marked by a new awareness of their own historical location and the political influences which mediate their understanding of early modern culture. As Stephen Greenblatt has helped to clarify:

> My own critical practice and that of many others associated with new historicism was decisively shaped by the American 1960s and early 1970s, and especially by the opposition to the Viet Nam War. Writing that was not engaged, that withheld judgments, that failed to connect the present with the past

seemed worthless. Such connection could be made either by analogy or causality; that is, a particular set of historical circumstances could be represented in such a way as to bring out homologies with aspects of the present or, alternatively, those circumstances could be analyzed as the generative forces that led to the modern condition.[5]

Shakespeare's works can thus be seen as an especially significant instance of imaginative writing which provides 'a context for' the present. Their extraordinary history of dissemination allows these texts to be investigated as a source which has helped ratify subsequent social norms and cultural values.

One way of beginning to evaluate new historical approaches is to perceive them as charting a new relationship between texts and *ideology*. For many critics, the latter term is understood as any social practices which construct the relationship between members of a society and their conditions of existence; often this implies the formation of a kind of false consciousness which germinates from and is sustained by the interests of a dominant class. The new agency discerned in Shakespeare's relationship to history turns on the ideological composition of his work and the influence it is deemed to exert upon existing conditions: its role in forming beliefs, naturalizing (or challenging) power-relations and legitimizing (or discrediting) the opposing forces involved in social conflicts. It is this issue which organizes critical consideration of Shakespeare's relationship to the variety of cultural issues which are being discerned as significant for his context and for ours. Such an approach has had important, and symptomatic, consequences for the interpretation of Shakespeare's plays which use history by drawing on sources concerned with the past. As new historical criticism frequently points out, earlier understanding of this genre tended to view its interest in the past as expressive of an assumed political consensus underpinning Elizabethan society: 'a conservative ideology of obedience, duty and deference to social and political hierarchy'.[6] Shakespeare's plays, along with their 'sources' in Hall and Holinshed, were seen to instil a patriotic attachment to English history as a royal, aristocratic and male spectacle, and to view threats against constituted authority in providential terms as a catastrophe for the disobedient and rebellious.

Contemporary discussion of the ideological import of Shakespeare's history plays has acknowledged that their political intentions and effects are far more complex than this. A broader sense of cultural context has ascertained the importance of conflicting interpretations of history and of opposing political ideas; such approaches recognize the ability of the stage to enact 'ideological contestation as much as it mirrored or reproduced anything that one could call the dominant ideology of a single class, class faction, or sex'.[7] One mode of analysis would perceive Elizabethan theatricality itself as a medium of great critical potential in offering a socially variegated audience an opportunity to judge the sphere of public action: 'The drama gives people images to think with, and thus reinforces confidence in their own ability to understand and discuss conflicts of state.'[8] If Shakespeare's plays are seen to contribute to history by inviting specific forms of perception, they do not necessarily reconcile an audience to dominant political norms. The history plays, in particular, have been seen to inculcate a practical awareness of the force and fraud intrinsic to the political process and of the constructed nature of social authority. In an influential appraisal of *Richard II*, for example, David Scott Kastan has argued that the 'history plays inevitably, if unconsciously, weakened the structure of authority: on stage the king became a subject – the subject of the author's imaginings and the subject of the attention and judgement of an audience of subjects'.[9] Kastan interprets the office of monarchy as being demystified by the play, exposing 'rule as role' and presenting kingship as a theatrical category, rather than an essential one: 'power passes to him who can best control and manipulate the visual and verbal symbols of authority'.[10] Other critics have explored the historical context of the plays as illuminating, retrospectively, the contradictions and ideological pressure intrinsic to their composition. In Dollimore and Sinfield's analysis of *Henry V*, the play is interpreted as bearing the marks of historical conflict: 'the play is fascinating precisely to the extent that it is implicated in and can be read to disclose both the struggles of its own historical moment and their ideological representation'.[11] To achieve its image of social unity, the play represents the marginalization of forces that run counter to monarchical design in a 'powerful Elizabethan fantasy' where all opposition to order is appeased. The existence of regional and national divisions, dynastic antagonisms, and the memory of regicide are evoked, only to be effectively controlled; any anxieties concerning internal political threats are displaced on to demonized foreign forces. Even the presence of such disturbing potentialities demonstrates, however, that real historical conflicts do exist and are quelled only through struggle. Critical awareness of the play's political context, therefore, reveals that the ideological coherence of its 'imaginary resolution' is only achieved in a precarious manner.

There are, then, many valuable analyses of how either the political realism of Shakespeare's history plays, or a 'contextual' reading of their ideological significance, are potentially disruptive of a 'false consciousness' fostered in early modern culture and perpetuated in long-enduring traditions of performance and interpretation. However, there is a much more powerful consensus, especially within the critical tradition termed 'new historicism', which insists that Shakespeare's history plays were (and *are*) essentially conservative forms of expression and that their 'theatrical production served to confirm the structure of human experience as proclaimed by those in authority'.[12] From this perspective, Shakespeare's history plays commemorate English heroes and traitors, idealize important components of the national temperament and traduce opposing nationalities; they celebrate the masculine vigour of chivalric kingship and the loyal service it should command and endorse the need for strict social discipline over unruly subjects. Often, such readings are predicated upon a thesis of power derived from Foucault, which discerns how a social order reproduces itself and secures subjection 'by producing and containing its own controlled subversion'.[13] In this view, whatever critical insights do emerge into the realities of a turbulent political process, either during their original performance or to critical hindsight, their ultimate effect is to convince an audience, perhaps more powerfully, of the necessity for hierarchical social order. This critical tradition analyses the inventive role of the plays in disseminating a social orthodoxy of rank, nation and gender through historical example.

Perhaps the most penetrating recent account of the ideological conservatism of Shakespeare's history plays is that provided in Richard Helgerson's essay 'Staging Exclusion'.[14] This account interprets the plays as a symptom of Shakespeare's desire to establish a more socially refined 'author's theatre' and as complicit with a much broader political animus towards the populace. For Helgerson, the history plays are a symbolic articulation of early modern exclusionism: a gathering intolerance among the elite for popular culture. The dramatic strategies of the plays work 'to efface, alienate, even demonize all signs of commoner participation in the political nation'.[15] In contrast to this (and, indeed, to Shakespeare's earlier practice), the history plays composed by the Henslowe dramatists are everywhere alive to the experiences and dilemmas of subjects; they display a much more inclusive conception of the commonwealth and emphasize the necessity for reciprocal social relations. Shakespeare's plays reinforce distinctions between social ranks and are preoccupied with the consolidation and maintenance of royal power: 'an infatuation that is often shadowed but never overcome by moral disapproval'.[16]

Helgerson's analysis draws much of its power from redressing the deficient critical attention paid to alternative forms of historical theatre. However, an initial reservation concerns the counter-intuitive attribution to Shakespeare of a snobbish disdain for the theatre to which he committed his professional life. More substantially, the opposition drawn between an 'inclusionary' and 'exclusionary' theatre needs more careful scrutiny. Many of the Henslowe dramas do include popular attitudes and experiences, but not in a positive or progressive manner; Andrew Gurr, for example, argues that 'the whole Henslowe repertoire was mainly inspired by its citizen and conservative allegiance'.[17] In addition, ascribing to Shakespeare a calculated exclusion of the populace from his works ignores that this is often foregrounded as an enterprise which raises questions over the construction and defence of the social order. Another problem with Helgerson's approach is not untypical of much new historicist practice in offering an abbreviated analysis of the plays. A more sustained account of complete dramatic compositions might lead to less assured convictions about their ideological effects. As James R. Siemon reminds us, part of the power of Shakespeare's writing lies in its iconoclastic commitment to 'an art that insistently surprises and frustrates by its incongruity of elements and violation of premises'.[18] In this respect, *Julius Caesar* is interpreted suggestively by Siemon as sharing the ambition of its source in

Plutarch to 'create the *effect* of history by the way in which the
text repeatedly interrupts its progress and violates its nascent
patterns with reminders of…gaps and discrepancies, discord
and disagreement, confronting one with the necessary burden
of interpretation'.[19]

One way of interpreting the history plays is to argue that they
inquire into the political premises upon which their narratives
are founded – premises which may still inform the society surrounding their production – and that this impulse is often overlooked in summaries of their uniform ideological direction. To
demonstrate this, the example of the 'garden scene' in *Richard II*
helps to indicate how the historical process represented in Shakespeare's plays is mediated through a play of shifting perspectives
which encourage critical reflection; the scene is also useful in
displaying the ambivalence which attends the exclusion of subordinate groups from political involvement.

In the 'garden scene' the play deviates from its depiction of the
political struggle between the king and elements of his nobility. At
the outset, the queen is seeking diversion from the crisis which
has overwhelmed the court: Richard's authority has collapsed as
Bolingbroke's insurgency grows in popularity and military
strength. None of the traditional pursuits that would normally
embody the ease and self-confidence of an assured court order
are sufficient: dance, song, storytelling, even bowls would make
the queen 'think the world is full of rubs / And that my fortune
runs against the bias' (III.iv.4–5).[20] In such pressured conditions,
any form of activity is saturated with unwelcome political implication. However, in eavesdropping on the gardeners' discussion
'of state', the queen expects that their conversation will be trivial
enough to provide distraction. In fact, in his directions for the
care of the land, the gardener elaborates a political allegory of
considerable power, deploying an eloquence which is comparable
to that of John of Gaunt earlier in the play. Although presumably
a servant of the Crown, his political instincts are governed by a
broader concern for the welfare of the land, and he stigmatizes
royal policy as reckless in failing to nurture natural resources and
ensure the equal 'supportance' of mature elements in the commonwealth: 'All must be even in our government' (III.iv.36). This
emphasis on 'even' government is also expressed in the actions
he recommends to preserve the integrity of the land: the need to

prune 'noisome weeds which without profit suck / The soil's fertility from wholesome flowers' (III.iv.38–9). The gardener has a strikingly 'inclusionist' vision of a commonwealth whose health consists of reciprocal and supportive relationships between its different elements. This perception is defined against those (like the 'wasteful king' and his favourites) who exploit the country in a wilful manner, as if one part of this interdependent whole had a right to proliferate at the expense of others. Such an opinion lends weight to recent critical accounts of the play which stress the breadth of its sympathy for the language and values of those who oppose the king and his followers, and argue that *Richard II* perceives the 'medieval past not as a lost world of symbolic unity but as the scene of a continual struggle between aristocratic and constitutional liberties and a monarchy that kept trying to appropriate public resources for its private interests'.[21] It is interesting to note in relation to Helgerson's argument that we are invited here to sympathize with a subordinate member of the commonwealth who perceives the necessity to 'exclude' any subjects or stewards of the land, regardless of their 'height', in the best interests of the whole. As Donald R. Kelley reminds us, the ethic of 'medieval constitutionalism' – which emphasized the ruler as steward rather than lord, and expressed the corporate character of government in an organic conception of the body politic – was a powerful component of Elizabethan political thought and is evoked in this scene in a manner more pressing than 'moral disapproval'.[22]

The political judgements demanded by the 'garden scene' continue to grow in complexity, especially in terms of deciding who is the best guardian of the realm's interests (a question integral to the play and here examined in a perspective detached from its main plot). The opposition drawn between royal policy and the values of subjects becomes more extreme as we witness the queen's intervention to exclude popular participation in political debate. What is particularly offensive to the queen is that the Gardener's 'harsh rude tongue' should dispense, and so have access to, information of which she is unaware, namely Richard's imprisonment and imminent deposition:

> King Richard he is in the mighty hold
> Of Bolingbroke. Their fortunes both are weigh'd;

In your lord's scale is nothing but himself,
And some few vanities that make him light.
But in the balance of great Bolingbroke,
Besides himself, are all the English peers,
And with that odds he weighs King Richard down.

(III.iii.83–9)

It is this material awareness of actualities which is as shocking to the queen as the political cognition the Gardener displays. In circumscribing the right of a 'wretch' to countenance such an appalling prospect, the queen makes use of a discourse made familiar by the king: projecting royal status as divinely exalted – here any threat to its continuance is compared to 'a second fall of cursed man'.

The ideological implications of this episode are complicated, but they certainly include a critical questioning of authority when its responsibilities are judged in relation to a broad conception of social needs. The speech of the Gardener is not without its own naivety and is heard only briefly in the play, but, in *Richard II*, none of the protagonists establishes a comprehensive historical understanding. Social subordinates, like their superiors (and, indeed, like a theatre audience), are surprised by events and by alternative political perspectives in a manner which evokes 'the effect of history' to demand difficult choices, rather than settled responses. The 'garden scene' blurs social and political distinctions between 'high' and 'low' reactions, not least in foregrounding the censoriousness and prejudice of the queen's reactions to her servant. *Richard II* is in part about the entitlement (or otherwise) rival forces have in claiming political prerogatives, and the dismissal of the Gardener is consistent with its illumination of the sectional motives that can inform assertions of natural right by the elite. In a recent article, Martha A. Kurtz has argued that non-Shakespearean history plays present a more complex and diverse view of female identity than canonical texts, and she instances the character of Richard II's Queen Anne in the anonymous, and very radical, *Woodstock*.[23] The queen's portrayal in the 'garden scene' may be consistent with a restricted conception of female identity in Shakespeare's history plays. From another perspective, however, the decision not to emphasize her charitable, 'commonwealth' instincts may be a sign that the dramatist is more,

rather than less, radical in his sympathies. Stressing royal intolerance for popular political debate, and her antipathy for an
'inclusionist' understanding of the realm, is consistent with the
detachment the play encourages towards the spectacle of royal
anguish and aristocratic ambition. This scene helps identify
important principles of *Richard II*'s design in satisfying popular
curiosity concerning the hidden motivations of elite struggles
and a scepticism concerning their nature. Like the garden, the
play 'gives people images to think with'.

Analysing this scene allows some reservations to be formulated
concerning the ideological relationships pertaining between
Shakespeare's history plays and history. It gives enough pause
to consider the force of Adorno's insight that 'Shakespeare was a
dialectical dramatist who . . . looked at the *theatrum mundi* from the
perspective of the victims of progress.'[24] The dramatic method
by which Shakespeare orchestrates historical material expresses
his interest in arresting shifts of perspective, in complicating the
distinctions between competing social groups and value-systems,
and in sustaining a questioning attitude towards the political
process rather than a consistent ideological resolution of it.
Recognizing the interrogative spirit of the plays helps identify
their *critical* attitude towards the divergent political mentalities
they depict and to the distinct ways in which relationships to
reality are defined and contested within them. The potential of
Shakespeare's history plays to release such insights can be aug-
mented by considering their form.

One way of forwarding an understanding of how Shakespeare's plays create the 'effect' of history and present a political
analysis of its content, is to return to the issue of ideology in terms
of the rhetorical composition of the texts. New historical
approaches tend to explore this issue by perceiving the truth-
claims made within literary works or, about their nature or context, as rhetorical in the sense of being constituted by partisan
interests. One might return to the issue of texts being rhetorical
constructs, however, in a manner more fully informed by early
modern conceptions of rhetoric as an activity of practical reasoning, rather than simply a method of persuasion. Hanna Gray
reminds us of the crucial importance of dialogue for humanist
aspirations: 'how questioning was essential to the illumination of
truth'.[25] Such an emphasis on disputation and dialogue as a

method of rhetorical inquiry has proved to be of real explanatory power in understanding habits of dramatic composition. As Joel Altman's landmark study of the 'Tudor play of mind' has demonstrated, early modern theatre was an art of exploration, an orchestration of alternative perspectives on its subject matter in the interests of making active an audience's powers of judgement. In this view, dramatists are perceived as dialectical rhetoricians, rather than ideologues, who provoke awareness of contrary viewpoints as well as disclosing similarities between apparent opposites.[26]

It is worth revisiting this earlier critical interest in theatre as a medium for dialogues over value in the light of more recent research on early modern rhetoric and in terms of contemporary critical debates concerned with ideology. One useful analogy for the interpretation of Shakespeare's practice has been offered by Victoria Kahn's analysis of Machiavelli. Kahn argues that Machiavelli offered an influential example for Renaissance political writers in conceptualizing and responding to the contingency of history. The form of his texts (as much as their content) sought to induce a flexible faculty of judgement, a rhetorical approach to politics which 'can be usefully equated with dialectical thinking when it involves the internal critique and negation of positive claims to authority'.[27] This offers a suggestive approach to the implications of Shakespeare's attitudes towards history and to the issue of ideology. Political interpretations of the plays need to recognize their structures as a form of dialectical inquiry where the adequacy of forms of power and belief are held up to scrutiny by their (apparent) opposites. A methodology for this, strangely neglected by contemporary Renaissance criticism, is available in the debates engendered by the work of the Frankfurt School.[28] The value of a renewed interest in this body of critical work, which can only be suggested here, is engendered by its attention both to the connections between culture and power and in the capacity of artworks to maintain modes of critical reflection, disputation and negation. For Adorno, particularly, the capacity of art to explore the conflict and contradictions between antithetical values and, hence, to test the adequacy of their relationship to reality, was a key factor in the complex relationship between art and ideology: 'Profound works of art ... are those that try both to highlight divergences or antagonisms and to settle them by forcing them into the open... thus making arbitration possible. Figuration of antagonisms is not the same as reconciliation or a definitive overcoming of antagonisms.'[29]

New historical criticism has often been defined in terms of an opposition between those who believe that 'the display of ideological contradictions is completely consonant with the maintenance of oppressive social relations' and those who 'emphasise that the text is a site of subversive potential and that the critic's job is to activate it'.[30] One way of rephrasing this debate is to return to both the complexity of rhetorical form in the plays and to the interest of Benjamin and Adorno in the capacity of art to be both constituted by ideologies, but also able to achieve a critical perspective upon these. Shakespeare's history plays may be one example of works which show the consequences of political and social values in the *process* of their becoming, and also the contradictions and dialectical relationships by which they are defined. As Shakespeare's changing relationship to history demonstrates, we live in a period of shifting boundaries and changing trajectories: in this spirit, it may be that early modern critics need to return to Frankfurt more frequently than Paris.

FURTHER READING

Claire Colebrook's *New Literary Histories: New Historicism and Contemporary Criticism* (Manchester, Manchester University Press, 1997) is the most insightful and comprehensive introduction to the intellectual premises and practices that characterize new historical criticism. There are now several anthologies which have gathered a range of representative work; two useful texts are *New Historicism and Cultural Materialism: A Reader*, ed. Kiernan Ryan (London, Edward Arnold, 1998) and *New Historicism and Renaissance Drama*, eds Richard Wilson and Richard Dutton (London and New York, Longman, 1992). Much consideration has been given to differences between 'new historicist' work and 'cultural materialist' approaches: a lucid introduction to some distinctions between these methodologies is provided by John Brannigan's recent *New Historicism and Cultural Materialism* (London, Methuen, 1998). The collection of essays edited by Jean E. Howard and Marion O'Connor is also a useful introduction:

Shakespeare Reproduced: The Text in History and Ideology (New York and London, Methuen, 1985). Two recent monographs address Shakespeare's practice as a writer of history: Phyllis Rackin, *Stages of History: Shakespeare's English Chronicles* (London, Routledge, 1990) and Paola Pugliatti, *Shakespeare the Historian* (London, Macmillan, 1996).

The 'new historicism' associated with the work of Stephen Greenblatt has attracted much critical debate. Examples of critical appraisals of the movement from scholars of a more traditional temper can be sampled in Edward Pechter's *What Was Shakespeare? Renaissance Plays and Changing Critical Practice* (Ithaca and London, Cornell University Press, 1995); Brian Vickers, *Appropriating Shakespeare: Contemporary Critical Quarrels* (New Haven and London, Yale University Press, 1993), especially pp. 214–71; Graham Bradshaw, *Misrepresentations: Shakespeare and the Materialists* (Ithaca and London, Cornell University Press, 1993); T. McAlindon, 'Testing the New Historicism: "Invisible Bullets" Reconsidered', *Studies in Philology* 92 (1995): 411–38. Critiques from other viewpoints might start with the essays by James Holstun and Janet Clare noted below, and Theodore B. Leinwand, 'Negotiation and New Historicism', *PMLA* 105 (1990): 477–90; Alan Liu, 'The Power of Formalism: The New Historicism', *English Literary History* 56 (1989): 721–71; and Richard Wilson, *Willpower: Essays in Shakespearean Authority* (London, Harvester Wheatsheaf, 1993), especially pp. 1–21.

II Shakespeare and National Identity

6. 'Home, Sweet Home': Stratford-upon-Avon and the Making of the Royal Shakespeare Company as a National Institution

COLIN CHAMBERS

Based in the town of Shakespeare's birth, itself in the heart of England, the Royal Shakespeare Company (RSC) cannot avoid being cast in the role of the nation's Pythian serpent, guardian of the Bard's flame and anointed declarer of prophetic utterance. The RSC has welcomed and exploited this destiny but knows there is also a damaging price to pay. The Company nurses a peculiar double burden of privilege and responsibility that reflects the contradictory position it finds itself in: it is nationally subsidized, with a local, national and international audience, presenting in Britain and abroad the works of the supreme icon of national as well as international writing in ways that aim both to honour authoritatively the truths of texts that are four centuries old, and at the same time to find meanings in them that resonate for its diverse audiences today. Like the playwright whose name the company bears, the RSC has to be both particular and general in appeal; it has to be 'authentic' and represent continuity, yet continually be new and embody change, if it is not to die.

Clearly the RSC occupies a special place at the centre of the intricate worldwide web of Shakespeare's contemporary presence. It is, however, a contested place, not simply because of the vicissitudes inevitably experienced by any theatre company, but more importantly because of its claim to a representative status. At the formation of the company, this claim was supported by but surpassed the politics of location, the accumulated cultural significance that is derived from association with the accident of the Bard's birth in Stratford-upon-Avon. The RSC's claim was made on a bolder basis: a linked geopolitical and artistic project to be a company of the nation and of the nation's playwright 'in the market-place of Now... expert in the past but alive to the present'.[1] As the categories of nation and text are notably unstable and fluid, this invocation of national unity intertwined with textual interpretation rooted in scholarship shaped the site of contestation.

The international importance of Shakespeare is not in doubt as far as the RSC is concerned. 'The company believe that the Elizabethan theatre – and especially Shakespeare – offers a dramatic richness unequalled in any other epoch or language', reads a note printed in the programme of the inaugural 1964 World Theatre Season hosted by the recently formed RSC.[2] Two decades later, with the RSC firmly established, its artistic director Trevor Nunn could write that Stratford-upon-Avon 'was the acknowledged world centre for Shakespeare studies and for the continuous performance of his plays'.[3] Shakespeare is the universal standard, and the theatre that emanates from his birthplace takes on the guarantee of his unremitting and seemingly unassailable global status.

This, however, was not always the case. When Shakespeare was elevated to the status of national icon in the eighteenth century by the literary establishment, the proper place for his plays was deemed to be the library and not the stage, where only suitably cleansed and tidied versions of selected plays in the canon appeared. It took until 1769 – 150 years after Shakespeare's death – for the town council in Stratford to organize a Shakespeare Festival there, and it was not until Shakespeare's house was bought for the nation nearly one hundred years later, in 1847, that calls were heard for the creation of a permanent celebration in the shape of a theatre dedicated to the Bard. This idea was realized by Charles Flower, a Stratford brewer, who oversaw the building of a theatre on the banks of the River Avon in 1875 and called it the Shakespeare Memorial Theatre. The opening was greeted not with acclaim, but with consternation and even contumely, by certain influential commentators who believed that the nation's capital was the only location fit for such a shrine. The Bardolators compared the prospects of the

Midlands market town unfavourably to those of Bayreuth, like-wise small and removed from its capital, but which enjoyed royal support for its temple to Wagner; furthermore, they were dis-satisfied because the Stratford festival was too short at a week long.

Campaigners seeking constant devotion came together in the early 1900s when the lobbyists for a National Theatre and those wanting to erect a lasting monument to Shakespeare formed the faction-ridden Shakespeare Memorial National Theatre (SMNT) Committee, and thereby firmly yoked Bardolatry to the national interest. Stratford was drawn in when the Committee agreed to pay a small subsidy to the director William Bridges-Adams to run a resident company there, although the money would be avail-able only for a limited duration. By the time Charles Flower's nephew Archie, who served on the SMNT Committee, won a Royal Charter for the Stratford theatre in 1925, the Committee's grant had ended. Insofar as the monarch was then seen to stand for the nation, the theatre had taken a step beyond its provincial status towards a national profile. However, when fire gutted the Victorian theatre in 1926, of the £306,000 raised by public subscription to build a new theatre for the nation, none came from the SMNT Committee and nearly half – £137,000 – came from Americans; more than half a century later, the RSC's Swan Theatre, a project once shelved through lack of funds, was finally built only through the generosity of an American benefactor.

Before the founding of the RSC in 1961, Stratford fought for the Shakespeare mantle with London's Old Vic, which, since the arrival there of Lilian Baylis in 1912, had made Shakespeare its mainstay. Before the Second World War, when the Old Vic was setting standards for the profession generally, Stratford (with some exceptions) usually lost out. The pendulum began to swing its way after the war under artistic directors Barry Jackson, Anthony Quayle and Glen Byam Shaw, and it remained with Stratford once the RSC was established, even following the even-tual launching of the National Theatre (NT) in 1963.

Relations between Stratford and the SMNT Committee/ National Theatre campaigners had remained distant until 1959, when at last there appeared a real likelihood of a National Thea-tre being established. Stratford became involved in Byzantine machinations with the NT group, at one juncture agreeing to a merger and then pulling out. The outcome of these joint discussions affected the speed of transition from the old, self-sufficient Stratford set-up to the new RSC structure, as well as its future share of public subsidy relative to the NT (the NT in its first year received five times more than the RSC). For Peter Hall, who created the RSC, the plan was to stake a claim before the NT opened. He wanted to form a theatre company that was a permanent ensemble performing modern and new plays as well as those by Shakespeare, and to do this he needed a London outlet and, crucially, state subsidy. Acquiring the 'royal' tag was an important tactical advantage over the NT, which did not stage its first production for another 18 months; it gave the RSC a claim to national status before the NT even existed, and the RSC has held on to that status ever since, though not without a struggle.

Stratford's competitiveness with the Old Vic, in which Shakespeare had been the common ground, was replaced by a symbiotic rivalry between the RSC and the NT, in which both institutions offered a broad repertoire in their various auditoria. As for Shakespeare, the RSC exerted a formidable and dominant grip, becoming in marketing terms the 'brand leader', with attendant proprietorial attitudes and practices. The BBC TV series of Shakespeare productions begun in 1978, the only comparable body of work to stand alongside the RSC output, was judged against standards set by the RSC, albeit in a different medium. Ironically, when Hall took over the NT and discussed planning co-operation with Trevor Nunn, his chosen successor at the RSC, he remembers in mild pique Nunn behaving as if 'in effect the 37 plays of Shakespeare belonged to the RSC'.[4]

The RSC justified its national legitimacy by reference to the centrality of Shakespeare and, more justifiably, the reception of its work, pointing to both an increase in audience figures and a plethora of critical praise. After winning public subsidy in 1962 for the following season – abetted by a well-nurtured and supportive media – this legitimacy was confirmed by an annual juggernaut of statistics: ever more productions playing to ever more people at ever less subsidy per seat. It was an approach forced on the RSC by the funding climate, and revealed a picture of quantitative achievement which bears comparison with any publicly subsidized company. In the late 1990s, for instance, the

RSC was selling over one million tickets a year and generating around 60 per cent of its annual income from ticket sales and commercial activities.

While aiming, though not being able, to alter significantly the sociological make-up of its audience, the RSC over time did meet its national responsibility by touring. In 1977, it established an annual Newcastle residency, and in 1978 a regular regional small-scale tour visiting locations that did not have easy access to professional theatre. When in 1997 the RSC added Plymouth to Newcastle as another annual residency, and reduced its commitment to the Barbican in London to six months instead of twelve each year, the company was at pains to point out that it had now become 'a truly national Company with 80% of the population able to see a performance by the Company within an hour's drive'.[5]

As well as visiting abroad, it was touring widely to large-, middle- and small-scale theatres within Britain, yet there were still complaints from certain quarters that the RSC was not fulfilling its national obligations; its audience was drawn from a narrow social base, and how often did it play in Northern Ireland or Scotland, for instance? But how would one judge its national legitimacy, or that of any nationally subsidized company, following devolution of the Arts Council of Great Britain into four national Councils and political devolution at state level, making national identity more elusive still, and England's synecdochic role as representative of Britain even weaker? In terms of national representation, if class and geographical considerations were important, then other factors, particularly lack of ethnic diversity, would have to be included and related to assessment of what was being represented and seen on stage. As an organization, it was certainly reflecting – if not representing – the nation insofar as it embraced a post-Thatcher, top-heavy management model and in being overwhelmingly white, middle-class and male-led.

Given the context of its existence, the RSC could never represent the nation, just as, beyond symbolism, the monarch does not, nor, for that matter, beyond the limits of current electoral arrangements, does Parliament. Nevertheless, the desire for and claim to national representation is paramount for all three institutions, as a necessary factor in their very survival. In this regard, it is instructive to look at the conditions that prevailed when the RSC first appeared and made its initial, successful, attempt at assuming such a national role.

When Hall learned in 1958, aged 27 and just five years out of Cambridge University, that he would become Stratford's Director, it was a time when religion had declined and become secular, and the empire had been 'lost'; consequently, the arts were able to be seen as a source of national pride and moral value. It was the period of Prime Minister Harold Macmillan's 'You've never had it so good' consumer society, which, for some sections of the population, was leaving post-war austerity behind. The Tories, trounced in terms of the number of MPs returned in the 1945 general election, had won the election of 1951, though with fewer votes than Labour; they had increased their majorities in 1955 and 1959. But in the first few years of the RSC, as pressure built up within society for a break with prevailing paternalistic Victorian values, the Tories lost their political touch and were defeated by Labour in 1964.

Hall was a self-declared radical and Labour supporter (though he later voted for Thatcher's Tories while regretting that he felt forced to do so). Stratford regularly returned a Tory MP. From 1950 to 1963 it was John Profumo, whose own fall from government as War Minister in the Christine Keeler sex-and-spy scandal accelerated his party's decline. When Hall took over the RSC, its President was Lord Avon, Tory MP for neighbouring Warwick and Leamington (1923–57) and, as Anthony Eden, Prime Minister (1955–57) during the Suez debacle. The chairman of the Board of Governors, who was old enough to be Hall's father, was still another Flower (called Fordham), a Sandhurst-trained ex-officer who had once considered standing as a Tory MP. Stratford was establishment to the core and the theatre there was commercially successful, but that did not prevent Fordham Flower from backing Hall to the hilt. Without Flower's support and drive, the RSC would never have survived, let alone been anything more substantial than the dream of an ambitious Cambridge graduate from an upper-working-class background.

Despite Hall's desire to create a popular theatre, in terms of audience background he only managed to make shifts within the middle class, appealing especially to the younger, university-educated 'upwardly mobile' section from whence he came. Hall did open up the RSC to its audience through a members' club, and in the mid-1960s launched Theatregoround to take work into working-class areas and schools. (The educational slant of Theatregoround soon took precedence over its social intent.) In contrast, Theatre Workshop – a radical ensemble whose style influenced Hall – did find a working-class audience, in the East End of London. But, unlike the RSC, the company was not to be favoured by the patrician grant-distributing body, the Arts Council, with anything approaching an equivalent public subsidy, despite the internationally recognized value of its pioneering work.

When Hall leased a London theatre for the RSC, he did not follow Theatre Workshop's example or, before that, of Lilian Baylis at the Old Vic – or of the Théâtre National Populaire (TNP) in Paris, another important influence on Hall, even to the point of his liking the initials RSC because they reminded him of the felicitous abbreviation TNP; he did not set up in a working-class district as they had done; he went into the West End. Hall was fighting for the RSC to receive public funding at the moment when the putative NT was engaged in a similar struggle and he wanted to strike a high profile. In Paris the TNP and the Comédie Française, which had been established in the seventeenth century, were both handsomely supported by the French government. In Hall's first year in charge at Stratford, before any subsidy came his way, the Comédie Française received the equivalent of £300,000 and the total Arts Council grant to drama amounted to £184,000.

In the British context, which had no secure tradition of state support for the arts and no mass Communist or left-wing party, the concept of the nation was different to that in France and elsewhere in Europe, and it remained locked into a representative rather than a participatory definition. While Shakespeare was thought to be as English as pre-BSE roast beef, public subsidy of the arts was not, yet without it the RSC would not have lasted more than a few seasons because Stratford's reserves would have been used up. The RSC's fight for state subsidy was of national significance, and its securing a public grant – to become one of the four companies along with the NT, the Royal Opera House and the English National Opera that is centrally funded – means it is necessarily of national concern.

The notion of an ensemble, which inspired Hall to create the RSC, was also a foreign idea. Nevertheless, it had animated Stratford since Charles Flower had read reports of the Duke of Saxe-Meiningen's German theatre company in the 1870s. For Hall, 80 years later, Europe remained the key. France had become for the British the theatre-centre of the early 1950s. The legacy of Stanislavsky and the Moscow Art Theatre was being felt more widely, as was that of Brecht and the Berliner Ensemble. Hall described the latter's visit to Britain in 1956 as the most influential since the war.[6] Hall brought the eminent French director and teacher Michel Saint-Denis into the RSC artistic direction alongside himself and Peter Brook, who is of Russian descent. Brook drank from many a foreign cup, among them that of the Polish critic Jan Kott, the Irishman living in France, Samuel Beckett; the French visionary Antonin Artaud; and the radical director Jerzy Grotowski, also from Poland, who worked with Brook in rehearsal at the RSC. The company's repertoire in London was international, primarily European, and the RSC hosted the enormously potent World Theatre Seasons. This English company was, after all, decidedly foreign.

But in the absence of any public subsidy at the time when Hall launched the RSC with a theatre in the West End as well as in Stratford, the London base had to secure a commercial hit in order to survive, and thus the very principle for which he was fighting was undermined at the outset. Even with the advent of state money, the sums were inadequate to support the work being produced and, as a consequence, the RSC was always anxious about the box office (whilst achieving returns that would have made the most hardbitten theatre manager melt with envy). Subsidy did allow certain experimentation in the 1960s, but the scope for this became ever more restricted as the RSC was forced to increase the volume of work simply in order to sustain the level of its subsidy, a process which led to over-expansion, consequent loss of focus and damage to its artistic standards. The subsidy level that was set initially could be read as a desire by the authorities to force the RSC out of London and thereby remove it as a threat to the preferentially subsidized National Theatre. Unlike in France, the British national establishment found it difficult to contemplate the nation paying for two national theatres in the capital, though ultimately it was forced to do so. This reluctant agreement was accompanied by a clear warning from the Treasury via the Arts Council that if the RSC found it necessary to 'operate at a National Theatre level' there would be no qualms artistically, but the state was not going to pay for it.[7]

There were further complications in the equation because the RSC's ascendancy was marked by a perceived subversion of certain British institutions and a portrayal of some of Shakespeare's plays that stood in contradistinction to the prevailing view of Shakespeare as the repository of transcendent spiritual beneficence. Hall's decision to cease playing the national anthem at every performance, for example, caused local uproar, and he recalls in his *Diaries* a Stratford alderman who defended the ritual as 'remembering the privilege of being British'.[8] The RSC was also frequently at loggerheads with the censor, the Lord Chamberlain, and helped to end his powers. During one tussle concerning *US*, a collective response to the Vietnam war which the Lord Chamberlain considered to be anti-American, the chairman of the governors thoughtfully advised the RSC president Lord Avon to bring forward his intended resignation from the RSC to avoid embarrassment as the fracas was about to become public. When an RSC experimental programme made fun of the censor, it was an outrage too far for one RSC governor, because the censor was a member of the Queen's household and the RSC operated under royal charter. Similar arguments were used by a group of blimpish governors in what became known as the 'Dirty Plays' row when they complained about the nature of some of the modern plays in the RSC repertoire and then broadened the attack to other plays in the West End, such as Joe Orton's *Entertaining Mr Sloane*.

The RSC's early anti-establishment character was noted by the Arts Council, itself on the receiving end of vigorous RSC public campaigning. Some years later, the radical tag was still being applied when in 1972 the then Stratford Tory MP Angus Maude resigned from the RSC governing body over a letter in *The Times* from the company's artistic director Trevor Nunn and associate director David Jones. It dealt with a dispute the company was having with two radical playwrights. As part of the RSC's defence, the directors described the company as 'basically a left-wing organisation'.[9] In truth, however, it was much more a microcosm of the dominant culture, which can accommodate those who challenge or oppose it.

The RSC at the beginning did set out, to quote Hall, to 'question everything and disturb its audience'.[10] It eschewed doctrine and theory, even if both could be found at play in its work. It established an identity capable of embracing antithetical positions: Brook's experiments in the Theatre of Cruelty season were in essence anti-word, while Hall was demanding reverence for the word. His production of *Hamlet* based on close textual scrutiny could play in the same year (1965) and in the same theatre alongside Brook's production of *Marat/Sade*, a visceral aria of passions that arose out of his Artaud explorations. Nevertheless, both these theatrical opposites became landmarks in the RSC saga.

Hall achieved a unity at the RSC by sheer force of will, allied to his ability to provide conditions of work – rehearsal and preparation time, size of company, workshop resources – matched in the British theatre only by the National, which could not, however, offer the campus life of Stratford existence. As is common in many artistic organizations, and most that are successful, the taste of the person in charge defines the output, and for a number of sometimes complex and sometimes simple reasons – it could be politics, personality, sexuality, artistic approach – Hall found and defined the group with whom he wanted to work by excluding or dropping those with whom he did not wish to share. Tony Richardson had directed at Stratford, but Hall saw no point in asking him back as he had a completely contrary view of verse-speaking to Hall's; Joan Littlewood was invited to direct *Henry IV Parts I* and *II* but did not fit in and never worked for the RSC; Bill Gaskill briefly brought Royal Court epic, poetic simplicity to Shakespeare at the RSC with *Richard III* (1961) and *Cymbeline* (1962), but then saw the new NT as a more conducive home. There was room for only one loner, and that was Peter Brook, the master of legerdemain who learned his craft in the commercial hothouse that Hall was now wishing to supplant, and who was now enjoying the fruits of subsidy and proving its worth.

A unity of sorts was maintained by the company until 1991 when the incoming artistic director Adrian Noble removed the associate directors from the payroll and went over to a free-lance system. Whatever had been perceived as an RSC style under Hall and the subsequent artistic regimes, dissipated with the departure of the associates and its free-fall into a market-driven ideology.

When it came to the language of Shakespeare, Hall focused on verse and later described himself as an iambic fundamentalist, insisting on the sanctity of the line.[11] RSC actors were directed to breathe in order to support meaning and were only allowed a breath at the end of a line. In his attitude, Hall combined two central traits of two bitterly antagonistic Cambridge University celebrities; from F. R. Leavis, who disdained theatre, he took a 'puritan' analysis of meaning through a fierce focus on the words, and from George Rylands, who was a confidant of the most powerful theatrical figures of the day, he took a 'cavalier' love of fine performance through an equally fierce focus on the form, shape and rhythm of a text.

Hall believed, rightly, that actors needed training for Shake-speare, and his chief of verse-speaking police was John Barton, a friend and academic from Cambridge University, who, more than any other director, was responsible through classes and his own productions for inculcating the desired habits in the en-semble. Nevertheless, while Hall was able to combine his 'Eng. Lit.' and university experience with the ancient craft prejudices and practices of actors, the traditional tension between stage and study did erupt from time to time where Barton was concerned. His egalitarian neglect of special treatment for the leading players in his first-season production of *The Taming of the Shrew* contributed to his removal by Hall at their behest, and he was not to direct at Stratford for another three years. Rehabilitation, however, was then complete.

As well as having to cope with the demands of verse, there were other obstacles to overcome in building a company of actors; despite a widespread willingness to work collectively, there was no tradition of ensemble playing, and Shakespeare's plays did not offer an even-handed gender mix or distribution of parts. Salaries were low because of the inadequate subsidy, but Hall attracted leading players by offering the first long-term contracts in the British theatre, and the challenge of new ways of working that could pay tremendous artistic dividends. Hall, however, considers his main achievement at the RSC not so much the cre-ation of a company but the creation of a coherent verse-speaking style.[12] Notwithstanding his zealotry, he recognizes that the emotional temperature of stage speaking does change, with successive generations seemingly acting more 'realistically' than their predecessors yet themselves becoming outdated within a decade or so. He was not surprised that the cool, rational style he had instigated gave way to a more romantic sweep under Trevor Nunn and Terry Hands.

Ironically, this basic issue of how to speak Shakespeare's lines throws up another anomaly concerning contemporary claims to Shakespeare's essential English-ness, an area of national debate in which the RSC is often used as a benchmark. There is a huge chasm between the English of Shakespeare's plays, the 'standard' English demanded by the National Curriculum in schools (illogically validated by reference to Shakespeare) and the English of 1990s multicultural Britain, where public discourse has declined and 'soundbite' speech no longer recognizes nor relishes rhetoric. It could perhaps be argued that those brought up speaking English have a head start where understanding Shakespeare's English is concerned, but the English of the plays remains a learnt language, just as is the idiom of 'cybertalk'. Hall implicitly acknowledges this when, while blithely ignoring the vast diversity of accents spoken in the USA, he writes in his autobiography that Americans would come closer than the British to how Shakespeare's plays might have sounded in their own day if only Americans would cease either emulating the 'received pronunciation' of an English accent or playing the lines naturalistically and thereby losing their form and shape.[13]

Supporters of Shakespeare's Englishness, usually right-wing or establishment figures, define that quality against the standard of an imaginary 'real' England now lost or debased beyond recognition. They have a habit of quoting references from Shakespeare's plays to national characteristics and chain-of-being cosmic order, regardless of dramatic context. Shakespeare lived in a dangerous, cruel world, dependent on the Court for patronage, and was no stranger to political machination, especially if he was, as seems likely, a secret Catholic admirer. He rewrote riot passages in *Sir Thomas More* for the censor but the ban on the play was still not lifted. His patron was an Essex conspirator, and on the eve of the Earl's rebellion, Shakespeare's company performed *Richard II* and ran into serious trouble even though the play, it could be said, presents a sympathetic picture of the Divine Right of Kings. A contemporary of Shakespeare's, John Hayward, was imprisoned in the Tower of London for having written about the deposed king.

Hall felt the twentieth century had similarities with the late sixteenth/early seventeenth centuries that Shakespeare knew – a time of change, of confusion, of conquest, of scientific and philosophical discovery and of an historic shift in class power, which, in the earlier period, led to a rising bourgeoisie decapitating the king. Hall believed the tension between past and present was crucial in performing classical plays and saw it occupying the heart of the RSC's work; it determined the taking of a London theatre in order to present modern work and allow the cross-fertilization within the company between the classic and the contemporary.

Central to this concern was Shakespeare's group of plays known as the histories and, within that group, the trilogy of plays Hall called *The Wars of the Roses*, the three *Henry VI* plays compressed into two along with *Richard III*. It was this trilogy rather than the comedies (the subject of Hall's first season in charge at Stratford), the tragedies, the late plays or even the 'difficult' middle plays that came to epitomize the fledgling RSC.

The histories have a special place in Stratford, and particularly RSC, lore. The new theatre was launched in 1932 with *Henry IV Parts I* and *II*, as was the RSC's new London base at the Barbican Centre in 1982 and Adrian Noble's reign as artistic director in 1991. They reappeared in 2000 to mark the millennium. Anthony Quayle's finest moment in charge of Stratford is generally regarded as his breakthrough four-play history cycle in 1951, showing (possibly for the first time) *Richard II*, the two *Henry IV*s and *Henry V* as part of a continuous story and thereby posing the important questions – 'what is history?' and 'how do we make it culturally?' Shakespeare is clearly writing about his own time, not the past, both socially (for example, the Falstaff milieu) and politically (exploring the Tudor settlement), and, famously, is putting the nation on the stage. As he progressively breaks with the standard chronicle play, it is possible to read a critique within the very structure of the plays (for example, in

Henry V, the use of a chorus and the verbal contrasts between countries and within a country).

In *The Wars of the Roses*, the RSC drew on the specificity of history but emphasized its generality: history – and the making of the nation – was a power struggle then and is one now, and, like the working-through of a curse in ancient drama, there is not much anyone can do about it. With *Henry V*, the most jingoistic of the plays according to tradition, the RSC in its productions that formed part of the complete 'history cycle' of 1964 and more especially in 1975 (directed by Terry Hands) not only played down the bombast and pageantry but questioned the notion of heroism and the meaning of nation.

Hands, ultimately, invoked an idealized 'one-nation' sensibility at a moment of national anxiety – 'who runs the country?' had been the theme of the last general election held against the backdrop of the oil crisis. He exploited the play's internal dialectic of debate to show that all coins have two sides: 'good' and 'bad' are interlocked. Henry is lauded but he is not king by right, the war is just but also a convenient diversion for monarch and Church, God is the commander, yet un-Christian massacres are still perpetrated, Henry the strong soldier-king challenges his own motives and blames others, troops question the reason for fighting but wage battle ferociously, the king becomes a commoner but also despises the common man, he unites the nation but without transgressing the hierarchy of rank or racial prejudice. This approach did not prevent some critics from responding enthusiastically to what they saw as 'patriotic tub-thumping' (*The Times*) and a 'reminder of national greatness' (*Daily Express*) – the inscription of the Shakespeare myth goes deep indeed.

The RSC was keen to play off the myth and simultaneously to show that it stood at a discreet distance from it, an ambiguity that affected its relationship to the repository of the myth itself, the text. Hall, who at college studied not only Elizabethan verse-speaking but punctuation, printing practices and the authenticity of different versions, placed great emphasis on textual fidelity, despite the fact that we have no way of knowing what that means. Four centuries of textual alterations by players and commentators alike should have been warning enough. Whether by Nahum Tate or Thomas Bowdler, David Garrick or Henry Irving, Donald Wolfit or Laurence Olivier, the texts have been hacked or trimmed constantly to suit the views of the time and of the perpetrator.[14]

Texts were no more sacrosanct at Stratford than elsewhere. (Bridges-Adams flew the flag for uncut Shakespeare early on but soon surrendered, and his successors followed suit.) Hall was going to make a stand on loyalty to the text, yet in *The Wars of the Roses* (1963) and another defining production, Peter Brook's *King Lear* (1962), the directors took blatant textual liberties and were attacked by senior academics for so doing. Hall later regretted the editing of the three *Henry VI* plays, in which one-fifth of the lines came not from the pen of Shakespeare but that of John Barton, with a little help from Hall himself. Barton, then the stricter of the two on verse-speaking, never recanted, believing these early plays to be dramaturgically brave but flawed and over-ambitious. The success of the RSC's resulting pastiche was due not only to the theatrical excitement of the productions but to their apparent contemporary relevance, which was underlined by the vigour and physicality of the design, staging and delivery of the verse. The success of the 'relevance' approach, in turn, owed much to the fact that the originals were virtually unknown.

Peter Brook, the presiding spirit hovering over post-war Stratford, criticized this directorial practice of massaging a text to make it 'relevant'. Yet in his now-legendary Beckettian version of *King Lear*, he manipulated the text to suit his preconceived view. He blocked the possibility of human conciliation (as he had done years earlier in *Romeo and Juliet*) by cutting the passage showing the servants' horror after Gloucester's eyes are plucked out. By the time Hands was directing all three *Henry VI* plays virtually uncut in 1977, 'relevance' had become an outmoded idea and romantic aesthetics had removed politics and history altogether – a trend that continued through to the emblematic *Plantagenets* (1988), Adrian Noble's version of *The Wars of the Roses*.

After the 1960s, the radical culture within the RSC had moved with Buzz Goodbody into the studio theatre The Other Place, and it stayed there after her suicide in 1975 until the political and funding climate changed hue in the wake of Thatcherite government. Main stage productions became lavish in the 1980s and, as the RSC moved into the Barbican in the City of London and was forced to court private sponsors to survive, experiment with the Bard faded. Innovation was left to groups outside the RSC, inspired by new performance cultures and theatre practices abroad.

By the end of the millennium, the RSC flag under Adrian Noble's stewardship had become, in his words, a 'quite reactionary' one.[15] He still believed, as Hall had, that Shakespearean production should be publicly funded because Shakespeare was good for the nation, but now the crusade was not to challenge and to question but to defend. In the face of rapid technological change and a merciless global economy, the nation generally was in decline, and the RSC, feeling ever more the repository of Shakespearean virtue, would take its responsibility seriously on the high ground of a conservative cultural populism that would try to stop the rot and bind the nation together again. Text and nation intertwined, Stratford was back to where it had been in the 1950s.

The early years of the RSC had transformed Stratford and the way Shakespeare was produced, but institutions ossify and need reinventing. Since then there had been many changes in society, including ideas about the nation and the texts of Shakespeare's plays. The time had come for reinvention. Ripeness is everything.

SELECT BIBLIOGRAPHY

Addenbrooke, David, *The Royal Shakespeare Company: The Peter Hall Years*, London, William Kimber, 1974.
Beauman, Sally, *The Royal Shakespeare Company: A History of Ten Decades*, Oxford, Oxford University Press, 1982.
Chambers, Colin, *Other Spaces: New Theatre and the RSC*, London, Eyre Methuen, 1980.
Dollimore, Jonathan and Sinfield, Alan (eds), *Political Shakespeare: New Essays in Cultural Materialism*, Manchester, Manchester University Press, 1985.
Drakakis, John (ed.), *Alternative Shakespeares*, London, Methuen, 1985.
Fay, Stephen, *Power Play: The Life and Times of Peter Hall*, London, Hodder & Stoughton, 1996.
Goodwin, John (ed.), *Peter Hall's Diaries: The Story of a Dramatic Battle*, London, Hamish Hamilton, 1983.

Hall, Peter, *Making an Exhibition of Myself*, London, Sinclair-Stevens, 1993.

Hawkes, Terence, *That Shakespearean Rag: Essays on a Critical Process*, London, Methuen, 1986.

Holderness, Graham (ed.), *The Shakespeare Myth*, Manchester, Manchester University Press, 1988.

Joughin, John (ed.), *Shakespeare and National Culture*, Manchester, Manchester University Press, 1997.

Shaughnessy, Robert, *Representing Shakespeare: England, History and the RSC*, Hemel Hempstead, Harvester Wheatsheaf, 1994.

III Shakespeare, Performance, Sexuality and Race

7. *Twelfth Night*: 'One face, one voice, one habit, and two persons!'

JANICE WARDLE

> One face, one voice, one habit, and two persons!
> A Natural Perspective, that is and is not.
>
> (V.i.213–14)

In the twentieth century the evolution of performance criticism, or stage-centred criticism, as it was first known, was one of the major developments in the academic study of Shakespeare. Performance criticism provides students of Renaissance texts with evidence of how the modern theatre negotiates the often paradoxical critical dilemmas which the plays embody. In the case of comedy, it has confirmed and reinforced critics' sense of the contested and problematical nature of this genre.

In this chapter, two productions of *Twelfth Night* by the Royal Shakespeare Company (RSC) will be examined. Like all Shakespeare's plays, *Twelfth Night* was afforded a wide range of interpretations by both academics and theatre practitioners in the twentieth century. I wish to use the methods of performance criticism to show that both academic criticism and theatre performances have been involved in a parallel, and often complementary, exploration of two potentially contradictory impulses within the text of *Twelfth Night*. My title highlights the important scene at the heart of the play which reunites the separated twins in a moment of platonic harmony. (The play is preoccupied by ideas of doubleness and complementarity.) I have used this metaphor of twin 'persons' to reflect the attempts by both academic and theatrical interpreters to achieve a harmonious balance between two movements in the play. Much of the play is light-hearted in character, with the comic potential of concealed and mistaken identities running rife. But the other 'person' of the

105

play is altogether less frivolous: many critics argue that the dominant mood of the play is sombre and dark, with its emphasis on self-deception and the transience of life and love. In the early twenty-first century this dual personality of the play continues to be negotiated by academic readings, and has to be confronted by all theatrical interpretations. The two productions of *Twelfth Night* examined here, although starting with the same textual 'face, voice and habit', do seem to produce 'two persons' and to expose the polarities of interpretation of this complex play.

Although all productions of a Shakespeare comedy will grapple with its contested meanings, it occasionally happens that because of a convergence of a number of historical influences, a production can become a benchmark of what seems to be a 'truthful' production to audiences, critics and practitioners for a considerable period. In 1969 John Barton staged a version of the play which was destined to become such a benchmark production for both theatre practitioners and academics. In 1997 Adrian Noble's production (eight RSC productions later) met with an animated but ambivalent critical response. Although these productions were nearly thirty years apart, because both were produced under the auspices of the one of the leading British theatre companies, the Royal Shakespeare Company, which consciously attempts to forge an evolving tradition of Shakespearean production,[1] it is possible to identify areas of influence and self-conscious comparison between productions as part of an ongoing corporate theatrical discourse.

John Barton's production of *Twelfth Night* opened in August 1969, and in the following three years it was performed on 202 occasions. The interpretation offered by Barton and his cast established in the minds of critics and audiences a standard of theatrical excellence against which to assess productions of Shakespeare's comedies, and not just this play, for the next 30 years. Barton's own assessment of his production was that 'he got more of *Twelfth Night* "right" than anything else he had done'.[2] Part of Barton's stated objective was to remove the accretion of previous interpretations and, in effect, defamiliarize the text. ('The text is so familiar, I think, to everyone that there's a danger of staleness. I suppose I started out with the idea that the play should as far as possible emerge uncluttered: free from previous conceptions, clichés, traditional interpretations of specific characters or scenes.'[3]) This desire to rethink the play is, as Stanley Wells notes, 'one of the most valuable characteristics of the post-war generation of university-trained directors'.[4] While professing a desire 'to avoid imposing an ostentatious directorial hand; it's very much an actor's play',[5] Barton added: 'the text contains an enormous range of emotions and moods and most productions seem to select one – farce or bitterness or romance – and emphasise it throughout. I wanted to sound all the notes that there are.'[6] Perhaps unsurprisingly, Barton did not succeed in his quest to sound all the notes. The majority of first-night critics were surprised by the melancholic 'dying fall' of the production, and the interpretation was regarded as a startling, innovative one. Judi Dench, who played Viola in the production, remarked: 'John Barton was the one who said it's such a bittersweet play, that if you do that [i.e. play it purely for comedy] it tips over. It's not pure comedy.'[7] The emphasis on the play's bittersweet notes and its melancholy may have owed something to Peter Hall's 1958 RSC production of the play. Barton's production, like Hall's, was described as Chekhovian by many critics, including Stanley Wells:

> When I think in retrospect of this production, it is its beauty that I remember. Not especially – though partly – a visual beauty, but a beauty of communication, of sympathy, understanding, and compassion. It had a Chekhovian quality, and I know John Barton would regard that as a compliment.[8]

This Chekhovian quality also chimed particularly well with academic criticism of this period, during which, as Mahood notes, 'unnumbered critics stress the underlying sadness of *Twelfth Night*'.[9] Most likely the major academic influence on John Barton's production was the work of his wife Anne Barton, who later edited and wrote the introductions to *The Riverside Shakespeare*,[10] and published extensively on Shakespeare. Anne Barton, in fact, wrote a substantial piece for the production's programme in which she claimed that '*Twelfth Night* links the two halves of Shakespeare's writing life' – which, in her view, was the half containing the comedies and the half containing the romances. She also claimed that the play contained within it an essential confrontation between artifice and reality, where the romantic

world of the play, that is, Illyria, is seen to be both festive and
artificial; there is a poignancy at the play's conclusion as some are
excluded from this world of romance. Anne Barton notes in the
programme: 'By its very nature, holiday is not eternal. It is only
an interval in the everyday, destined to yield in the end to the
sober order it has momentarily overthrown. In the final act of
Twelfth Night, fantasy fights against the cold light of day.'[11]

The influence of Northrop Frye and C. L. Barber on this
interpretation is fairly obvious.[12] The methodology employed
by Frye in his exploration of the comic genre led him to find
parallels, motifs and archetypal similarities between texts in
order to expose deep-seated structural similarities. A tripartite
structure for Shakespearean comedy was suggested, which
involved a move from 'normal world to green world and back
again'.[13] Frye, like Anne Barton, had suggested that because in
Twelfth Night the action of the play occurs in one place, and is thus
more like *The Comedy of Errors*, *Pericles* and *The Tempest*, it should
be classified as a 'sea comedy', where 'the entire action takes place
in the second world'.[14] This 'second world' is a mutation of Frye's
'green world' where, he argues, the metamorphosis of comedy
takes place, and a new society begins to crystallize around the
newly married lovers. Anne Barton's addition to this interpretation was the idea that the characters, as much as the audience,
were to be aware of the artificiality of this romantic location:

> For some characters, it is true, holiday perpetuates itself. Viola,
> Orsino, Olivia and Sebastian remain, by the special dispensa-
> tion of art, in a romance world that never falters. They recover
> their sanity. They have gained a certain self-knowledge from
> their experiences. But it is clear that they remain privileged
> inhabitants of Illyria: that place of idealistic friendships and
> sudden irrational loves, where people are shipwrecked into
> good fortune, and the dead return..... The other characters
> of the comedy, by contrast, are exiled into reality. For most of
> them, holiday is paid for in ways that have real life con-
> sequences.[15]

The world of Illyria is thus romantic, artificial and inherently
melancholic for the audience who, like the non-romantic characters, experience a parallel 'jolt into reality':

Only in the theatre can some people be left in Illyria. For the rest of us, at a certain point, the play is done and we return to normality along with Sir Toby, Aguecheek and Malvolio. *Twelfth Night* is over, and we have been dismissed into a world beyond holiday, where the rain it raineth every day.[16]

The conclusion of John Barton's production followed this interpretation in a particularly literal fashion, with Sir Toby, Aguecheek and Malvolio all leaving the stage by exits nearest to the audience. Anne Barton's critical attempts to equate the audience's reality with the harsher reality that she identifies within *Twelfth Night* owes much to the ideas explored in her earlier study, *Shakespeare and the Idea of the Play*.[17] In this reading of *Twelfth Night*, the relationship between artifice (which is taken to be art) and reality is deemed to be confrontational. Anne Barton has adopted Frye's basic structure for this comedy but altered the thematic spirit which underpins it. For Frye, 'Shakespearean comedy illustrates, as clearly as any mythos we have, the archetypal function of literature in visualizing the world of desire, not as an escape from "reality" but as a genuine form of the world that human life tries to imitate.'[18] Frye finds in Shakespearean comedy a harmonious aspiration for the real to imitate the world of desire, but for Anne Barton, 'fantasy fights against the cold light of day'.[19] As well as focusing on the individual's experience confronting the artifice versus reality paradox, she seemed also to be modifying the concept of the 'festive' explored by C. L. Barber in his seminal text. Anne Barton and Barber both emphasize the parallel between the artificial nature of the festive world and the audience's experience in attending the play, because performance and festive moment have a definite time span and must end. The difference between Barton and Barber is that although both critics recognize the ephemeral nature of the festive, Barber's understanding of this concept is far more positive than Anne Barton's. Primarily this is because Barber proposes that the festive is a *social* movement 'which involve[s] inversion, statement and counter-statement and a basic movement which can be summarised in the formula through release to clarification'.[20] Anne Barton, and also the production which was complemented by her programme note, rejected this 'through release to clarification' formula because 'holiday is paid for in ways that have real life consequences'.[21] The production appeared to employ the festive as an example of an artificial situation that encapsulated a heightened mood and emotion in which the behaviour of individuals could be explored. Thus there was a significant shift in focus from Barber's understanding of festive comedy in terms of its optimistic social ramifications to the production's definition, which focused on the fate of individuals, who even while participating in the revelry are pessimistically aware of the limitations of the festive moment.

For much of the twentieth century this focus on individuals and characters was of course a mainstay of academic Shakespearean criticism.[22] However, the focus on character was also an essential underpinning of twentieth-century theatre practice. In 1984 Barton defined two traditions which have shaped modern theatrical presentations: the 'modern' and the 'Elizabethan'. The 'modern' was located as follows:

> Our tradition is based more than we are usually conscious of on various modern influences like Freud and television and the cinema and, above all, the teachings of the director and actor, Stanislavsky. I suspect he works on us all the time, often without our knowing it.[23]

The reference to Stanislavsky is significant here, and it highlights not just a theatrical working practice,[24] but a theoretically derived practice which has shaped the way in which Barton and many other twentieth-century theatre practitioners perceived Shakespearean comedy. Barton has also affirmed that this 'exploration of character... is at the heart of the acting tradition in England'.[25] For Barton the source of this 'modern' tradition lies in an earlier 'Elizabethan' tradition:

> I believe our tradition actually derives from him [Shakespeare]. In a sense Shakespeare invented it, with his teeming gift for characterisation and his frequent use of naturalistic language, though he didn't of course know that he was doing it at the time.[26]

The foregrounding of the significance of character in a Shakespearean text, together with a commitment to Stanislavskian exploratory techniques, constitute the essence of Barton's perception of Shakespearean comedy.

In Barton's production of *Twelfth Night*, the romance world of Illyria, which provided the context for this exploration of character, was realized partly through the set design of Christopher Morley. It consisted of 'a long receding wattle tunnel decorated by four stately, flickering candlesticks, but lit from outside, sometimes a sombre twilight umber, sometimes soaring into sunburst brilliance',[27] which the designer had inserted into the basic white box structure that had served for other productions that season. This description illustrates how the lighting of the set was one of the keys to the design's success. Not only did it contribute to the evocation of the magical mood of the production, it also enabled the director and his designer to create a permanent framework for the play while also retaining a degree of flexibility in establishing the different locations within Illyria. In the opening scene, for example, the perspective created by the receding latticed walls was employed to suggest Orsino's baronial hall. The lighting, together with some pre-performance business, involving a lutenist playing on stage and leading into a song by Dowland, evoked the languid melancholy of Orsino's Court. This music was reprised before each of Orsino's entrances as an aural reminder of the character's mournful infatuation. Sound-effects were also used to create the mood of Illyria and to suggest a web of cross-references and thematic links. The most significant of these were the sounds of the sea: waves were heard crashing on to Illyria's shore during Orsino's opening speech, and the scene concluded with the noise of screeching gulls accompanying Valentine's description of his failed suit to Olivia, as Orsino sat 'dashed'.[28] Some critics, such as Stanley Wells, saw this dramatic notation through sounds as being akin to Wilson Knight's academic interest in the 'symbolic significance of sea imagery'.[29] Yet others found the sea-noises spurious and intrusive, and appeared not to make the connection between them and the programme note which identified Illyria as a 'world elsewhere, [and] a mysteriously benevolent providence associated with the sea'.[30]

The stage setting and design were used to forge connections between important moments in the play. For example, Viola's arrival in Illyria in I.ii was linked to the moment of *anagnorisis* in V.i when Viola and Sebastian are reunited. The first episode was undoubtedly crucial in establishing Barton's interpretation, as the audience needed to recognize Viola as the somewhat bewildered representative of a world beyond Illyria's shore. Viola entered the stage, and Illyria, from the rear of the latticed tunnel. Two large doors were flung back, and to the accompaniment of loud crashing waves, Viola was ushered slowly down the slightly raked stage by the sea captain. As she did so, the stage was filled with smoke, intended perhaps to suggest sea-spray, but which in the murky darkness also created an atmosphere reminiscent of a dream-world. This was an interesting embodiment not only of Frye's sea-comedy, but also of his statement that the 'green-world has analogies, not only to the fertile world of ritual, but to the dream-world that we create out of our own desires'.[31] Viola, played by Judi Dench, was bedraggled and barefooted, and in her long frilly dress and waist-length fair hair 'there was a touch of Alice in Wonderland in her appearance as she looked wonderingly about her and asked "What country, friend, is this?"'[32] Wells may have just taken his cue from Anne Barton's programme note,[33] but the stage presentation had undoubtedly conjured up the dreamlike strangeness of Illyria. Moreover, the sound of crashing waves, which accompanied Viola's arrival in the play and Illyria, encouraged the audience to make cross-references to the first scene, where Orsino's longing for love has also been expressed to the accompaniment of sea-sounds. Thus the audience was encouraged to make the connection between Orsino's desire for love and Viola as the potential recipient of his affections, born from the sea like Aphrodite. Once the thematic pattern had been established in this way, the sea was used, almost cryptically, to reassure the audience that all would be well. For example, it was heard in I.iv.9ff and repeatedly in II.iv, reaching a crescendo on Orsino's line 'But mine is all as hungry as the sea, / And can digest as much' (II.iv.99–100), and then underlining the following interchange between himself and Viola–Cesario, where she surreptitiously reveals her love for him.

This underscoring of climactic moments with sound-effects was a realization of Anne Barton's programme note, which insisted on the regenerative power of the sea both for the romantic aspirations of its inhabitants and for the reunion of Viola and Sebastian. Barton's staging of this moment of recognition and reconciliation in V.i was generally agreed to be one of the most emotionally powerful moments of the production. As Orsino spoke the line 'One face, one voice, one habit and two persons!' (V.i.213), the sound of the sea was heard. This, together with the swirl of sea-mist and the shafts of mellow light filtering through the side walls, created a magical, still, dreamlike centre to the scene, in which there was 'a sudden freeze of motion and sound as lost brother confronts lost sister with all the other characters forgotten save the enigmatic Feste framed in the background between them'.[34] With the twins placed downstage, and the sexual innuendo of Olivia's 'Most wonderful!' played down, Sebastian's tentative enquiry 'Do I stand there?' was charged with emotion. This staging of this moment of *anagnorisis* was obviously intended to echo Viola's first entry into Illyria. In terms of the plot it is the casting aside of the disguise first assumed then, but thematically it is a moment where Viola and Sebastian reaffirm their rebirth from the sea. Significantly, one of the few excisions Barton made to the text occurred during this interchange, when the following lines were cut:

> ... which to confirm
> I'll bring you to a captain in this town
> Where lie my maiden weeds; by whose gentle help
> I was preserved to serve this noble Count.
> All the occurrence of my fortune since
> Hath been between this lady and this lord.
>
> (V.i.251–6)

The characters in Barton's interpretation did not need any such 'empirical' evidence: they, and perhaps the audience by this stage, were bewitched by the regenerative powers of the romance world of Illyria, which possessed its own internal logic.

The presence of Feste in this reconciliation scene was again an amendment made by Barton. While the *New Cambridge* text[35] used in the production does not include Feste in this scene, his inclusion framed between brother and sister was necessary for Barton's interpretation, which afforded him the role of choric commentator who exposes the artificiality of Illyria and its romantic inhabitants. Feste was dressed simply and somewhat raggedly in neutral colours of cream and beige, and he merged chameleon-like into the prevailing autumnal colours of the set. He was presented as an observer-figure commenting on the fragility of the festive moment. Feste was employed to affect the 'mood' of the play primarily through his songs. Snatches of his songs became associated with specific characters: as the Dowland air had become Orsino's leitmotif, so 'Hey Robin' became associated with Olivia, 'Farewell, Dear Heart' with Sebastian, and 'What is love? 'Tis not hereafter' with Sir Toby and Sir Andrew. The songs were also used by Barton as a major device to explore character. In II.iii additional songs were included as part of the night-time revels, and as Feste sang the other individuals frequently joined in, repeating phrases and humming the tune. In this way the suggestion was made that this was a regular occurrence, creating the 'impression of a shared background among the members of Olivia's household'.[36] The songs were also made relevant to the character's predicament. Sir Toby substituted Maria's name in the Tudor Ballad 'Constant Susanna' included in the scene as part of a mock-courtship of Maria. The melancholy mood which the song generated owed much to Sir Toby's advanced age and also Maria's obvious aspirations to marry this lukewarm suitor. In this scene Maria's overtures of friendship were brusquely rejected by Sir Toby, and his line "'tis too late to go to bed now' was directed to Maria as a rejection of her sexual favours. Presumably these details were included in agreement with the view of the programme note that their marriage was 'the coldest of off-stage bargains'.[37]

The scenes of festive revelry thus tended towards the serious in Barton's interpretation. This was largely because the actors had been led through their exploration of character to demonstrate to the audience their own awareness of their predicament as ageing individuals trapped in an artificial festive world. In the representation of Malvolio the paradoxical twinning of the comic and serious elements was left far more open. The early scenes saw him as almost ludicrously comic in his appearance as a 'Victorian cartoon Humpty Dumpty, all bald, ruffled and painfully etched sneer lines'.[38] The confidence and arrogance of the character attired in yellow stockings was such that 'when he glances down from his watch to the sundial he has been honouring with his elbow it is the sundial he alters',[39] physically lifting it from the ground. Several critics commented that such comic stage business seemed to be at odds with the production's darker undercurrents.[40] Arguably because the audience were often laughing with the character rather than at him, they were more predisposed to pity his plight when imprisoned like 'a great black bull, tethered and roaring from his pen: and then half-emerging, white-faced and disconcertingly human, to rail'.[41] This sympathy was increased because Feste demonstrated a world-weary distaste as he put aside his Sir Topas disguise. However, ironically it seems that the audience did not side completely with Malvolio because all of the characters in this production had exerted a pull on the audience's sympathy. Judi Dench, who played Viola, was particularly praised. Many critics believed the strength of her performance was her ability to present both sides of her dual personality to the audience simultaneously. The conflict of her assumed fictional role and the 'reality' was central to Barton's reading of the play. Stanley Wells describes her delivery of 'I am all the daughters of my father's house / And all the brothers too' (II.iv.119–20):

> A tiny pause followed by a catch in the voice as he said 'brothers' took us movingly from the fictional situation of Viola speaking equivocally to conceal her own disguise, to the reality of the situation in which she genuinely believed that she had lost her brother. This was truly poetic acting.[42]

Poetic acting, certainly, and also acting firmly established within the dominant British tradition of psychological exploration of character. It is this aspect of Barton's style that also affords his production of *Twelfth Night* the descriptive term 'Chekhovian': first in its 'beauty of communication, of sympathy, understanding and passion',[43] but also in the way that Barton explored

> [the truth] in the most intimate moods, in the most secret corners of the heart. This truth moves us by its unexpectedness, by its mysterious links with our forgotten past, by its inexplicable foreknowledge of the future, which baffles commonsense, which seems to mock or even play malicious tricks on human beings, at times perplexing them utterly and at times making them laugh.[44]

Although this would be an apt assessment of Barton's production of *Twelfth Night*, it is, of course, Stanislavsky's description of Chekhov's drama. The parallel extends to Stanislavsky's analysis of the subtle mixture of 'serious' and 'comic' moods, and the implication that there is a logical consistency in even the most random events. Yet what is more interesting is the important parallel here between the Stanislavsky–Chekhov and the Barton–Shakespeare relationships. Chekhov accused Stanislavsky of ruining his play *The Cherry Orchard* and converting what Chekhov thought was a 'comedy and in places a farce'[45] into what the director Stanislavsky thought was 'a great tragedy of Russian life'.[46] Primarily this was the result of Stanislavsky's applying his quite distinctive production techniques to create a 'mood'[47] that would assist his actors, yet in the process altered Chekhov's comedy into a tragedy. It would seem a similar criticism could be levelled at Barton's treatment of *Twelfth Night*. Barton's application of Stanislavskian-based techniques led him to implant detailed character analysis within accepted anthropological structures, derived from Frye and Barber, which had primarily displayed the social, and not the individual's function in comedy. Arguably, tensions would inevitably result and, as in the case of Stanislavsky's exploration of Chekhov's individuals trapped within a limiting social system, the prevailing mood would be melancholic.

Nevertheless, despite these reservations, John Barton's production of *Twelfth Night* was a great critical and box-office success and a highly influential production. The measure of its stature may be seen in the influence it has exerted on both literary criticism and theatrical presentation. In 1974, for example, Alexander Leggatt's comments on the play in *Shakespeare's Comedy of Love* seem to be operating within a Bartonian frame of reference.[48] Yet it is perhaps in terms of theatrical presentation, especially within the RSC, that Barton's influence is most clearly seen. Terry Hands's 1979 production of the play, set in a winter landscape, drew heavily upon and also intensified the darker aspects of Barton's production. In 1983, John Caird's production echoed the 1969 costume designs and also followed Barton in having a pathetic, elderly Sir Andrew and Sir Toby. Most recently, Trevor Nunn's 1996 film version seemed to take many of its cues from Barton's production. This may be seen in details, such as Nunn's Malvolio exposing his arrogance by trying to alter a sundial, and a malicious, drunken Sir Toby rejecting the besotted advances of Maria. Yet the comparison runs deeper: and despite the difference in setting, within Nunn's Victorian *Twelfth Night* there is a very similar commitment to an exploration of the psychological complexity of the characterization, coloured again by the Chekhovian context.[49] Paradoxically, it could be that Barton's persuasive interpretation of *Twelfth Night* has now become hardened into the very kind of critical cliché that Barton wished to question in 1969.

Adrian Noble's 1997 RSC production of *Twelfth Night* may in some respects be seen as an attempt to re-evaluate such theatrical and cinematic readings of the play. The visual style of the production was very different, described by critics as being 'bright, circus-like, almost cartoonish',[50] and a production 'that's apparently a co-production with the National Theatre of Teletubbyland . . . with its dayglo primal colours and giant rubber props'.[51] The set by Anthony Ward was dominated by a large arch which traversed the stage. As the play progressed, a large luminescent globe moved along the track of the arch from one side of the stage to the other. The design seemed to have symbolized in this dominant image the play's fascination with the passage of time and the inexorable role of fate, as well as helping to mark seasonal changes suggested in the production. The action of the play was performed beneath this arch. Particular locations were suggested by stage properties either carried on to the basically bare playing space, or else appearing up through trapdoors or flown in. In this way the production gained pace and continuity, and the design of the properties gave a sense of quickly sketched-in context. For example, the late-night carousing of Sir Toby Belch and Sir Andrew Aguecheek in II.iii took place in a basement kitchen (a staircase was wheeled in from stage left), dominated by a giant fridge which was laden with large bottles and an extravagant amount of leftover food. This image of plenitude was redolent of the post-Christmas period of the play's title, and was further suggested by the drunken singing of the half-remembered song 'The Twelve Days of Christmas'. Yet the scale was exaggerated, comic and non-realistic. The suggestion of winter in the first half of the play gave way in later scenes to spring, as a cuckoo and, later, other songbirds were heard in the grounds of Olivia's house. Unlike Barton's use of birdsong, however, this sound-effect was not designed to give layers of meaning to the mood being created, but rather to act as a jokey self-conscious indicator of a change of season. The gardens of Illyria's house were also caricatured and larger than life. The scene was brightly lit in sunshine yellow and the garden was suggested by a vivid green box-tree which was obviously artificial and studded with brush-like plastic nodules. It was either raised, to reveal two dark pillars (the tree trunks of a child's drawing), or parted in the middle to create different locations within the grounds. These rather quirky cartoon-like locations were contrasted with other scenes created with realistic detail. For example, in I.ii Viola was discovered in a hospital bed, recounting her tale to the sea captain, who was wearing pyjamas and dressing gown and had his arm in a sling. It was more *Doctor in the House* or *Carry on Nurse* than *Casualty* (though many first-night theatre critics alluded to the latter), with a starchily crisp nurse in attendance exuding annoyance at the pipe-smoking Captain, before Viola made her escape disguised as a doctor. The design of this scene and several that followed often seemed to take the 1950s (perhaps as perceived through *Carry On* films) as its historical cue. Maria's costume and that of Feste were suggestive of this post-war period: Maria sported high heels and a tight-fitting skirt, and there were suggestions of the teddy-boy in Feste's DA hairstyle, drainpipe trousers and crêpe-soled shoes. Nevertheless, the overall costume design was eclectic, and incorporated motifs from a number of twentieth-century styles, ranging from the velvet-suited aesthetes of Orsino's circle to the loud check suit of Sir Toby. The design of the production was, in short, bold, brash and cartoon-like.

Many critics expressed disappointment at the interpretation of the play offered by Adrian Noble. Michael Billington in the *Guardian* noted that 'Adrian Noble seems born to direct *Twelfth Night*, the most Chekhovian of Shakespeare's comedies. But Noble's new production...is whimsically strange – a kind of pop-art Alice in Illyria with little emotional reality or erotic tension.'[52] In the *Daily Telegraph* Charles Spencer commented that 'one expects more from Noble than such a dumbly populist, churlishly unendearing approach to this wonderfully rich play'.[53] In these remarks one senses the disappointment of first-night critics denied much of the psychological richness of character seen in earlier productions. As the critics cast around for something to praise which was within the range of their usual expectations of this play, they seized on a variety of different performances which fulfilled their wishes in terms of moving characterization. Some selected Malvolio, played by Philip Voss, who displayed a 'sensuality behind his monolithic grandeur, a defencelessness that exposes itself in sudden sobs of joy when he decides that his desirable employer desires him'.[54] Others chose Feste, played by Stephen Boxer, who 'suggests that Feste's word-corrupting obsession is a cover for his loneliness: his final solace-seeking stare at the audience was the most touching thing of the evening'.[55] Some even, perhaps clutching at straws, singled out Fabian: 'played as a chauffeur, Malcolm Scates puts in a masterly cameo, alive with social and psychological nuance'.[56] The performances given by Noble's actors and the playful, quirky, self-referential visual style of the production had certainly challenged these particular members of the audience.

The programme for the 1997 production gives further clues to the interpretative style adopted by Noble. As with the production, there was something rather eclectic about the material included. There was an essay entitled 'Sadness is All' by Dr Trevor Turner, a consultant psychiatrist, an essay on 'Shakespeare's comedies' by Professor Stanley Wells, a stage history of the play with photographs of past productions, and the usual cast lists and résumés. The bulk of the programme was taken up with 'character studies'. However, these were character studies with a difference. The preamble commented:

> Early Shakespeare criticism was generally much concerned with character, particularly the identification of dominant traits and the 'fatal flaw'.... Today the business world thrives on psychological profiling – systems of character identification that management consultants use to promote self-awareness and help employees interact more successfully with each other. One of the most popular of these is the 'Enneagram', which sorts people into nine personality types, with corresponding positive and negative characteristics.
>
> Putting the two schools of thought together, we subjected the inhabitants of Illyria to the Enneagram.[57]

What followed were a number of character sketches constructed out of quotations from academic critics, mainly from the late nineteenth century to the 1960s. Each character sketch was accompanied by an enneagram report.[58] While thanks were offered to the production's sponsor, Allied Domecq, for the idea, the presentation of these character sketches was humorous and playful, with each study accompanied by a Steadmanesque caricature of the actor playing the part in the production. This format seemed to be a direct parody of the programme for the 1969 production, which had also favoured character studies. It is interesting to note that the 1997 programme used not just the same critics, but also many of the identical quotations from the 1969 programme. While it is most unlikely that Noble himself devised the programme, it is likely that he would have had to agree to its design as one which complemented his production. Both programme and production, with their eclectic, parodic styles, challenged the received notions of both early twentieth-century character criticism in academic studies of *Twelfth Night* and the Stanislavskian techniques which had often underpinned these ideas in the theatre.

It was not just characterization that was challenged by the playful style of the production. The critics were generally unhappy with its treatment of the play's mood. Michael Billington commented that 'Noble's strenuously bright version misses its peculiar weave of comedy and sadness, reality and fantasy',[59] and Peter Kemp noted that 'the two poles of the play are wrenched wider apart. Instead of shot-silk ripplings between light and dark, there are lurchings between farce and something harsh.'[60] If we accept a recent definition of farce as a theatrical form whose 'premise is that of a wacky world without much sense, inhabited by lot of zany people, where logic and reason have no function',[61] then Noble's production had numerous moments of farce. They were seen both in scenes where farce may be expected, such as III.iv, where the two reluctant 'swordsmen' are brought together (the promptbook note for Sir Toby's line 244 reads 'Bilko impersonation', which indicates the frame of reference here), and somewhat bizarrely in I.iv, where the interpolation of a short game of basketball and a shower scene was used to exploit the comic sexual tension of Viola's disguise. There was often much farcical business with clothes and stage properties, such as Maria's collecting Sir Toby's drunkenly discarded clothes in I.iii, and all Feste's worldly goods falling out of his large holdall in I.v. This seaside postcard humour continued in III.iv, with Malvolio transformed from sober black into tennis shorts, white boater and yellow striped socks, with his tennis racket suggestively held between his legs. The tormenting of Malvolio was one of the harsher moments alluded to by Kemp. Malvolio was imprisoned in a dog-kennel, where first smoke and then excrement were rained on him while he was tethered by a dog collar and chain. The harshness was emphasized by the clinical detachment of those involved in his tormenting or torture. When Malvolio appeared in V.i he was a pathetic figure with a stammer, taunted by Feste and his speech impediment mimicked by Olivia.[62] This stark presentation of the two polarities of mood in the play indicates that Noble made little attempt to reconcile the paradoxical impulses within the text, but instead chose to emphasize the play's discontinuity and its contradictory nature. Unlike Barton, he favoured neither of the 'persons' of the text and was prepared to allow it, if necessary, to display a 'split' personality.

The aim of this chapter has not been to suggest that Barton's production of *Twelfth Night* was better, or got more aspects of the play 'right', than Noble's.[63] The Barton production did show that the psychological analysis of character could result in poignant character vignettes in the theatre. It also, following Stanislavsky, employed music and lighting to give a general emotional colouring to the play, and create a mood which acted as a correlative to the melancholic thematic undercurrent which has been identified in theoretical analyses of the play. Yet one could perhaps concur with Stanley Wells's comment that 'a danger of Mr Barton's production methods... [is] that at their extremes, they were directing their audience what to think, instead of stimulating their imaginations to think it'.[64]

My main aim has been to show that a particular production, whatever one's judgement of its merits, may become a benchmark when a number of historical influences converge. Barton's production of *Twelfth Night* was influenced by academic analysis and could be seen to be articulating its concerns, and it occurred at a moment when academic analysis and twentieth-century theatre practice were in step because of their fascination with characterization. This agreement chimed also with the traditions of English drama (as expounded by Barton), and was supported by the corporate discourse of the RSC which at that moment was imbued with the Cambridge ethos of its university-trained directors.

It is also clear, from my analysis of Noble's production and its reception, that benchmark productions like Barton's persist in people's minds for many years and through many intervening productions. Yet Noble's *Twelfth Night* demonstrates how such benchmarks can begin to be erased by new cultural developments. With its playful postmodern pastiche of styles, it challenged the Bartonian 'psychological' frame of reference and released some of the inherent comic energy of *Twelfth Night*. Noble's depiction of a more anarchic and farcical version of festivity allowed some of the comic stereotypical attributes of the characters to enliven the play. The textual 'face, voice and habit' of these productions was, like the twins in Shakespeare's play, nearly identical,[65] but the directors' exploration of the paradox of its two 'persons' produced very different interpretations of this complex play.

8. Shakespeare and the Homoerotic

MILES THOMPSON AND IMELDA WHELEHAN

In the 1990s theoretical explorations of Shakespeare have included a cluster of studies of homoeroticism in the plays. The more recent emphasis on exploring contradictions and subversion in the 'political' Shakespearean text, as opposed to unities and singular meaning in the works, means that critics are alive to the possibilities of performance overlayered by contemporary meanings, as well as revisiting dominant interpretations of the past. Of course, such investigations are vulnerable to accusations of historical relativism and of the wilful application of modish speculations to a previous era; as Peter Smith observes, 'Tillyardian uniformity is long gone and we fashion the Renaissance in our own fragmented image.'[1] To some extent we are trapped by the meanings circulated within our own time, and certainly the meanings of homoeroticism cannot simplistically be applied to Renaissance drama when we speculate on the impact of boy players, audience responses to the spectacle of theatre, sexual references and innuendo. Yet the concerns of the anti-theatricalists confirm that the subversive potential of the homoerotic content of Renaissance drama was a live issue in Shakespeare's own day, and that cross-dressing was a practice that extended beyond the confines of the stage. In our own time charges of homoeroticism in Shakespeare can be as emotive as those of the anti-theatrical polemicists, and the most cogent analyses are occasionally reduced to questions of Shakespeare's own sexual orientation – resulting in anxious attempts to protect the reputation of the Bard from 'corruption'.

This chapter aims to offer an introduction to representations and receptions of the homoerotic in Shakespeare. We will begin by examining the Elizabethan context and the claims of the anti-theatricalist critics, and then go on to look at how critical perspectives on the dynamics of the homoerotic in performance

produced insightful contributions to the debates about interpretation, culture and performance during the twentieth century.
Such work has arguably widened the possibility for the plays to be
read as rendering a plurality of meanings which include questions of gendered performance in relation to sexuality. It is clear
also that the response to homoeroticism, and attempts to repress
such 'improper' inflections, tell us much about the ways Shakespearean texts are made to mean today, and how the homoerotic
charge of some of the plays can still prove to be incendiary as a
topic for critical discussion.

As the theatre represents a space of metaphoric potential that
can take advantage of the possibilities for disturbance and anarchy, so the stage provides a space for performances which include
a homoerotic perspective. The exclusion of women from the
Elizabethan stage meant that boys played women's parts, a tradition that stretched back to the medieval period and the mystery
plays, and in the Elizabethan period boys were apprenticed to the
theatre just as they might be to any respectable trade. Shakespeare would therefore have understood the boy heroine as a
natural phenomenon within the theatre, as this was a feature of
the public playhouses and of all-boy companies. Although it was a
reality of which Shakespeare took full dramatic advantage, we
have no hard evidence about the methods which he used to
achieve a credible performance style from the boys themselves.

The aesthetic of the boy heroine relied on effeminization and
cross-dressing, allowing circulations of sexually explicit references, including homoerotic ones which would have been understood by the audience, as well as prompting criticism from
commentators who were opposed to the theatre. It is difficult to
understand how cross-dressing was organized in terms of performance, yet it is clear that the style of acting which the Elizabethan
theatre demanded was different from the earlier period of mystery plays, with their renditions of biblical characters as stock
types – for example, Noah's wife becomes a nagging shrew with
echoes, perhaps, of the twentieth-century pantomime dame.[2]
The contemporary children's companies were attached to the
chapel choirs of noble households and their performance spaces
came under the protection of the Church; for this reason the
two major London companies were not subject to sudden closure
by the Lord Mayor.[3] This was opposed to public purpose-built

theatres, which attracted a much more heterogeneous audience, exposed to the elements. The works which boy companies performed perhaps did not require such emotional depth, with masques and light entertainment being the staple fare of these companies. In comparison, skills which were required by the boy actors playing the roles of women in the plays of Shakespeare and his contemporaries were markedly advanced, as characterizations for their works demanded greater depth and range, with an understanding of heroic and romantic women's roles which included demonstrations of female emotion and sexuality.

It is worth examining the skills which they may have possessed in order to have a clearer understanding of their abilities, but the content of the plays themselves attests to a style of performance which demands complexity and emotional conviction. Characterizations would have been completed through the voices and gestures of the performer, and it is possible that the physical presence of the cross-dressed boy actor would have presented a phenomenon which was both believable and convincing, demonstrating that they would have possessed the necessary skills to undertake the female roles that Shakespeare wrote. In *Twelfth Night* Duke Orsino comments to Viola:

> Thy small pipe
> Is as the maiden's organ, shrill and sound,
> And all is semblative a woman's part.
> (I.iv.32–4)

One could assume from this comment that the boy actors' voices needed to be unbroken, yet this should not rule out the possibility of them attempting roles which required greater depth of characterization such as Cleopatra, as a boy's voice is still capable of considerable range and shading. The voice would have issued from an actor who had the appearance of a woman, and it would thus be an integral part of the overall phenomenon presented on the stage. Equally, it is probable that some of the more famous boy actors continued to portray women into their maturity.

Costumes would have also helped complete the picture. Roger Baker, in *Drag: A History of Female Impersonation on the Stage* (1968), notes that the boy actors would have appeared on stage in attire which would have reflected the status of the characters that they played, as well as being in the style of the period. They would probably have been bought by the theatre company from the servants of aristocratic families, who were presented with these hand-me-downs by their employers.[4] Elizabethan costume included wide skirts, ruffs, padded sleeves and rigid corsets, and could have made expansive gestures and movement difficult, making costume and voice arguably the most important features.

Furthermore, the contemporary appearance of the boy actors wearing fashionable clothes may have added to the erotic spectacle which the anti-theatricalists feared would arouse the male audience. As one contemporary critic of the theatre, John Rainolds, remarks: 'what sparkles of lust to that vice the putting on of woman's attire on men may kindle in unclean affections'.[5] Rainolds's objection to the boy heroine may have included a concern that the potential effect on the male audience would have been enhanced by the resemblance to women of fashion. His statement is a good example of the obsessive interest which critics of the period expressed concerning the effects which the apparel of the cross-dressed boy actors could have on those who viewed the phenomenon, and this reflects wider anxieties about breaches in dress codes where costume very rigidly demarcated class and gender status in society at large.

Jean Howard observes that 'crossdressing, like other disruptions of the Renaissance semiotics of dress, opened a gap between the supposed reality of one's social station and sexual kind, and the clothes that were to display that reality to the world'.[6] She also notes that cross-dressing occurs beyond the confines of the stage and cites examples of women dressing as men in public, which, in the case of lower-class women, would link them automatically to prostitution or sexual incontinence.[7] In the case of theatrical cross-dressing, however, a true understanding of the Elizabethan audience's reception of performances is difficult to gauge, due to lack of information – particularly about the mechanics of the plays – and as the perceptions which surrounded both the theatre and plays in performance are hugely different to our own. Of course, measuring audience response, even from our own period, is especially difficult; the possibility of gauging or articulating the nature of desires provoked by performance seems remote. Nonetheless, desire (and its suppression) is the focus of the anti-theatricalists' attack; similarly, explorations of homoerotic desire, even in current analyses of Shakespeare, are often viewed with hostility.

In *Desire and Anxiety: Circulations of Sexuality in Shakespearean Drama* (1992), which looks at tensions between sexuality and gender in Shakespearean drama, Valerie Traub investigates this difficult question, commenting that 'individual desires and anxieties, fantasies and fears complicate the experience of spectatorship', yet speculates that 'desires were encoded along gender status lines'.[8] This view suggests that the various personal interests, and the different understanding of performances by individual audience members, make it difficult to generalize about their reception of possible homoerotic perspectives within the plays the audiences would have witnessed. Here Traub proposes a perspective which further problematizes the issue of spectatorship. After having noted the importance of the different spaces where plays were performed, such as public playhouses and the more exclusive private theatres, she proposes that 'erotic desire may sometimes *exceed* gender constraints',[9] so that erotic spectacle and sexual desire were perhaps a transgressive force in the theatre which fragmented certainties of a self governed by gender, sex and status identity, not least because of the need to stage representations of women in a context controlled by men.

The ideological shifts that have occurred between the Renaissance and today also present problems of interpretation. As Susan Bassnett comments: 'we can only with great difficulty imagine how the Renaissance mind worked';[10] never more so that when we try to re-create their attitude to sex and sexuality. Therefore it is difficult to comprehend the way in which the Elizabethans would have viewed cross-dressed performers on the stage, and any of the possibilities which their presence suggested, as the terms through which both the audiences and the anti-theatricalists criticized them expressed different meanings from those same terms today. During the Renaissance the terms 'gay' and 'homosexual' had no currency. Yet as Kate Chedgzoy reminds us, 'to say that the modern form of homosexual identity did not exist before the word "homosexual" was coined in 1869 is not necessarily to say that same-sex relationships or sexual practices had no cultural meaning before that time'.[11] Sexual encounters between men would have been discussed under the umbrella term of 'sodomy', which could also include popery, bestiality and sorcery,[12] and were therefore gathered together as heretical practices. 'Buggery' and 'sodomy' were acts one could perform upon persons or animals which were not assumed to comprise a person's sexual identity as they might be seen to in the twenty-first century. As Michel Foucault observes, re-marking on the insertion of the 'homosexual' as a category into nineteenth-century medical discourse, 'the sodomite had been a temporary aberration; the homosexual was now a species'.[13] Although highly-charged sexual relationships between men must have existed, it is misleading to believe that the Elizabethans would have conceived of them as homoerotic, as this term is understood today. Instead they would have discussed male same-sex encounters as sodomitical practices, with the emphasis on the act rather than what it said about the person performing the act. This should not imply that we are unable to understand Elizabethan social arrangements or make contrasts with contem-porary reflections on sexuality; Valerie Traub asserts: 'despite the absence of a specific discourse of sexuality, within early modern culture there circulated significations that, however incommen-surate, can be usefully brought in tension with modern meanings'.[14] Late twentieth-/early twenty-first-century under-standings of circulations of homoeroticism express very different ideas, connoting erotic practices and desires which are same-sex directed, but which may also include relationships within this perspective: in other words, we now perceive homosexuality as a sexual identity.

Rainolds's remark, quoted above, suggests the inflammatory style of the highly vocal group of anti-theatrical critics who inveighed against cross-dressed performance as it was practised in the sixteenth-century theatre. Cross-dressing caused consider-able comment from these critics, often exposing their anxieties and concerns about homoeroticism and its effects within their tirades against the theatre. It could be argued that whilst the Elizabethan stage was not the site of depravity which this group insisted upon, their writing provides a window through which it is possible to observe the major concerns that cross-dressing generated. Given that several critics (such as Jean E. Howard) have affirmed the existence of same-sex encounters within the space of the theatre and beyond, one could argue that this *was* a key space for 'depravity'; but whether cross-dressing can be seen itself to *generate* a homoerotic desire which would otherwise not be expressed is another matter. Howard cautions that it might be 'a mistake to romanticise the period as one in which the unfettered experience of polymorphous desire reigned supreme'.[15] She further notes that:

> the very fact that antitheatrical tracts were so wide-ranging, that they often constituted general anatomies of social folly, suggests that the public theater was not viewed in the period as an isolated phenomenon, but as part of an ensemble of cultural and social changes disturbing enough to warrant various forms of intervention and management.[16]

Much of the vehemence of such attacks against the theatre seem bound up with its capacity in performance to disrupt the dominant social order, and playfully suggest the viability of social and even sexual alternatives. Rainolds was one of a group of respected academics and formidable scholars (he eventually became president of Corpus Christi College, Oxford), who produced a constant stream of pamphlets that attacked cross-dressing and its supposed effects upon the stage. Other outspoken commentators included Barnabe Riche, George Gascoigne, Stephen Gosson, Phillip Stubbes, William Prynne and William Rankins, who all joined the debate, writing treatises and books which objected loudly to the appearance of boys playing women's parts upon the Elizabethan stage.

Effeminacy is another term that is used to identify behaviour which is often associated in the late twentieth century with homosexual behaviour, but prior to this, as Alan Sinfield notes, it meant 'being emotional and spending too much time with women',[17] and that to be manly in Elizabethan England 'was of course to go with women, but in a way which did not forfeit mastery'.[18] Both Sinfield and Phyllis Rackin point out examples from Shakespeare's plays where, for example, Romeo and Antony are 'unmanned' by love, and where virility and physical prowess are 'not only depicted as consistent with men's erotic desire for other men, it also seems to be expressed in it'.[19] The obvious example of this male erotic identification is of course Coriolanus's expression of his admiration for his old enemy, Tullus Aufidius. Sinfield's interpretation of effeminacy suggests that the criticisms which were levelled at the boy actors also included their desertion of a traditional masculine role which withheld emotion, but held power over women. William Prynne concentrates on the possible blurring of the roles of the sexes, producing a theatrical spectacle that induced boys to 'effeminate their manly nature, being both effeminate men and women, yea being neither men nor women if we speak truly'.[20] Stubbes, in *The Anatomie of Abuses* (1583), condemns the theatre outright, making quite clear his belief that the theatre breeds homosexuality and that costume and spectacle obscure status and gender identity in such a way as to prompt social anarchy. After having witnessed a performance he notes: 'they play the sodomites or worse. And these be the fruits of plays and interludes for the most part.'[21] His tract suggests the extent of paranoia about the consequences of masquerade and the politics of appearance where sumptuary regulations lay down clear guidance about who was permitted to wear certain colours, fabrics and forms of adornment. To twenty-first-century eyes the rhetoric which the polemicists used to express their opinions appears melodramatic in tone. However, their assertions are a valuable indicator of the fears which surround the potential erotic interest of Elizabethan theatrical texts, and of the performances themselves. One of their main fears was that the transgressions of the boy actors would destabilize existing categories of gender and sexuality, and the outcome of watching the transgressive act of cross-dressed performance would lead to sodomy. The intention of condemning boy actors appearing as women on the stage is very clear – not only covering their onstage performances but their possible off-stage activities. Stubbes also comments on the highly performative and suggestive nature of the behaviour of the actors upon the stage, thus causing conjecture as to the effects on the male audience watching such a performance, 'where such wanton gesture, and bawdy speeches, such laughing and fleering, such kissing, and bussing, such clipping and culling, such winking and glancing of wanton eyes, and the like, is used as is wonderful to behold.'[22] As Laura Levine indicates, there seemed to be among the anti-theatricalists a very real fear that the putting on of costume could transform men into women, arguing that 'At stake in the fear of effeminization must be a basic doubt: "What am I?"'[23] Levine's reading of the anti-theatricalists suggests a concern that the categories of man and woman are themselves unstable enough to be liable to slippage, and therefore need to be constantly under scrutiny. Here the connection of the world of the play to the outside world is debated and the effect of such cross-dressed spectacles upon the audience is assessed as the danger that the audience will go home and impersonate the actors – perhaps not just in terms of gender transformation, but because in the putting on of aristocratic costumes of fashion, the actors are presuming to be something beyond their own social standing.

Roger Baker remarks of some influential early twentieth-century critics that few 'can bring themselves to believe that their appearances were anything but odd and ruinous to the full effects of the play',[24] as they found it virtually impossible to come to terms with the phenomenon of boy actors playing women's parts. In this he demonstrates the impossibility of stripping away our contemporary perceptions of the meanings we ascribe to cross-dressing or drag, considering a convention organic to performance practice in a previous period. Sir Sidney Lee appears unable to believe that the boy actor could be capable of the range required to portray Shakespeare's major female characters: 'How characters like Lady Macbeth and Desdemona were adequately rendered beggars description', whilst Ivor Brown asks, 'Were there some full grown but sexually neutral types specially... retained for parts of this kind?'[25] These quotations acknowledge the critics' unease with the topic, but Baker does not analyse their reluctance to discuss the sixteenth-century cross-dressed heroine with any degree of seriousness. Nor does he note that the dismissive attitude of these once influential writers could have been due to pure homophobia, although Baker does admit that Brown may simply have associated homosexuality with effeminacy.[26] If anything, Baker is himself too willing to defuse the possibility of homoerotic tensions in the plays when he asserts: 'the female impersonators were completely accepted. There were no sly remarks or lecherous sneers, no passing moments of distaste or laughter, when a comely boy recited a feminine protestation of love or of deflowering.'[27] His main aim is clearly to make us understand how far our culture has shifted, and that to reproduce such stage practices today is, to Baker's mind, 'either distasteful or ridiculous'.[28]

In the light of later work, the apparent unwillingness of past writers to respond to cross-dressing and the homoerotic perspective within Shakespeare may be difficult to comprehend, but work by present-day theorists still attests to what Peter Smith calls the 'non canonicity of the subject'.[29] In offering this comment, Smith reminds us that in spite of the increased interest in gender and sexuality on the Renaissance stage, the importance of cross-dressing and the homoerotic within Shakespeare's plays is still not considered to be central to his work. Valerie Traub has argued how, in the case of Lisa Jardine's feminist text *Still Harping on Daughters* (1983), her emphasis on the boy actors' skilled mimicry of femininity dilutes the homoerotic effects of the spectacle and 'reconstitutes this interaction as implicitly *hetero*erotic'.[30] Peter Smith, after acknowledging that Lisa Jardine was one of the first theorists to investigate the erotic charge of the boy actor on the Renaissance stage, is also concerned by what he regards as her homophobia, where 'in her desire to address what she takes to be the sexism of an exclusively male acting company, Jardine begins to sound homophobic'.[31]

Particular interest in queer readings of the text, as well as examinations of homoerotic discourses which seem already contained within the text, is prompted particularly by one aspect of Shakespeare studies known as 'cultural materialism' (and latterly new historicism), which gained impetus in English departments during the 1980s – an accompaniment to the so-called 'crisis' in English studies, where theoreticians where supposedly battling it out with traditional literary scholars. Cultural materialism sees itself as an interdisciplinary approach to English studies which embraces theoretical perspectives in Marxism, psychoanalysis, semiotics and the developments of poststructuralist and feminist thought, combined with a sense of historicism and the wider cultural relevance of artefacts to the period in which they were produced.[32] In addition, such analyses are always critiques of ideology and aim to expose a society which is class-riven, gendered and whose political realities are precarious and suffer resistances at every level – such analyses afford a critique of the naturalizing effects of ideology itself. As Jonathan Dollimore observes, 'in the case of those who sexually transgressed in the early seventeenth century, what we recover may well tell us more about the society that demonised than about the demonised themselves'.[33]

Lisa Jardine notes the commonplace assumption that the well-known fact that female parts were taken by young male actors on the Elizabethan stage is of no consequence to the twentieth-century student of Shakespeare.[34] But as she goes on to assert, it *is* naive to assume that Elizabethan audiences accepted the practice as mere theatrical illusion, not least because of the sheer volume of contemporary comment on the convention occasioned by anti-theatricalists and others. Her essay further claims that playwrights were themselves well aware of the accusation that the spectacle of men in women's apparel would generate lust in male spectators and lead them into sexual perversion, and often exploited these fears within the dynamics of the drama itself. The knowledge that the female character who dressed as a boy *is* a boy allows for double-entendre and irony, and perhaps plays up the erotic possibilities of the boy in female dress rather than any attempt to naturalize the role. Obviously an awareness of the possible effect of more complex terms and their double meanings enriches our understanding of the plays, as well as highlighting the importance of historical context in such debate.

Stephen Greenblatt shows how in *Twelfth Night* the fulfilment of homoerotic desire is averted, but only just, and 'depends upon a movement that deviates from the desired object straight in one's path to a marginal object, a body one scarcely knows'.[35] Sebastian has little dramatic consequence but to emerge to unravel the transgressive possibilities of Viola's relationship to Orsino and Olivia. As Greenblatt says of Viola and Sebastian, 'with a change of a few conventional signals, the exquisitely feminine Viola and the manly Sebastian are indistinguishable: hence, perhaps, the disquieting intensity of Antonio's passion for Sebastian and the ease with which the confused Olivia is "betroth'd both to a maid and man"'.[36] The fact that Viola is not transformed into a 'maid' at the end of the play (in other words, she remains in boy's attire right up to the close) reminds us also that 'the only authentic transformation that the Elizabethan audience could anticipate when the play was done was the metamorphosis of Viola back into a boy'.[37] Moreover, this spectacle emphasizes the homoerotic man/boy bond between Orsino and Cesario-Viola which is not disrupted by marriage, suggesting that 'what is important is not the homoerotic or heterosexual nature of his desire so much as his maintenance of a position of superiority vis-à-vis either a wife or a male subordinate. Viola-Cesario, conveniently, stands for both.'[38] While Orsino reaffirms his dominant masculinity towards the close of the play, Viola, in common with other characters in the play, but particularly Antonio, represents the potential to subvert and thus undermine the status quo. The instability of the gender relationships in the play remains, despite the reassertion of control by the aristocratic male, and the continuity between Orsino's regard for 'Cesario' and Viola suggests a polymorphous perversity which supplants a fixed and regulated sexuality. This denial of heterosexual closure is further and more explicitly echoed in the epilogue to *As You Like It*, where Rosalind asserts:

> If I were a
> Woman I would kiss as many of you as had beards that pleased
> Me, complexions that liked me, and breaths that I defied not.
> (Epilogue, 14–16)

In its overt reference to the real gender identity of the actor this speech also takes the anarchic themes of the play beyond its confines; its address to the audience knowingly awakens all those anxieties expressed by the anti-theatricalists. It also reminds us that another of these critics' concerns was for the woman spectator who, thrust into the anarchic world of the theatre, may find herself inflamed by the performance as well as potentially subject to the lustful gaze of men. As John Northbrooke laments, 'what safegarde of chastitie can there be, where the woman is desired with so many eyes, where so many faces looke upon hir, and againe she uppon so manye? She must needes fire some, and hir selfe also fired againe, and she be not a Stone.'[39]

Just as we have seen how anxieties about the homoerotics of performance conjoin with wider concerns about social order in a time of change during the early modern period, so contemporary homophobia often parades itself in the guise of social welfare. Nowhere is this better displayed than in recent parliamentary debates about lowering the age of homosexual consent to 16, couched to an extent in terms of the need to protect the vulnerable from exploitation. While this may be a laudable aim as applied to young people in general, it is clearly situated in such

a way within this debate to enable the representation of homosexual relationships in terms of proselytism and exploitation.
Jamie Cann's (MP for Ipswich) speech betrays the central anxieties of many that 'If it were true that one cannot help being
homosexual and one is born that way, there would be no point in
trying to fight against it. However, that is not always the case.'[40]
Whereas in the early modern period, homosexual acts were
conceived as a lapse from upright moral behaviour, in the
twenty-first century, where homosexuality is seen as theoretically
an identity of its own, there is still the suggestion that transformations can be enacted, just as the anti-theatricalists' underlying
fears about cross-dressing seemed to be about the potential fluidity of gender signification.

In relation to Shakespeare studies in the twenty-first century
there are two issues at stake: the question of Shakespeare's own
sexual identity – most anxiously debated with reference to the
sonnets – and the exploration of homoerotic themes in the plays
themselves. Simon Shepherd's essay 'Shakespeare and Homosexuality' explores these issues and their impact on Shakespeare
scholarship in the twentieth century. This has led to instances of
where 'Homos have been spotted' – to coin Shepherd's phrase –
in several of the plays. He goes on to suggest that 'queerness
helpfully links things together'[41] by means of explaining some of
the more motiveless or malign actions of characters in the plays;
yet as Shepherd suspects, with good reason, the depiction of
homosexuality in plays is quite another matter from calling into
question the sexuality of the Bard. There is realistically little to be
gained from discovering Shakespeare's sexuality, particularly
since sexual identity was not inscribed in such terms during the
Elizabethan period, whereas much can be produced from readings of the plays which embrace recent theoretical explorations of
homoerotics in performance. Kate Chedgzoy asserts that 'while
the possibility that something we call homoerotic desire is represented in some of the plays has achieved a measure of general
acceptance, the idea that the *Sonnets*, read as autobiographical
documents, inscribe Shakespeare's own homoeroticism remains
troublesomely central to the debate'.[42] In other words, questions
of authorial sexual identity clash with excursions into the mut-
ability of sexual identity, the possibilities of which are represented
by the performances of boy actors on the Renaissance stage.

Nonetheless, these potentialities are rarely exploited in the modern theatre. Shepherd further claims that productions since the 1960s have offered representations of homoerotic desire through eroticized depictions of the male body which pander to the covert homoerotic fantasies of a nation – thus debates about Shakespeare's homosexuality are closed off as far too incendiary, and alternative expressions of sexual desire are consigned to the margins, as the product of ingenious over-determination of the text. Elaine Hobby turns to Section 28 of the Local Government Act 1988 in order to ponder the fate of Shakespeare studies in education. This Act had a clause forbidding the 'promotion' of homosexuality in schools and local authorities, which itself impacts on the way Shakespeare is taught to schoolchildren and young adults even today.

The representation of 'Shakespeare' in popular culture reinforces the heterosexist discourse which generally surrounds criticism of his work. The blockbuster *Shakespeare in Love* (John Madden, 1999), while bringing to popular film the 'realities' of the Renaissance theatre, simultaneously obscures the homoerotic potential of performance by inserting a further instance of cross-dressing (Gwyneth Paltrow disguising herself as boy actor Thomas Kent) which enables a purely heterosexist reading of *Romeo and Juliet* (and by extension, Shakespeare's entire *oeuvre*) to be established. The exchanges between the two principal boy actors rehearsing their lines forestalls any homoerotic inflection, because of the means by which the spectator's attention is on Paltrow as woman in disguise being observed by her lover in the wings, Shakespeare. Paltrow's incursion on the stage may at best offer a quasi-feminist intervention into Renaissance theatre practices, but just as Lisa Jardine has been accused of obscuring homoerotics in her concern for feminist rereadings, so Paltrow's 'radical' position as girl–boy actor evacuates other tensions from the play. Paltrow's character is aptly named Viola, but she fails to live up to the subversive potential of her namesake, and it is surely notable that the play being performed is not one of Shakespeare's sexually transgressive comedies.

Mainstream performances rarely celebrate the homoerotics of Shakespearean drama, and it is telling, if ironic, that in 1994 a primary school headteacher banned her pupils from seeing a ballet version of *Romeo and Juliet* because, allegedly, she felt it to be a heterosexual love story.[43] She certainly would have found this to be the case had she been faced with sending her pupils to see *Shakespeare in Love*; and even in the Globe Theatre, where an all-male performance of *Antony and Cleopatra* was staged in 1999, some of the homoerotic potential of such performance is already forestalled by lead actor Mark Rylance's assertion that his Cleopatra will be playful rather than camp.[44] Although, as camp includes an element of parody, camp may itself dilute the homoerotic in performance. Where cross-dressing emerges as part of the dynamics of performance, as it certainly does in this case and in the case of *Shakespeare in Love*, there seems to be a compulsion to consign its effects to historical speculation, with little attention to the impact of such gender uncertainties on the spectators and players themselves.

9. Shakespeare and Race: *Othello* I.iii

DEBORAH CARTMELL

Translating Othello's self-defence for marrying Desdemona to stage or screen presents a number of difficulties. Even though more likely to wink at Othello's misdemeanour because he is so needed in the war, the Duke is remarkably 'liberal' in siding with Othello over Brabantio, that is, with a black man over a white man. What seems a magnificent, even unbelievable, success will be considered within the context of recent readings and the two mainstream film adaptations of the play: those of Orson Welles (1952) and Oliver Parker (1995).

Othello enters in I.iii ready to face the charges of Brabantio before the Duke and his senators. Brabantio accuses Othello of witchcraft, of unnatural behaviour, to which Othello replies (with the utmost reverence to those present) that although 'rude' in speech, he will attempt an explanation. Brabantio further glosses that Desdemona must be bewitched to 'fall in love with what she fear'd to look on' (98).[1] Othello requests that Desdemona be summoned and proceeds with his love story, the eloquence of which, as if frequently commented on, contradicts his former claim to being unschooled in the art of rhetoric, or in Iago's words, an 'erring barbarian'. Ian Smith has suggested that Othello is able to persuade his audience through his eloquence, that is, his narrative performance 'declares his *cultural whiteness* and hence his innocence'.[2] As Smith has demonstrated, in early modern England, barbarism means to speak gibberish; it's defined in the *Oxford English Dictionary* as 'rudeness or unpolished condition of language'.[3] Crucially, Othello must be proficient in white discourse in order to succeed in white society.[4] But it is not only how he speaks, but what he says that is music to the white men's ears.

Othello proceeds to account for why a white woman of quality could fall in love with a moor by retelling his account of the story of his life. As Karen Newman has pointed out, Othello communicates 'through the ascriptions of European colonial discourses',[5] by pandering to European tastes for such travellers' tales, like *A Geographical Historie of Africa*, by the black convert to Christianity, Leo Africanus (translated into English in 1600). Such tales as Africanus's text, confirming that blackness reflected sinfulness (resulting from the mythic progenitor, Noah's son Ham), and relating all kinds of unruly sexuality, were clearly a source of fascination for the English.[6] Jyotsna Singh has since argued that Newman oversimplifies the case by collapsing race and gender and claiming that Desdemona and Othello are similar types of victim.[7] In the scene under scrutiny, Desdemona is anything but a victim. Although Othello clearly plays the game and succeeds in his narrative performance, Desdemona does not, and in this sense they are diametrically opposed.

Race is an important feature in Othello's tale. Not only do we learn he was 'sold to slavery', but that he encountered

> cannibals that each oth...
> T... whose heads
> ... ...rs.
>
> (142–4)

It is at this ver... point that Desdemona does 'seriously incline', and at this poin... from Othello shifts his focus from himself to Desdemona. The wonders are ... im F. Hall has identified in her discussion of t... in early modern England, in 'not only . . . the myste... strangeness" they describe but in the yet-untold wonde... they offer the future traveler',[8] wonders which reveal h... den attitudes to the body and to sexuality. Stephen Greenblatt has gone so far as to read the earliest English tract on America (1505) – where everyone is naked, men have sex with sisters, mothers, daughters, they eat their wives and children – as 'an almost embarrassingly clinical delineation of the Freudian id'.[9] Such representations, according to Greenblatt, provide a screen for Renaissance Europeans to 'project their darkest and yet most compelling fantasies'.[10] Indeed, Othello himself, at this point in the play, can be interpreted as Desdemona's 'newfoundland' – like Donne's mistress – an embodiment of the exotic cultures which he describes.

In the second half of the speech – following 'This to hear /
Would Desdemona seriously incline' – Othello largely replaces 'I'
and 'my' for 'she' and 'her'; he becomes the object, she, the
subject of his discourse. By implication, I suggest that Desdemona is attracted to Othello by his racialist discourse – that is,
his revelation of the existence of racial inferiority, including
promise of a voracious sexual appetite – and by his linguistic
and (real) substitution of her for him.

In this scene, Desdemona never defends her own remarkable
action (overruling her father and marrying a Moor), save for her
famous statement 'I saw Othello's visage in his mind.' Although
we are accustomed to thinking of Desdemona as pure and self-
effacing (perhaps based on a nineteenth-century tendency to
beautify her),[11] here, she is remarkably self-assertive. Bewilder-
ingly, critical accounts of her elopement fail to take into account
the overwhelming dominance fathers held over their daughters.
Even Eldred Jones, in his analysis of the perpetuation of racial
stereotypes in Renaissance drama, takes Desdemona out of context, remarking that her love is unequivocally 'full and perfect in
every way'.[12] Yet surely her articulation of desire goes much
against the grain. Unlike Othello, she rarely misses an opportunity to mention herself. To her father she responds,

> *My* noble father,
> *I* do perceive here a divided duty:
> To you *I* am bound for life and education;
> *My* life and education both do learn *me*
> How to respect you.You are the lord of duty –
> *I* am hitherto your daughter; but here's *my* husband,
> And so much duty as *my* mother show'd
> To you, preferring you before her father,
> So much *I* challenge that *I* may profess
> Due to the Moor, *my* lord.
>
> (179–88; my italics)

The speech contains a striking number of personal pronouns and
possessives. Desdemona defines everyone in relation to herself:
'My noble father', 'my mother', 'my husband'. If this is interpreted as innocent and modest – that is, if she can only see herself
as the property of others – it is modesty in the extreme. Even

more startling than her continual self-referencing is her interjection in the second half of the scene, where she speaks without being spoken to first. To the Duke's suggestion that Desdemona reside with Brabantio while Othello is away, Brabantio replies: 'I'll not have it so.' And as if, not to be upstaged by her former master, Othello answers: 'Nor I.' Most surprisingly, Desdemona imposes herself on to the debate, insisting that she have the final word:

> Nor would I there reside,
> To put my father in impatient thoughts
> By being in his eye. Most gracious Duke,
> To my unfolding lend your prosperous ear,
> And let me find a charter in your voice
> T'assist my simpleness.
>
> (240, 241, 242–7)

The Quarto texts of 1622 and 1630 feature a more emphatic Desdemona than the Folio text quoted above. Instead of 'Nor would I', Desdemona places herself on an equal level with Brabantio and Othello, echoing Othello with 'Nor I, I would not...'. Her insistence on speaking her desires (like Eve in *Paradise Lost*) forecasts her ultimate fall. She is doomed for what she calls herself a 'challenge that I may profess'. Not only does she challenge and overrule her father, she overrules and subdues her husband, who puts himself beneath her, elevating her to the level of the Duke, to whom Othello asks 'Let her have your voice.' In this scene, she is Othello's opposite: her articulation of desire ('if I be left behind... The rites for why I love him are bereft me') is strikingly contrasted by Othello's unsolicited assurance that lust – for him – is not a problem:

> I therefore beg it not
> To please the palate of my appetite,
> Nor to comply with heat.
>
> (261–3)

Eldred Jones finds Othello 'ungallant' here but defends him by insisting that Othello is fighting against a racial stereotype (thereby reinforcing his cultural whiteness) and that the Moor later 'shows an enthusiasm for Desdemona's body which he had deliberately concealed from the senate'.[13] But while Othello might be fighting against the racial stereotype of the innately lascivious Moor, Desdemona is not; in fact, she can be seen as wilfully perpetuating the stereotype of the oversexed, corrupt white female whose 'evil' is manifested in an alliance with a black man. The difference in declared sexual urges is striking in their responses to the Duke's statement that Othello must leave 'tonight' (and therefore the consummation of their marriage be delayed). Desdemona replies (first, and out of turn again): 'To-night, my lord!', while Othello's response could hardly be more different: 'With all my heart.' Uniquely, Desdemona is able to speak her own desire within the male-controlled discourse of Venice.[14] Her disruption of Venetian patriarchy clearly sets off alarm bells and shocks and humiliates Brabantio, who ultimately sides with the Moor rather than his daughter, who 'worse' than being black, betrayed both her class and her gender in marrying Othello. Significantly, Brabantio speaks to Othello, not to Desdemona, as he exits: 'Look to her, moor, if thou hast eyes to see: / She has deceiv'd her father, and may thee.'

The self-assertion displayed here is cruelly punished by Iago, who manipulates her into a position of extreme subservience and passivity. Yet Desdemona, in the aggression which she displays and in her attraction to Othello, is more likely to recall someone like Tamora from *Titus Andronicus* (whose evil is reinforced by her 'perverse' sexual attraction to a Moor) than to Juliet or Cordelia, as has been previously argued.[15] Certainly, I would suggest that the general seventeenth-century reaction to her – especially if you left the theatre at this point – could be very much in line with that of Thomas Rymer, who in 1693 interpreted the play as 'a caution to all Maidens of Quality, how, without their parents' consent they run away with Blackamoors',[16] a reading which is too often swept aside as being grossly insensitive to the play.

For most of the twentieth century, critics have found the relationship between Desdemona and Othello unsettling and baffling; one way of dealing with it was to ignore or minimize the issue of race, while another, more recent, approach is to see the play as Eldred Jones does, as anachronistically championing the cause of black men (and by 'men', I mean to exclude women).

Jones praises Shakespeare for his 'complete humanization of a type character who for the most of his contemporaries has only decorative or a crude moral significance'.[17] There is in this reading a 'belief' in Othello's humanity corresponding to a belief in Shakespeare as timeless educator. The Arden editor, M. R. Ridley, on the other hand (the text was first published in 1958, reprinted in 1962 and the Arden text until 1996), opts for a reading which, rather than valorizing, minimalizes colour. He responds to Coleridge's repugnance to Othello's colour and Miss Preston's infamous remark that 'Shakespeare was too correct a delineator of human nature to have coloured Othello *black* if he had personally acquainted himself with the idiosyncrasies of the African race',[18] with the statement: 'There are more races than one in Africa, and that a man is black in colour is no reason why he should, even to European eyes, look sub-human.'[19] He goes on to describe a black man who he encountered in an American Pullman car who, although black, had features not unattractive to European eyes and, therefore, could have played Othello. Instead of shutting one's eyes to Othello's blackness (as Miss Preston did), Ridley suggests here that he should be 'only a little' black.

Ridley, surely unknowingly, implies that the more black, the more dangerous, subscribing to a colour hierarchy which was taken for granted in the sixteenth and seventeenth centuries. (I am using the word 'black' as Homi Bhabha has defined it, 'not to deny [racially maginalized groups'] diversity but to audaciously announce the important artifice of cultural identity and its difference'[20].) Ania Loomba has described how, from the sixteenth century onwards, black men are increasingly stereotyped as naturally lascivious, a myth which is undeniably behind the racialist discourse of Coleridge, Preston and Ridley. As Brabantio informs us, for a woman of quality, that is, 'A maiden never bold, / Of spirit so still and quiet that her motion / Blush'd at herself', she has behaved unnaturally to fall for the very thing she should fear to look on. In *The Tempest*, Miranda passes the test in her rejection of Caliban, calling him a 'villain' who she does 'not love to look on' (I.iii.312–13). In *The Two Gentlemen of Verona*, Julia expresses her repugnance of black men, thereby confirming her chastity (or lack of sexuality) and her consequent eligibility for marriage:

Proteus: But pearls are fair; and the old saying is,
                   'Black men are pearls in beauteous ladies'
                   eyes'.
Julia [aside]:   'Tis true, such pearls as put out ladies' eyes,
                   For I had rather wink than look on them.
                                                        (V.ii.11–14)

Toni Morrison, in her introduction to *Race-ing Justice, En-gender-ing Power: Essays on Anita Hill, Clarence Thomas and the Construction of Social Reality* (1993), reflects on how white descriptions of black people invariably refer to the black person's body, a feature which undoubtedly has its origins in white culture's obsession with the black body, especially with the black male organ.[21]

Miss Preston's repugnance to Shakespeare's black protagonist can be seen within such a context, yet seemingly perversely, Dymphna Callaghan, writing in 1996, agrees that 'Othello was a white man.'[22] Callaghan discusses the use of blackface and white-face paint on Shakespeare's stage and the ways in which it is used to construct representations of blackness and femininity; and, as she points out, Desdemona too-'whited up', 'smooth as monu-mental alabaster' – was also, like Othello, a white man.

Critics have been quick to applaud the progressiveness of the theatre, compared to the cinema, in employing black actors in the part of Othello. The first black Othello appeared on the London stage in 1833 (Ira Aldrige), while the first black Othello didn't appear in the mainstream cinema until 1995 (Laurence Fishburne).[23] The fundamental conservatism of Hollywood is now a well-worn topic and, as James Monaco has remarked, racism, too, 'pervades American film because it is a basic strain in American history. It is one of the ugly facts that the landmark *The Birth of a Nation* (1915) can be generally hailed as a classic despite its essential racism.'[24] In the film, black characters were played by whites in make-up, not unlike representations of Othello on the Jacobean stage. In later, more 'progressive' films, such as *Gone with the Wind*, black actors actually played black parts; yet Butterfly McQueen, who played 'Prissy', deeply regretted her endorsement of a racial stereotype, and Hattie McDaniel was doomed to replay the role of 'Mammy' for the rest of her acting career. We need to ask ourselves, what is worse:

a white or a black representation of a racial stereotype? In hindsight, it may be better to be a maid than play one. As Butterfly McQueen stressed, a black actor playing a racial stereotype endorses it, confirms it as true, in a way that white actors cannot. I will end with a comparison of the two major film versions of *Othello* (Orson Welles, 1956, and Oliver Parker, 1995), looking especially at their readings of I.iii, and the impact of a black actor and a white actor playing Othello.

Welles's *Othello* was shot between 1948 and 1952 in Morocco and Venice. The black-and-white cinematography makes Welles's Othello appear only 'a little black', and his reading, like Ridley's, seems to minimalize the colour issue. Suzanne Cloutier's Desdemona, on the other hand, is visually very white indeed; blonde and very fair-skinned, she forms a contrast to Welles's Othello. Blame is taken away from individuals and cast, instead, on the society as reflected in the *mise-en-scène* inside the claustrophobic castle; the interiors are prison-like, the barred windows cast shadows on the faces of the *dramatis personae*, indicating that they are trapped, doomed through no fault of their own. Brabantio is old, decrepit and ineffectual; he whines out his lines 'My daughter, O, my daughter' in a manner we would expect from the materialistic Shylock after discovering the departure of Jessica. Welles's Othello's bulky presence appears in a rapid cut, immediately after Brabantio's lines (transposed from I.ii.64): 'Damned as thou art, thou hast enchanted her.' From this moment on Othello dominates – in no way does he reveal any sense of inferiority. He is viewed as head and shoulders above the rest of the cast (indeed, in this sequence, this is all we see of him). With the exception of Desdemona, the rest of the cast are almost always filmed from above (Othello's vantage point), and are thus dwarfed in comparison to the protagonist. Most of the references to race or colour are omitted. Instead of describing Desdemona being swayed after hearing of the cannibals and the anthropophagi, she 'seriously inclines' to Welles's Othello upon his mention of being taken in slavery. In this respect, she comes across as more sympathetic, full of pity rather than lust. The Duke, likewise, is persuaded by Othello's eloquence, and Welles's text, unlike Parker's, keeps 'I think this tale would win my daughter, too.' Cloutier's Desdemona retains only one-third of her lines; in fact she speaks only her reply to her father; her disruption of the male discourse and her assertion of desire are excised entirely from this version. While Oliver Parker retains more of the scene than Welles, Laurence Fishburne's Othello retains five lines less than Welles's Othello – and as a result he is far less dominating. Brabantio, unlike the Brabantio in Welles's film, is a twisted and dominating figure and Desdemona, played by Irene Jacob, keeps four-fifths of her lines (compared to Cloutier's third). Without doubt, Parker subordinates Othello while Welles elevates him. While Welles eliminates most references to race in his adaptation, Parker retains these (the cannibals and the anthropophagi, Desdemona's 'I saw Othello's visage in his mind' and the Duke's compliment, 'Your son-in-law is far more fair than black' are all kept).

Instead of closely scrutinizing Othello's face during the 'Her father loved me' speech, as Welles does, Fishburne's Othello's speech is accompanied by flashbacks to the love scene between Othello and Desdemona. The visuals dominate, distracting us from the words, emphasizing Desdemona's physical attraction to Othello. In fact, in the flashback sequence it's hard to imagine much talking going on as the camera lingers on Fishburne's body. It is his body rather than his words which clearly attracts Desdemona. In the flashback sequence, Parker locates the gaze in Desdemona; she appears the instigator of the love affair, and her visual articulation of desire is further emphasized by her outspokenness later where she is allowed the 'That I did love the Moor to live with him' speech.

While race is hardly perceptible in Welles's film (partially through the minimum use of make-up and his *film noir* approach), it's hard to avoid it in Parker's. In retaining lines which Welles deleted, Parker not only calls attention to the thematic importance of race, he also reinforces it through the emphasis on Fishburne's body (unlike Welles's version, this Othello is seen from head to toe) and in Desdemona's verbal and visual articulations of desire. Barbara Hodgdon has read the film as distorting the play in its demonization of Desdemona; certainly the repetitive imagery of Desdemona's body in the film is reflected in the publicity poster in which the warm tones minimalize colour differentiation and Desdemona is positioned above Othello, whispering in his ear. According to Hodgdon, the image aligns her with Iago, or even Satan; and, while she is demonized,

Othello is pictured as victim.[25] But, I would suggest, Parker's representation of her is not at all a departure from the playtext; but rather confirms the myth that women with 'unhealthy appetites' are attracted to black men; and that by using a black actor in the part, Parker's film endorses the racial stereotype.

Just as Leo Africanus's blackness provided validity for his popular *Geographical Historie of Africa*, Othello's blackness serves to validate and enhance his own traveller's tale. It is possible that the use of a black actor in the part of Othello has a similar impact. Ultimately, Parker's film reinforces my reading of I.iii: it is Desdemona who can indeed be seen as 'the cause' of the racial tension within the play. Instead of 'representing' Othello, the film brings 'him to life' and while seemingly fighting against racism, it ultimately endorses the racial stereotype which the play – possibly – challenges.[26] It has taken almost a century to produce a mainstream film with a black Othello – it may take another century to film Othello as a white man playing the part or, perhaps, to decide that the part is, alas, unfilmable.

SELECT BIBLIOGRAPHY

Barthelemy, Anthony Gerald, *Black Face Maligned Race: Representations of Blacks in English Drama from Shakespeare to Southerne*, Baton Rouge, Louisiana State University Press, 1987.

Dabydeen, David (ed), *The Black Presence in English Literature*, Manchester, Manchester University Press, 1985.

D'Amico, Jack, *The Moor in English Renaissance Drama*, Tampa, Tampa University Press, 1991.

Erickson, Peter, 'Representations of Blacks and Blackness in the Renaissance', *Criticism* 35 (1993): 499–527.

Hall, Kim F., *Things of Darkness: Economies of Race and Gender in Early Modern England*, Ithaca, Cornell University Press, 1995.

Hendricks, Margo and Patricia Parker (eds), *Women, 'Race', and Writing in the Early Modern Period*, London and New York, Routledge, 1994.

Hunter, G. K., *Dramatic Identities and Cultural Traditions: Studies in Shakespeare and His Contemporaries*, New York, Barnes & Noble, 1978.

Jones, Eldred D., *Othello's Countrymen: The African in English Renaissance Drama*, London, Oxford University Press, 1965.

——. *The Elizabethan Image of Africa*, Charlottesville, University Press of Virginia, 1971.

Loomba, Ania. *Gender, Race, Renaissance Drama*, Manchester, Manchester University Press, 1989.

Newman, Karen. ' "And wash the Ethiop white": Femininity and the Monstrous in *Othello'*, in *Shakespeare Reproduced: The Text in History and Ideology*, ed. Jean E. Howard and Marion O'Connor, New York, Methuen, 1987, pp. 143–63.

Orkin, Martin, 'Othello and the "Plain Face" of Racism', *Studies in Philology* 38 (1987): 166–88.

Smith, Ian, 'Barbarian Errors: Performing Race in Early Modern England', *Shakespeare Quarterly* 2 (1992): 168–86.

Tokson, Elliot H., *The Popular Image of the Black Man in English Drama, 1550–1688*, Boston, G. K. Hall, 1982.

IV Shakespeare, Film and the Future

10. The Unkindest Cuts: Flashcut Excess in Kenneth Branagh's *Hamlet*

BERNICE W. KLIMAN

In December 1996, rumours of a drastically cut version to be released later propelled serious viewers to Kenneth Branagh's uncut, four-hour *Hamlet*, which was soon to be withdrawn in favour of a trimmed version.[1] Those were heady times for filmed Shakespeare, of long queues and tickets that had to be purchased in advance. But many of us were impatient for the two-hour film. We wanted to see what Branagh would cut and what that would reveal about his interpretation. Now the two-hour version has appeared, and although I believe viewers in the USA and Canada have not seen it yet, it was shown on Spanish television in summer 1999 – a version which I have seen thanks to the timely help of Jesús Tronch-Perez (University of Valencia) and José Ramón Díaz Fernández (University of Málaga). Fortunately, I am disappointed in what is cut;[2] – 'fortunately' because that gives me an opportunity to do my own editing. My long-range project is twofold: first, in this chapter, to excise what I think mars the four-hour film – much of which the two-hour film retains; and second, in a future article, to explore the artistry of what remains. Although at present I am concerned mainly with the film's defects, I aim to be 'cruel only to be kind', to enable me to put aside everything that occludes this film's many excellences.

If I were to make a shorter version of Branagh's film, I would eliminate every one of the 'flashcuts', as the published script calls them. In a flashcut the film splices a very brief inset scene into the main scene. I would also remove many of the longer spliced-in scenes – anything that diverts attention from the speakers. Surgical removal of all the additional scenes, fat in and between the lines obstructing the film's arteries, should bring the film to little more than three hours instead of four. Samuel Crowl speculated that removing spliced-in scenes would be the way the two-hour film would be created from the four-hour version,[3] but I think a little more might be necessary. Since the film's control text is the Oxford, Folio-based edition, I would also remove the lines Branagh added from the Second Quarto (1604), as well as any other lines that conflict with screen images, further reducing the film to less than three hours. To respect his original intention to film the complete *Hamlet*, I would not delete any scenes.

Shakespeare films, typically, substitute visual pictures for verbal ones; Branagh daringly wants it both ways – the pictures *and* the words, piling visuals on top of verbals. During filming, some of the planned excess disappeared. For example, Russell Jackson says that Hamlet and Horatio originally were to make their way to the play-within-the-play through a throng of dancers; this was shot but not used,[4] and it is not missed. Laertes's scripted departure by boat after farewells to Polonius and Ophelia was not filmed at all, 'dropped before we went on location', says Russell Jackson, owing to weather problems. As might be expected, the shooting script called for a scene of Ophelia's drowning, meant to illustrate Gertrude's willow speech in voiceover, but thankfully the flashcut sequence was reduced to the final image of the dead girl seen below the surface of the water – which I would cut as well. As Irene Dash points out, Ophelia drowning in an icy stream as Gertrude (Julie Christie) describes summer flowers is absurd, but somehow Gertrude's speech is acceptable if it stands alone, without illustration.[5] Christie holds our attention for this long speech, revealing what the film could have been if Branagh had been more confident about Shakespeare's words. The choice seems clear: either do what Grigori Kozintzev does – suppress the words and show the extratextual images, or keep the words without the images – or when combining both, make sure there is a good reason to do so. Branagh set himself a daunting problem – almost an oxymoron – to create a film with a full text – and the flashcut is his principal method.

Some flashcuts are excellent things in themselves – and critics have praised them; director Michael Kahn, for example, calls them 'brilliant'.[6] But in my opinion they do very little good and much harm to the film. First, they extend the perception of time.

Space *is* time, and when a film takes its audience to a new space it also lengthens its sense of the extent of time. Even when the flashcut coincides with speech, the time stretches with each variation in space. This ill effect cannot be overestimated; it's deadly, especially in a film that retains an overfull text. The very large number of these flashcuts chops the film into bits. While every film is made of thousands of shots, an editor rarely calls attention to seams as do these flashcuts – and when the contrivances of film *do* show, it is usually for a good reason. Emrys Jones points out that what we most enjoy in *Hamlet* and other great Shakespearean plays is the tempo; we can enjoy the play repeatedly in performance after performance, much as we can enjoy a loved symphony over and over again.[7] Branagh's film, with these flashcuts and other added scenes, disturbs and distorts the play's tempo and sabotages itself because it cannot be viewed over and over again with renewed pleasure and awareness. It yields less rather than more. With its flashcuts, even the two-hour version seems slow.

Second, it is often difficult to understand the point of view of what the screen displays. To make sense, a film usually establishes a code that an audience can absorb automatically, as, for example, having a character exit through a space at the right of a frame and then, after a cut, reappear again at the left of the next frame – to create an illusion of, say, going through a door. Or the camera focuses in close-up on a character, then dissolves or cuts to what that character is thinking, and then back again to the close-up. But Branagh does not code the flashcuts consistently. Some of them are flash*backs*, that is, representations of a past event, while others illustrate what the character is thinking in the present time, and many are uncertain. During the Player's speech, for example, flashcuts of Troy's destruction augment the Player's verbal picture – and, not so incidentally, pay homage to John Gielgud as Priam and Judi Dench as Hecuba. These ambiguous insets are either the Player's images, that is, the mental images that inspire his histrionics; or they arise from his on-screen audience's (perhaps Hamlet's) visualization of his verbal images; or they are the filmmaker's helpful aid to a long speech – what I call an omniscient flashcut. While Branagh appears from interviews to have meant them to be Hamlet's images, they *feel* like omniscient images. In his *Hamlet* film,

Olivier tried dramatic insets for narration, but kept them to a minimum so that, though the same question of point of view arises, his four did less damage than Branagh's countless insets. The thought creeps in that the flashcuts are fancy footwork to hide the barrenness of Branagh's cinematic imagination.[8]

Three groups of insets – for the Ghost, for Ophelia, and for Fortinbras – will illustrate, I think, the flaws in the flashcuts. The first group dominates the opening third of the film, the second the middle, and the third the ending.

THE OPENING: GHOST

The flashcuts and visual interpretations of the Ghost, though Brian Blessed is an outstanding actor, seriously detract from Branagh's ghost scenes, severely damaging the film. Branagh may have his reasons for undermining the Ghost: the less compelling the Ghost, the less we care about Hamlet's lack of responsiveness to its command. But the message is so mixed, one almost has to posit a psychological struggle within Branagh between himself and Blessed, one of his father figures, who has played a key role in Branagh's films and his career.

Every successful *Hamlet* film I know creates a Ghost that is dramatically, theatrically and cinematically impressive, one way or another – Zeffirelli's very human Ghost or Kozintsev's majestic and terrifying figure – the exact form that it takes does not matter if it compels a response that advances the production. Branagh offers confusion. Is that close-up view of old Hamlet's statue removing its sword from its scabbard Francisco's fevered thought? Or is the statue coming to life even before Bernardo arrives? What a strange Ghost this is, something out of *Don Giovanni*, as Norm Holland suggests, rather than the richly ambiguous figure that Shakespeare's text limns. The anachronism of an armoured ghost in a late nineteenth-century setting is not as disturbing as the filming itself. Rather than a chilling confrontation, this looks like clumsy animation, a technical manipulation, replete with a brief, unlikely moment when the Ghost's face is lit – possibly to accommodate Horatio's assertion that he saw its face (I.ii.230). It would not be difficult to cut these shots because the camera never shows the ghost-statue and the men together in a single frame. They were undoubtedly filmed apart from each other,[9] and the disjunction shows. Since many films choose non-material Ghosts (Tony Richardson's and Ragnar Lyth's, for example), yet expertly create a frisson of dread and fear – effects that Branagh wants to achieve, as evidenced by the reaction shots he films – the reaction shots alone could have made us see the Ghost if the camera had remained fixed on their faces in close-up and bodies in long shot. This armed floater has to go. Making the Ghost the old King's statue come to life (as the script says) is also a blunder, because it vitiates the identification of the Ghost with old Hamlet – of *course* it would look like him, being a statue *of* the King. It's also absurd that Horatio, in describing the apparition to Hamlet, does not mention the statue. One has to be careful about adding images that then require added language to go with them. Far better in *this* film to see the Ghost for the first time when it speaks to Hamlet alone, when we see its human face with its weird blue eyes. Someone recognized, it seems, the awkwardness of the first appearances of the Ghost, because the two-hour version eliminates the first scene altogether.

In Shakespeare's script, upon the Ghost's first appearance to Hamlet in Scene iv, Hamlet addresses his first words 'Angels and ministers of grace defend us' to heavenly powers, and then 'Be thou a spirit of health, or goblin damn'd', and so on for another twenty-odd lines (I.iv.39–57), to the Ghost. But as shot, all these words are interior monologue. Branagh transposes this whole Scene iv speech to follow rather than precede Hamlet's breaking away from Horatio and Marcellus. The transposition was a late decision, says Russell Jackson, 'to avoid a static episode in what needed to be a rapid response to the apparition'.[10] Originally, says Jackson, the shooting script contained no transpositions at all. I suspect that filming Hamlet speaking to a ghost who remained floating off camera (the method to which Branagh had tied himself) caused the static quality, which Branagh perceived at the editing table. There is nothing inherently static about this speech said to a *manifest* apparition; great actors have made it their signature speech. There is everything ridiculous about this speech said on the run, with no ghost visible. Movement at high speed (too frequent a device in this film) does not animate what is inert. The running makes voice-over necessary because sprinting and speaking are incompatible. Since soliloquies pose a special problem for a filmmaker because they can remove film's main resource, the reaction shot, it seems perverse of Branagh to convert dialogue, with its potential for reaction shots, into a soliloquy. Since Branagh shot most scenes several ways, and since the transposition was a late decision, I assume that Branagh also shot the sequence showing Hamlet speaking to the Ghost, off camera, with Horatio and Marcellus reacting. I would, in my shortened film, substitute that unused footage.

Once the Ghost appears again to Hamlet – announced by no tender gesture but by the Ghost's hand roughly pushing him against a tree – ragged filming, including strange camera angles and flashcuts, continues to undermine the scene. The two actors would have to be shot individually, of course, when the camera takes the place of the other in the scene, when one actor speaks to the camera standing in for the other actor, but usually such scenes alternate with two-shots. In Branagh's film the two Hamlets are disconnected, except for a very few moments when parts of the two appear together in the same frame.

In this scene, Branagh layers three or four levels of flashcut. Some of them are so short that they have, if anything, a subliminal effect. Split-second cuts of a screen-sized, plastic-looking ear with blood pouring out of it alternate with the Ghost's face from a variety of angles. The plastic ear and blood come before the Ghost's revelation of the poisoning and thus cannot be Hamlet's image. The Ghost could not have seen this view. This is the omniscient narrator, telling us something we do not need to know at this moment, but presenting it so quickly that we cannot tell what it is. The extreme close-ups of a mouth and later, of an eye, do no good, either. With the excesses gone, Blessed and Branagh might have made the Ghost's revelation an intense moment. The Ghost is so important to the first third of the play that its mishandling is enough, almost alone, to sink the film. Branagh admitted, during an interview reported in the *Shakespeare Newsletter*, that his main motive for introducing the insets is uncertainty about audience tolerance of talking heads: 'Because the Ghost's narrative is so long, it seemed to cry out for illustration.' He thought that 'some visual aids would help the audience "feel the urgency of Hamlet's mission"'.[11] No work of art can be made solely on the basis of what the audience might need or want

– or at least, if the audience is a constraint, it is one that should function like the rules of a sonnet – a necessity that forces the best from an artist. Perhaps, however, Branagh aimed for the alienation effects that Anthony Dawson perceived in the 1992 Adrian Noble/Kenneth Branagh production – and Branagh's rationalizations, in interviews, serve the purposes of public relations.[12] But one can judge only by the insets themselves.

Silent films, which did not have much choice, typically showed the poisoning in the orchard – images in lieu of words. The difficulty is that anything we *see* we tend to take as what really occurred. The Ghost's narrative must be believable to Hamlet, but one that he might question later (unless a director wants to problematize Hamlet's questioning). But as Branagh presents the flashcuts, the possibility of omniscience is always present: what we see *is* what happened rather than what happened filtered through the Ghost's perception.[13] Claudius's horror at his deed does not seem part of what the Ghost would notice. Later, Branagh repeats views from the orchard scene – one being Claudius's recollection, during the play-within-the-play, of his crime. There the flashcut is psychological, an emanation from Claudius's mind,[14] pre-empting, as Graham Bradshaw says, the audience's decision about the efficacy of Hamlet's test.[15] In the prayer scene, the film cuts again to an image from the orchard scene – Hamlet's father falling, grasping his head in pain. The visual image of his father's suffering hardens Hamlet's heart towards Claudius – but this is just what the *words* say.

Another flashcut during the prayer scene has Hamlet envisioning his dagger piercing the lattice wall of the confessional to kill Claudius. But unlike the flashbacks, this flashcut is an unrealized moment, expressing Hamlet's unfulfilled wish. This may be the only flashcut that serves such a purpose, and it is one I would keep; it shows Hamlet confronting the bloodthirstiness of his longing, unafraid. This is an *interpretive* rather than a redundant image.

To return to Scene iv, Branagh intercuts into the orchard flashback a domestic scene when Claudius was perhaps a too-loving brother to the Queen, and further intercuts the flashback with Hamlet's pained and shamed expression. By ordinary film codes, this image should signal Hamlet's own recollection of uneasiness at the affection between his mother and his uncle.

The sequence culminates in an image of a hand hurriedly loosening the laces of a woman's corset as the Ghost speaks of preying on garbage – a flashcut the published script does not mention. This could be an illustration of the Ghost's words. Or it could be the omniscient narrator, solidifying what in the text is ambiguous. Or, since it is preceded and followed by images of Hamlet's face, it could be his mental picture of Claudius and his mother. In all these cases it's expendable: the play has enough *words* to convey the Ghost's and Hamlet's uneasiness and even disgust – his obscene imagination. It's crude to have him mentally uncover his mother's nakedness – especially since Branagh minimizes the Oedipal theme.

Worst of all, underlying the various flashback levels during Hamlet's encounter with the Ghost, the film has illustrations of hellish emanations from the earth, both before and after the Ghost appears. As Hamlet runs through the woods, flashcuts show flames spouting out of the ground, dry ice roiling away, and other 'supernatural' manifestations. These artificial images of the rocky earth grating open provide a backdrop to Hamlet's thoughts. In the prayer scene, when Hamlet thinks of his father's suffering, he again sees the splitting of the jaws of Hell (as Branagh in his script refers to these images of sliding earth), and then when he thinks of Claudius doomed to Hell he sees them close. Both images appear to reflect his thoughts, but again they could be omniscience at work; Branagh obscures with these visual images what is apparent in the text: Hamlet forgets that Claudius too has a soul immortal like his own, and that he has no power over that soul, whatever he does to the body. In Scene iv, if the hellish images are Hamlet's own thoughts, he is placing his father in a perilous state before he ever hears of the horrors of the purgatorial punishment. Finally, during the swearing on the sword, the ground under the feet of Horatio, Marcellus and Hamlet *is* heaving. The film here makes these hellish images part of the present reality rather than something either Hamlet or the Ghost conjures up. The images might have been worse: Russell Jackson (privately) said that the special effects were going to be more elaborate, 'ground splitting, flames, &c., but didn't look right' and so were toned down. But not enough. In addition to difficulties in point of view, the hellish images are silly. I fear that Branagh did not entirely get out of his system the giggles about *Hamlet* that he meant to allay with his delightful *Midwinter's Tale* – his 1995 film send-up of a troupe of actors performing *Hamlet* in the British provinces.[16]

THE MIDDLE: OPHELIA

If Hamlet's relation to his father is the essential starting point for the action – a relation that the flashcuts and animations cloud – his relation to Ophelia is one that carries us through to the great middle of the play. Her betrayal of him in the nunnery scene is for many Hamlets their lowest point. While Kate Winslet makes an intelligent, sensitive Ophelia, the flashcuts and extra scenes mar the good she brings to her role. The two-hour version keeps most of them: Ophelia recollects nights and days of love with Hamlet at the very moment her father is sternly cautioning her about throwing herself away. Or are we seeing these scenes in the flesh (a flash*back* rather than a psychological flashcut)? Or is this image her wishful thinking, as some have conjectured? Strikingly, Hamlet never 'thinks' about Ophelia; we never see a flashback of lovemaking or of any connection between them during his speeches, whether to her or about her. This absence suggests that the images could be her fabrications. However, the fact that an intercut scene of lovemaking occurs during Polonius's reading of her letter from Hamlet shows that the love affair is objective reality, conveyed by an omniscient narrator. The flashback shows a naked Hamlet, writing, as Ophelia, in her nightdress, stands by. Polonius, voiceover, says the words of the letter as we see the scene, and then, in an aural dissolve, Hamlet himself says the words most feelingly. As the letter concludes, the soundtrack dissolves to Polonius's voice again, and then the camera cuts back to the main frame, Polonius's disclosure to the King and Queen. By conventional film codes the focus on Polonius before and after the intercut scene should indicate it is his view, but Polonius cannot be imagining this scene because he does not know how far the affair has gone, and would not imagine it as a sweet interlude.

Ambiguities about their relationship are all proper to the play; no lovemaking scene is needed from either the unconscious or the omniscient narrator to de-ambiguate their scenes. *Any way* one takes the lovemaking images, the film is in trouble. Russell Jackson, in his 'Diary' of the production published with the script, tells us that Branagh intended Hamlet and Ophelia to be lovers because 'we want this relationship to be as serious as possible',[17] but acting alone could have shown the seriousness of their relationship – as is true for many many productions.[18] Hamlet has few enough opportunities to demonstrate his feelings for Ophelia in any version, and (however tenderly the film portrays their lovemaking) to make Hamlet equivalent to the woman-using Polonius or Laertes is to diminish him greatly. To take advantage of Ophelia without proposing marriage, Hamlet would be something less than most of us want him to be. The film substitutes '*almost* all the holy vows of heaven' from the Quarto for the Folio's '*all* the vows of heaven'.[19] I don't mind a film text that purports to be based on the Folio using a Quarto line now and then, but here, when we have seen Hamlet as lover, he should have made *all* the vows.

The time scheme of the film is not 1991 – when men and women go to bed without thinking of marriage – but 1901, when the double standard is fully operative, as we see from Laertes's advice and Polonius's demands in the third scene and from the latter's indulgence for himself and his son in the Reynaldo scene. As her Valentine Day song proclaims, scorn is what men who believe in the double standard feel about the women they bed outside marriage. Branagh, it appears, wants both Laertes and Polonius to be correct in their cautions. In interpreting Shakespeare's play, most have thought that Laertes's and Polonius's advice reflects their own narrow view of the ways of men with women, wrongly judging Hamlet by their own exploiting behaviour. To make Polonius and Laertes correct is to even out characterizations, to make Hamlet less high-minded, to make these other men more creditable: In this film they both care about Ophelia and want to protect her. If Hamlet has been Ophelia's lover since his arrival home, since the death of his father, his wish to return to Wittenberg seems odd. In this film, he agrees reluctantly to stay, as the script says and the film shows, out of princely decorum, without a thought for Ophelia. If they had been lovers his taunts at the play-within are too cruel. A tarnished Hamlet would be a plausible interpretation if the message were clearer, but I cannot help but feel that Branagh is at his most admiring of his Hamlet when he and Ophelia are making love, and for me, this is his Hamlet's least admirable aspect, given the attitude towards sexuality in this film.

If the lovemaking scenes have a problematic effect on the characterization of Hamlet, they are inconsistent with the characterization of Ophelia. She lies to her brother, with whom she is very close – to whom she is very dear and he to her – telling him 'I shall th' effect of this good lesson keep / As Watchman to my heart', but she has already violated the lesson. Yes, one lies about sex, but in retrospect this lie diminishes her, and her agreement with Polonius, 'I shall obey, my Lord', is even worse than usual if she is already Hamlet's lover. If she is willing to lie to her brother and father to protect their relationship, it seems inconceivable that she would lie to Hamlet or help others to spy on him. The two parts of her characterization do not mesh. An Ophelia can help her father and the King from various motives, but if she has been Hamlet's lover, none will work – not at the moment he asks her where her father is. Branagh's screenplay does confront this problem, saying that her decision is difficult for Ophelia, but that does not explain her betrayal or justify it aesthetically.

In the nunnery scene, although she had kept her distance from Hamlet since her father commanded her to do so, she nevertheless can accuse Hamlet of proving unkind (III.i.100). And, in this film, unkind indeed he is; after Hamlet kills her father and before he is hustled into Claudius's presence, she runs to him, appealing to him for comfort, she knows not yet for what. But seeing her, he turns and runs, crying – 'Hide fox and all after' – with her unheeded calls of 'My Lord, Lord Hamlet' echoing.[20] He abandons her, but so does the production. Branagh has guards keep her from her dead father for no good reason except to make everyone appear as cruel as possible, and, as a mad-woman, she is hosed down by a guard – unaccountably, since our last view of her before this was of her standing, motionless and silent, in her cell. These are more of the added scenes that are not only expendable but also actively deleterious. On the positive side, they counter the prettified images of Ophelia mourning sweetly for her father, the sugar-coated image of her death, as related by Gertrude and eagerly embraced by many nineteenth-century productions. A grittier view of Ophelia is all to the good – as in the Lyth production (1984), for example. But Branagh's added images go too far in the other direction, distracting by their ugliness. Hamlet's unbelievable rejection of her after he has murdered her father make a hash of Hamlet's declaration of love at graveside and of his boast. Forty thousand lovers like him would not equal one brother like Laertes, who does love his sister. Hamlet is volatile; just as quickly as he mourns over Yorick and then, without a further thought, tosses the skull to the grave-digger, so does this Hamlet wallow in sentimentality over Ophelia's grave and then just as readily toss her aside. With such a diminished Hamlet, the film means, it seems, to create something different from the noble, sensitive, generous prince of nineteenth-century imagination. Branagh's prince is variable, intelligent, selfish, perceptive, philosophical, shallow, verbally acrobatic, quick to perceive slights by others and quick to give back as good as he gets. Some of these traits are what Branagh means to express with his added pictures of the Ophelia relationship. Remarks by Branagh in his published script suggest that he did mean to diminish Hamlet, but since this diminished Hamlet is one of the possibilities in Shakespeare's script it does not require any outside pictures to convey it. Hamlet's failure to mention Ophelia after he has killed her father, his failure to begin to understand what he has done to Laertes or to her, his failure to reflect on her death after his grandstanding at the graveside – all these are potential in the complete text. The text with appropriate acting would do it all, more efficiently and more cleanly. It's possible that Branagh wants it both ways – the noble *and* the caddish Hamlet – and these two contradictory impulses muddy the portrayal rather than, as intended, enrich it.

ENDING: FORTINBRAS

My third and final example of added scenes most affects the film's conclusion. Frequently, productions do not do much with Fortinbras – even going so far as to eliminate the role – but Branagh allows him a large amount of screen time through added scenes and through what the script calls 'flashbacks' rather than 'flash-cuts'. Plainly, the film does not trust the mass audience; Branagh perhaps doubts it will believe in Fortinbras without seeing him. The arty slow-motion shots, the silence of the first Fortinbras flashbacks, after Horatio's encounter with the statue-ghost, along with the voice-over by Horatio, give the inset scenes a surreal effect. The question, 'Whose vision does the screen show?' is answered, at one point, by the fact that the script calls for the reappearance of a segment of the same scene, Fortinbras tearing a map of Denmark, when Claudius tells the court about him. Either Fortinbras's specific action with the map is common currency (an unlikely possibility), or the inset is the product of omniscience. During that same speech by Claudius, the screen also shows the tetchy old Norway – the morose old man rejecting his nurse's babying. The latter vignette is very well done – with much information conveyed in small compass – as, from a pure filmic standpoint, are many others. But it contains no new or necessary intelligence, and solidifies what should remain *Claudius's* description of old Norway – not absolute truth. Later, when Voltemand returns from Norway, flashbacks show scenes that he perhaps witnessed – old Norway's rebuke of Fortinbras and the younger man's contrition and suit for forgiveness – but it is doubtful that Voltemand saw this scene. Again, more plausibly, the omniscient narrator is at work. An added shot, of Horatio reading about Fortinbras's invasions (inserted between II.i and III.ii), gives way to images of the warmongering Fortinbras in full career.

These Fortinbras insets, along with his image, played by Rufus Sewell as a cold, ruthless tyrant, skew the plot: Claudius, in this view, is not a good administrator and politician after all, because he fails to understand this threat. Hamlet diddles with internal problems when external exigencies are, as events unfold, more pressing. His admiration for Fortinbras in the fourth act shows how blind Hamlet is to political reality and how ill-fitted he is to be a king (and the filming of it makes no sense at all; where in that wide, wide view to which the camera booms are Rosencrantz and Guildenstern?).

Later, many crosscuts show Fortinbras invading Elsinore, revealing how paltry are the concerns of the Court, how insufficient its preparations, with poor Francisco, virtually alone, on guard duty. Where are all those blank-faced guards who are there in abundance to terrorize Ophelia when, looking for Hamlet, they surprise her in her bed? Is *everyone* watching the fencing match?[21] While crosscuts in general are a legitimate film device, since they further an interpretive point and depict two actions taking place at the same time, I question the value of Branagh's

idea; he wrenches the plot to turn it into the triumph of evil in
the form of Fortinbras, an evil that the ghost did nothing to
prevent. Retrospectively, the ghost is culpable for having come,
not, as Horatio had thought, on affairs of state, but concerned
solely about personal revenge. The ineffectuality of all three –
Claudius, Hamlet and the Ghost – lets Fortinbras happen. In a
coda, Fortinbras's men pull down old King Hamlet's statue (its
eyes weeping) – and thus the Ghost, but give Hamlet noble funeral
rites, perhaps in deference to Hamlet's dying voice for Fortinbras's
election, an ironically unnecessary gesture on Hamlet's part. Branagh could have made his point about the danger without all the
preliminary flashcuts and flashbacks of Fortinbras – a point made
by John Gilbert's nineteenth-century illustration of the scene; it's
also Lyth's interpretation, and Ingmar Bergman's for his 1987
stage production – all without any additions whatsoever, counting
on the manner of Fortinbras's entrance at the end. Bypassing both
the crosscuts and the flashbacks, my version of Branagh's *Hamlet*
would eliminate the Fortinbras diversions and – until the moment
he appears in Act V – keep attention focused on Hamlet.[22]

Without the Fortinbras flashbacks Branagh could have clari-
fied the scenic structure he attempts with the position of his
intermission. Emrys Jones believes that the end of IV.iv is the
appropriate climax of the play's first part. The Peter Hall stage
productions of 1965 and 1966 placed the interval there, with the
effect, Jones says, of 'unusual clarity'.[23] Each half ends, then,
with Fortinbras's entrance, the only two spots where the script
calls for him to be on stage. For Jones, this scheme works with
either the Folio or the Quarto text, but if Fortinbras has the last
word of IV.iv, as he does in the Folio, the parallel structure would
be even more apparent. Branagh obscures the design by introducing Fortinbras over and over through the flashcuts, flashbacks and crosscuts. Though I would cut all of the Quarto-only
lines, the fourth-act soliloquy particularly cries out for excision; it
makes no sense at all with this Hamlet, who does not delay and
who does not catch even a glimpse of the prince he describes,
inaccurately, as 'delicate and tender' (IV.iv.49). Eliminating the
soliloquy would have the added benefit of ridding the film of the
worst of its music (composed by Patrick Doyle, a frequent con-
tributor, as composer and actor, to Branagh's films, never before
to such ill effect). By including the Quarto's 'How all occasions'

soliloquy – and by filming it as he does – Branagh means to make Hamlet's encounter with Fortinbras's army a great climax, but it's as if Branagh's Hamlet commenting on Fortinbras is in a different film from Sewell's *playing* Fortinbras. The impetus to action Hamlet derives from his notion of Fortinbras is called into question by the falsity of his picture, but I think Branagh could have found a more direct way to convey the idea that Hamlet's decisive declaration, 'from this time forth / My thoughts be bloody or be nothing worth', is based on a false premise – if that indeed was the idea Branagh wanted to communicate.

Russell Jackson informs me that Branagh, thinking that something was not working after the intermission, decided to supply a review for an audience presumed to have short-term memory loss – a review not in the shooting script – with Claudius's speech to Gertrude in voice-over transposed to open the second act accompanied by flashcut illustrations.[24] These flashcuts, repetitions of what the film has already shown and new insets, are awkward and mechanical. The view of Laertes is particularly static, where the words and the image (which looks like something from a publicity shoot) utterly clash.

Without the inset scenes, Branagh's film would remain a '"paratext" – a version located "beyond, or contrary to" (from the Greek *para*) the ordinary written text while remaining broadly referential to it'. (I am here quoting Eric W. Mallin, who uses these words to describe the Arnold Schwarzenegger film *Last Action Hero*[25] – they can apply to Branagh's film as well.) This is a film that stands back from itself and asks the audience in the know to recognize allusions – to Gielgud's famous pose holding the skull at arm's length; to the celebrities, and the relation of some of them to Branagh; to the Adrian Noble/Branagh RSC production of 1992. These presumably are meant to function like Shakespeare's metatheatrical references. The actor-friends passing through this film – reprising Branagh's career – and the many celebrity actors, some who stand in a parental role to him – make for multiple texts, multiple significations. No amount of cutting is likely to strip the film of this paratextual element, shot through, so to speak, as it is with allusions. What will remain, then, after the elimination of flashcuts and all added scenes that fill unnecessary spaces between the words, and after pruning all the extra words from the Quarto, is still a quintessential Branagh film, and, I think, a better one. The residue would still convey Branagh's central idea that a flawed Hamlet ruins two families and the whole of Denmark. The production does have many fine things about it that I hope to write about at a future date. My cut version would preserve all of the best that is in the film: the homage to Chamberlain's *Hamlet* (1970) in details of setting; the clarity and tact with which the film shows the moment Gertrude turns away from Claudius in IV.v.145; the character-revealing details of Hamlet's book-lined study; the brilliance of the language, the multiracial casting. At its kernel are some grand performances – among others, by Jacobi, Winslet and Branagh. Removing the husk can only make the kernel more available. Whether that will be sufficient to raise this film into greatness remains to be seen. That's the second half of my continuing project.

BIBLIOGRAPHY

Andrews, John F., 'Kenneth Branagh's *Hamlet*', *Shakespeare Newsletter* 46, 3 (Fall 1996): 53, 62, 66.

Bradshaw, Graham, 'The "Encrusted *Hamlet*: Mousetrap in Text and Performance" ', in *Approaches to Teaching* Hamlet, ed. Bernice W. Kliman, New York, MLA, forthcoming.

Branagh, Kenneth, Hamlet *by William Shakespeare: Screenplay and Introduction by Kenneth Branagh*, New York, Norton, 1996.

Chamberlain, Richard, *Hamlet*, 1970. See Kliman, Hamlet, pp. 180–7.

Crowl, Samuel, 'Hamlet "Most Royal", An Interview with Kenneth Branagh', *Shakespeare Bulletin* 12, 4 (Fall 1994): 5–8.

——.'*Hamlet*', *Shakespeare Bulletin* 15, 1 (Winter 1997): 34–5.

Dawson, Anthony B., *Shakespeare in Performance*: Hamlet, Manchester and New York, Manchester University Press, 1995.

Film credits, reviews, and purchasing information: http://us.imdb.com/

Gilbert, John, illus., frontispiece for *Hamlet, The Globe Illustrated Shakespeare*, ed. Howard Staunton, New York: Greenwich House, 1851, distributed by Crown, 1983.

Holland, Norm, SHAKSPER: Electronic ListServ, 2 January 1997.

Jackson, Russell, 'Diary', in Kenneth Branagh, *'Hamlet' by William Shakespeare: Screenplay and Introduction by Kenneth Branagh*. New York, Norton, 1996, pp. 175–208.

——, 'Kenneth Branagh's Film of *Hamlet*: The Textual Choices', *Shakespeare Bulletin* 15, 2 (Spring 1997): 37–8.

Jones, Emrys, *Scenic Form in Shakespeare*, Oxford: Oxford University Press; 1971, rpt. New York: Clarendon Press, 1985.

Kliman, Bernice W., Hamlet: *Film, Television, and Audio Performance*, Rutherford, NJ, Fairleigh Dickinson University Press, 1988.

Lyth, Ragnar, *Hamlet: den tragiska historien om Hamlet av Denmark*, 1984. See Kliman, '*Hamlet*', pp. 202–24.

Mahon, John W., 'Editor's View' appended to Andrews, 'Kenneth Branagh's *Hamlet*', *Shakespeare Newsletter* 46, 3 (Fall 1996): 66, 76. See also Pendleton, 'And the Thoughts of the Other Editor'.

Mallin, Eric S., ' "You Kilt My Foddah": or Arnold, Prince of Denmark', *Shakespeare Quarterly* 50, 2 (Summer 1999): 127–51.

Nichols, Nina daVinci, 'Branagh's *Hamlet* Redux' *Shakespeare Bulletin* 15, 3 (Summer 1997): 38–41.

Pendleton, Thomas, 'And the Thoughts of the Other Editor', *Shakespeare Newsletter* 46, 3 (Fall 1996): 60.

Shakespeare, William, *Riverside Shakespeare*, ed. J. Blakemore Evans et al., 2nd ed. Boston, Houghton Mifflin, 1997.

Smith, Dinitia, 'Much Ado about Branagh: The New Orson Welles', *New York*, 24 May 1993: 36–45.

Walton, David, 'The Fortunes of Fortinbras in Three Film Versions of *Hamlet*', *Shakespeare Bulletin* 16, 3 (Summer 1998): 36–7.

11. Showing Versus Telling: Shakespeare's *Ekphraseis*, Visual Absences, and the Cinema

GABRIEL EGAN

Drama offers the storyteller a simple choice about how to communicate each element of the story to the audience: show it, or
have a character describe it. The use of both modes within one
work is what distinguishes drama from mime, at one extreme,
and from narrative recital at the other, but often we may sense
that at a particular moment the use of one mode or other is
conditioned by practical rather than aesthetic considerations. As
a narrative unit the 'car chase' is confined to works in the medium uniquely suited to conveying its tension, the cinema, and
we should expect drama's strengths to lie elsewhere. Although
physical playing space was limited, the theatre professionals of
Shakespeare's time did not shy away from attempting to represent events which are to be imagined occurring over large areas
of space such as a battlefield, and they found a number of techniques to counter the physical limitations of their stage. The
Chorus at the beginning of Shakespeare's *Henry V* appears to
apologize for the theatre's inability to do justice to the events to
be portrayed, but the rest of the play shows impressive ingenuity
at representing battles and sieges by jumping from location to
location, and by focusing on the Harfleur city-gate before which
Henry makes his demands in III.iii.[1] Occasionally, however, one
feels the strain of theatrical limitations when events are described
which one might prefer to see for oneself. Hamlet's remarkable
sea-adventure is a case in point, and film directors frequently
choose to show the audience the events which are merely
described in a letter read aloud by Horatio at IV.vi.12–30 and
subsequently related at greater length by Hamlet at V.ii.1–56.[2]

Technology now exists to show a cinema audience anything that can be imagined. An entire feature film can be made on computer and the images transferred directly to film without the intermediate forms of ink and paper, so there are no practical limits upon the director's freedom to show what previous storytellers could only have their characters describe. This freedom must be exercised cautiously, because in drama there is an epistemological difference between events that are shown and those that are described: in general we have to trust that the former are true (insofar as anything in a play is true), while the latter are necessarily mediated and suspect. Certain textual ambiguities have to be decided one way or the other in dramatic production. Concerning the appearance of Caliban in *The Tempest*, a theatre director has to make a decision which lies somewhere along the spectrum between Stephano and Trinculo's view (they call him 'monster' 45 times in all) and Miranda's implicit counting of Caliban among humankind ('This / Is the third man that e'er I saw', I.ii.447–8), although she will not admit as much to Ferdinand ('nor have I seen / More that I may call men than you, good friend, / And my dear father', III.i.50–2).[3] Other matters such as how green is the island do not have to be resolved, since a unlocalized playing space need confirm neither Gonzalo's 'How lush and lusty the grass looks! / How green!' nor Antonio's immediately succeeding contradiction, 'The ground indeed is tawny' (II.i.57–9). Where something is not shown, competing verbal accounts of it can be set in competition, and reality may be presented as inaccessible other than through the representations of characters whose motives must be sought and whose honesty must be questioned from moment to moment.

In adapting Shakespeare to the screen, total freedom of visual representation ought to force attention on to the original choices made by Shakespeare and others working in the medium of early modern theatre. Much twentieth-century theatre history can be fairly characterized as reaction to the Victorian taste for lavish theatrical spectacle which was predicated on a conviction that, had he the means at his disposal, Shakespeare would have shown his audience Hamlet's fight with the pirates and the heaped corpses at Agincourt. A guiding principle of twentieth-century theatrical asceticism – encoded most succinctly in the idea of a

Tudor 'bare stage' – has been that Shakespeare made virtues of dramatic necessities, and when choosing whether to show or narrate an event, he applied subtle artistic criteria. Quite possibly, the iconization of this principle in the notion of a Tudor 'bare stage' is misguided, since their stages were not naked: they were keen on colourful decoration and might well have used more furniture than mid-twentieth-century theatrical ascetics believed.[4] But despite this overstatement of the bareness of the Tudor stage, we should continue to inquire carefully whether Shakespeare chose narration over ostentation, telling over showing, for reasons other than practical necessity. Here I will be exploring a range of moments when Shakespeare's decisions to tell rather than show – to offer mediated accounts of reality – give an artistic effect which film directors easily lose in the transition to screen. Film offers ample compensations for these losses, but it is worth distinguishing those dramatic effects which must be foregone from those which might be retained.

In even the simplest cases where Shakespeare decided to tell rather than show the audience an event there is often a witty self-consciousness to the dramaturgy. The final chorus of Shakespeare's *Henry V* (V.Chorus.1–46) continues the theme of apology for dramatic incapacity which runs through the preceding choruses: 'admit th' excuse / Of time, of numbers, and due course of things, / Which cannot in their huge and proper life / Be here presented.' But what follows tests the audience's indulgence by requesting a series of imaginative leaps. First, 'bear the King / Toward Calais. Grant him there; there seen', then 'Behold, the English beach . . . So let him land', then 'solemnly see him set on to London', to 'imagine him upon Blackheath', whence 'in London place him' for the celebration of his military victory. Such imaginative effort is justifiable for scene setting, but the chorus repeatedly offers what might be the location for the next scene only to move us on again. Finally, the audience are enjoined to 'brook abridgement, and your eyes advance, / After your thoughts, straight back again to France', where we left Henry at the end of Act IV. So the repeated appeal to the visual imagination ('seen . . . behold . . . see him . . . imagine . . . your eyes advance') turns out to be gratuitous: we are back where we started, and the events might easily have been narrated. This pattern of raising and deflating expectation is a general principle throughout the play's choruses, as Antony Hammond demonstrated,[5] but it is worth noting that the apparently earnest requests for imaginative indulgence have, by the end, turned capricious. Shakespeare's choruses bear out the aphorism, often attributed to Hollywood studio boss Jack Warner, that the key to success is faking sincerity. Shakespeare's framing of the story with these devices should sensitize an audience to the rhetorical power of claims of inadequacy within the play, especially in Henry's final-act 'wooing' of Catherine.

The imaginative relocation of the stage enjoined by the Chorus in *Henry V* is necessary, because even the Globe's apparently wide stage could not contain the events of the drama on a 1:1 scale. Indeed, even within a particular 'location' the events depicted often occupy a larger area than that available in a playhouse. Spatial compression and spatial discontinuity were common on the early modern stage and were frequently discussed by its theoreticians. Philip Sidney's attack on the 'simultaneous staging' (E. K. Chambers's phrase) of plays which 'haue Asia of the one side, and Affricke of the other'[6] came early in the period, and Chambers thought such techniques a sign of dramatic art's immaturity. Shakespeare usually employed discontinuity rather than compression, but his simultaneous representation of the camps of Richard and Richmond in *Richard III*, V.iii shows how juxtaposition could be symbolically significant, especially as it allowed the two leaders to share a single dream or ghost visitation, their different reactions to which are indices of their relative virtues. Shakespeare made use of a third spatial technique besides compression and discontinuity: locating exciting events off stage and having them commented upon by characters on stage. Tim Fitzpatrick argued that the Shakespearean stage usually represents an intermediate space between two other locations reached via each of the two stage doors. One door, he argued, usually leads 'further in' to a more private chamber, and the other leads 'further out' to a wider world.[7] In Shakespeare's *Macbeth* the murder of Duncan takes place in a room imagined to be behind one of the stage doors, further 'in' to the Macbeths' castle, and the porter admits potential interferers from 'outside' through the other door. Communication between the world imagined to be just off stage and those on the stage can occur through sound effects. In the second scene of

Shakespeare's *Julius Caesar* Brutus fears that the 'Flourish and shout within' (I.ii.80) he hears is celebration at the election of Caesar as king, and his giving voice to this fear allows Cassius to broach directly the subject of rebellion.

As well as sounds coming from off stage, news of exciting events just out of sight can come by messenger's report. Shakespeare used this device for the combat of Arcite and Palamon in *The Two Noble Kinsmen*, reports of which reach Emilia from a messenger who rushes back and forth with news. Oddly, the messenger does not have direct visual evidence, only hearsay, to report: 'The cry's "A Palamon"' (V.v.67), 'Still "Palamon"' (V.v.71), 'They said that Palamon had Arcite's body' (V.v.79), and 'Nay, now the sound is "Arcite"' (V.v.90). Since the cries of 'Palamon' and 'Arcite' are clearly marked as offstage sounds in the 1634 Quarto text which is the only authority for this play,[8] we might wonder why Emilia needs these reports which put her at a double remove from the action. As we shall see with *Much Ado About Nothing*, the difference between first-, second-, and third-hand evidence is a recurrent theme when Shakespeare chooses not to show crucial events to the audience. Most editors add directions for Emilia to be holding and comparing pictures of her suitors throughout the fight, and it appears that here, too, Shakespeare self-consciously draws attention to the medium rather than the message of his story. We might suppose that something not shown to the audience retains a mystery which ostentation would dispel, but Shakespeare (the scene is his) seems interested in *ekphrasis*, which the Oxford Classical Dictionary calls 'an extended and detailed literary description of any object, real or imaginary',[9] but which is commonly used in the more precise sense summarized by Grant F. Scott as 'a verbal representation of a visual representation'.[10] Emilia first brings on her pictures of Palamon and Arcite in IV.ii and describes that of Arcite in terms which, as we shall see, recall Hamlet's description of his father:

> *Emilia*:   What an eye,
> Of what a fiery sparkle and quick sweetness
> Has this young prince! Here love himself sits smiling!
>
> (IV.ii.12–14)

Eleven more lines of similar praise follow. The inferior man is, amongst other things, darker than his rival: 'Palamon / Is but his foil; to him a mere dull shadow; / He's swart and meagre' (IV.ii.25–7). But Emilia changes her mind as she considers the pictures and decides 'Palamon, thou art alone / And only beautiful...What a bold gravity, and yet inviting, / Has this brown manly face?' (IV.ii.37–42). Changing her mind again, Emilia finally decides that she cannot decide because they are 'two fair gauds of equal sweetness' (IV.ii.53). One of the most fascinating aspects of drama is the degree to which spectators are prepared to accept a character's interpretation of reality, so long as it is not flatly contradicted by the evidence of their own eyes, and in the examples from *Hamlet* (considered more fully below) and *The Two Noble Kinsmen* (IV.ii is John Fletcher's work), the dramatists appear to be exploring the power of *ekphrastic* rhetoric. In such a case the film director who decides to show what is being described risks filling in the significant absences which give the scenes their power.

Palamon's dark complexion is one of the characteristics Emilia weighs up and cannot decide upon. Shakespeare's Othello is the period's quintessential dark man loved by a white woman, but the important *ekphrastic* rhetoric is his, not hers. To the senate Othello describes his courting of Desdemona with stories of 'battles, sieges, fortunes', 'disastrous chances', 'moving accidents' and 'hair-breadth scapes' (I.iii.129–35), and like all good rhetoricians he begins with a claim of rhetorical inadequacy: 'Rude am I in my speech' (I.iii.81). Oliver Parker's film of *Othello*[11] provided a flashback to Othello's wooing of Desdemona with stories, but the unpublished shooting script reveals that Parker also shot flashback-within-flashback scenes showing Othello's boyhood and adolescent military training. These would have given the audience the visual images supposedly conjured in Desdemona's mind by Othello's stories, and one particularly significant moment is Othello 'fighting side by side with IAGO. OTHELLO saves IAGO from a fatal blow. IAGO escapes through smoke. OTHELLO fights on. IAGO returns on horseback, picks up OTHELLO and they ride off though flames.'[12] Such bonding gives Iago's pique a tangible cause. This scene was apparently a late insertion into the script (it is a blue page, indicating second rewrite) and was removed in editing, thus restoring Iago's usual, and probably authorially intended, level of inscrutability.

The scene of Emilia's comparison of the two pictures in *The Two Noble Kinsmen* has a prototype in Shakespeare's *Hamlet*. In III.iv Gertrude is berated by her son for failing to see the essential difference between her first husband and her second, pictures of whom Hamlet shows her. First Hamlet Senior:

> *Hamlet*:   See what a grace was seated on this brow –
> Hyperion's curls, the front of Jove himself,
> An eye like Mars, to threaten or command,
>   (III.iv.54–6)

He continues in this vein for several more lines. By comparison, Claudius's picture moves Hamlet to fury: 'a mildewed ear / Blasting his wholesome brother' and 'Have you eyes? / Could you on this fair mountain leave to feed, / And batten on this moor?' (III.iv.63–6). At one level the imagery here is agricultural: Claudius's mildew blights (blasts) Hamlet Senior's fair pastures and leads Gertrude to feed (batten) instead on Claudius's marshy ground (moor), as G. R. Hibbard explained.[13] However, the outburst can also be read as impugning the faculties provided by Gertrude's facial orifices: hearing, speaking (blasting), seeing and eating. Hearing and speaking are inverted (an ear 'blasts') and fair Hamlet Senior is opposed to dark (moorish) Claudius. I assume that the pictures are held by Hamlet and are not large portraits visible to the audience. Hamlet's descriptions are *ekphrastic* and provide powerful emotional incentives to concur in his tirade, but the audience are not in possession of all the evidence. Portable pictures would be too small for the playhouse audience to judge them, so the audience must judge by the appearance of the actors. Hamlet Senior has appeared only as a ghost, so presumably the visual advantage is with his living rival. Perhaps indeed this is the point, that Hamlet's impassioned description counteracts the visual impressions made by the two actors. A cinema director has the opportunity to tip the balance in favour of either man by offering close-up views of the pictures. In the title role of his film *Hamlet* Kenneth Branagh gave himself two monochrome photographs in folding cases and the audience are allowed clear views of the pictures of Brian Blessed (Hamlet

Senior) and Derek Jacobi (Claudius), to the disadvantage of the latter. Laurence Olivier, on the other hand, kept the audience's point of view behind the hand-held pictures and retained what was presumably Shakespeare's intended ambiguity, and Franco Zeffirelli achieved the same effect by keeping the camera too far from the pictures for the audience to make out their details.

Branagh's provision of visual representations to supplement verbal representations in *Hamlet* is a unique case because of his decision to use every line of an editorial invention: a conflation of the Quartos and the Folio texts which brings together lines which were not spoken together in Shakespeare's lifetime.[14] The precursor to Hamlet's berating of Gertrude in her closet is illuminating in this regard. It appears that Hamlet's tirade to his mother is his reworking and extension of the Ghost's tirade on the same theme:

> *Ghost*:   O Hamlet, what a falling off was there! –
> From me, whose love was of that dignity
> That it went hand-in-hand even with the vow
> I made to her in marriage, and to decline
> Upon a wretch whose natural gifts were poor
> To those of mine.
>
>   (I.v.47–52)

As the Ghost makes a comparison of his former self and Claudius, the audience see a flashback of them, together with Gertrude and Hamlet, playing an indoor variant of the game of curling on the polished floor of the palace.[15] Here, too, Branagh evens up the odds concerning the audience's perception of the relative merits of Hamlet Senior and Claudius by giving views of the former's vigour which cannot be offered to the play's audience. These images, however, are not simply reality, rather they are Hamlet's recollections of his father ('remember me', I.v.91), and hence mediated through his necessarily partial mind. Because all the lines of Shakespeare's play, and more, are present, images cannot be used to replace dialogue, only to supplement it, and we should carefully consider the status of each of Branagh's invented images; they are not necessarily representations of reality. In every case the flashback – or rather 'flash-elsewhere', since what they have in common is representation of a time and place distanced from the utterance of the accompanying dialogue – might plausibly be explained as representation of what is in the mind's eye(s) of one or more characters on the stage. They are recollections or imaginings rather than unmediated truths, which is appropriate, since *Hamlet* is the only Shakespeare play containing the phrase 'mind's eye', occurring twice in the Second Quarto ('*Hora. A moth it is to trouble the mindes eye*' and '*Ham.* In my mindes eye *Horatio*'[16]) and once in the Folio text ('*Ham.* In my minds eye (*Horatio*)'[17]).

A particularly significant image is that of Hamlet and Ophelia having sex which, argued Carol Chillington Rutter, not only problematizes Ophelia's status – if she is sexually experienced she ought to spot her father's hypocritical 'drabbing' – but also 'den[ies] her subjectivity in the process of objectifying her'.[18] However, that the audience see Ophelia having sex does not make it real. The sexual images are first shown while Polonius questions his daughter about Hamlet's attentions to her (I.iii.98–136), for which Branagh has the father and daughter sharing the same side of a confessional booth. This booth is reused for the scene of Claudius at prayer (III.iii.36–98), during which Hamlet comes close to enacting his revenge, slowly inching his knife through the grille separating the two sides of the booth and reaching to Claudius's ear. The audience are shown the knife entering Claudius's ear and drawing blood, which is clearly a representation of Hamlet's fantasy rather than reality, since Claudius is unscathed a moment later. Planning to postpone his attack until a moment when Claudius is 'drunk asleep', 'in his rage', 'in th' incestuous pleasure of his bed', 'gaming' or 'swearing' (III.iii.89–91), Hamlet fantasizes each situation in turn and the audience are allowed to share his visual imagining. The images of Hamlet and Ophelia having sex may also be imaginings, the first of them occurring in the same confessional-booth location and being arguably the fantasy of either Polonius or Ophelia. Similar images recur at II.ii.109–19, the reading of Hamlet's love-letter, which Branagh reassigns from Polonius to Ophelia. Part-way through the recitation Ophelia breaks off, overcome with emotion, and as Polonius completes it we see Hamlet, half-dressed, kissing Ophelia as the words of the letter become their post-coital dialogue. It is hardly likely that Hamlet's letter is a transcript he made of this conversation, so presumably the accompanying sexual images are representations of the fantasies of Polonius, Gertrude and Claudius, are the events which they infer from the existence of the letter.

Rutter claimed that 'Almost every soliloquy or moderately lengthy speech is "imaged"' in Branagh's film, and I count twelve such 'imaged' speeches. For Rutter these images are evidence that Branagh 'perversely mistrusts both the word and the audience: he uses them to rush us over the language and supplies pictures to gloss the hard words'.[19] Taking them in turn, however, it is clear that what the audience see may easily be a character's mental image, not reality. As the First Player recites the Priam/Hecuba speech (II.ii.470–521), the audience are shown images of the classical story which clearly are not reality, but rather represent the effect of the speech upon the minds of its hearers. Likewise, during the performance of *The Mousetrap*, the flashback to the murdering of Hamlet Senior is Claudius's recollection prompted by the story's parallels with his own case (III.ii.242–52). The final image of Hamlet and Ophelia having sex occurs while Ophelia sings her bawdy song at IV.v.62–5, and again, to read this as unproblematic reality rather than a view of Ophelia's, or Gertrude's, or Claudius's mind's eye is to reduce the film's representational ambiguity. In Branagh's film, as in the play, recollections or imaginings have objective causes. The skull of Yorick brings the living man to mind, and all the more forcefully because the skull retains the famous protruding teeth of the comedian, Ken Dodd, who plays Yorick in a flashback showing Hamlet's recollection of his childhood playmate.

Three 'imaged' speeches concern Fortinbras's project. The first occurs as Horatio describes Fortinbras's raising of an army to take back the lands his father lost (I.i.94–103), and the audience sees him with his generals poring over maps and looking fierce. The second occurs as Claudius cheers his Court by announcing that he has sent Norway news of Fortinbras's intentions with a request to restrain his nephew (I.ii.27–33), and the audience sees Norway receiving the news with displeasure. Since Claudius still holds the letter and cannot know of its effect, the image is clearly a fantasy of the policy's success. The third image concerning Fortinbras accompanies Valtemand's report of Norway's recall and chastisement of his nephew, and it enacts the description (II.ii.61–75). The final example of 'imaged' speech, the twelfth in all, is a representation of Ophelia under water as Gertrude stares into space, having described the drowning at IV.vii.138–55. Branagh's decision to use a full text made these images inevitably supplementary, and there was no possibility of showing an event rather than narrating it. There was, then, no opportunity to make dramatically true what Shakespeare had written as merely one character's account of reality, and hence no way to represent definite falsehood either. Under these conditions, the truth of these images must be questionable, just as the truth of what a character reports is questionable. Several of my example images might be taken for simple reality by the cinema audience, but others – most obviously Hamlet's fantasy of killing Claudius – cannot be, and this throws doubt on them all. For his part, Branagh decided from the outset that Hamlet and Ophelia had been enjoying a sexual relationship.[20] From the directorial point of view, then, my reading of the images of love-making is simply a misreading, yet the fortuitous reuse of the confessional-booth location (originally Polonius's interrogation of Ophelia was to take place in the boathouse by the lake) and, more importantly, the visual economy entailed by the use of a full text, place the sexual images beyond narrative certainty. As we shall see, Branagh's visual technique in this film differs considerably from his technique in his earlier film of *Much Ado About Nothing*. This was more conventional in its use of standard 35 mm film stock and in its running time, in the version shown in the UK, of 111 minutes, which required heavy cutting of the text and hence encouraged the provision of images to replace, rather than supplement, dialogue.[21]

Zeffirelli's film of *Hamlet* runs for 129 minutes, which was achieved by cutting the text heavily, as is usual for film adaptations, and by showing events which are only described by characters in the playtext. A typical example is the execution of Rosencrantz and Guildenstern, which occupies only a few seconds of screen time, as Hamlet tells Horatio the pith of his faked letter to the English king (V.ii.45–7). Probably saving no time at all, Zeffirelli gave full cinematic realization to Hamlet's disorderly intrusion into Ophelia's chamber, instead of her account of it (II.i.78–101). Rutter complained that Branagh's failure to show this moment was 'a cheat' because 'Branagh, who explains everything else, withholds explanation here.'[22] But the incident is mysterious precisely because we have only Ophelia's account of it, and her relationship to Hamlet is a deliberate ambiguity of the play. Zeffirelli often invents time-saving and explicatory images with considerable style, but the opening moment of his film signally failed to 'suit the action to the word'. The film begins with an invented scene of grieving as Hamlet slowly drops soil over the body of his recently deceased father. The first words spoken are Claudius's '[Hamlet] think of us / As of a father' (I.ii.107–8), and we may suppose that the soil-dropping image was prompted by the unspoken line which immediately precedes this: 'We pray you throw to earth / This unprevailing woe' (I.ii.106–7). This is an economic substitution of image for speech, but it is quite inappropriate, since the point of Gertrude and Claudius's importuning Hamlet to stop grieving in I.ii is that he has persisted well beyond the required period. Asking Hamlet to give up grieving before his father is even in the ground is absurdly tasteless.

Where an important event is referred to in a Shakespeare play but is not shown, we may suspect that it has merely been lost from the dramatic text. The first three Quartos of Shakespeare's *Richard II* do not show the deposition that is central to the action, perhaps because it would have been dangerous to present such a scene on the stage. Alternatively, it might have been acceptable to show the scene but not to print it, and so the scene was cut only from the printed text. But it can also be argued that the play is stronger with this conspicuous absence at its core; not showing what all the fuss is about might have been Shakespeare's original intention. The Bishop of Westminster sees what he calls a 'A woeful pageant' (IV.i.311), which sounds impressive, but even without the abdication scene the line still makes sense as a comment, David Bergeron argued, on 'the arrest of Carlisle, the announcement of Richard's abdication, Bolingbroke's ascent to the throne, and his plans for coronation'.[23] Bergeron thought that the play works well without the abdication being shown, and the success of Quentin Tarantino's *Reservoir Dogs* proves that, for all the claims that visual culture is supervening our verbal/written culture, modern audiences still find aesthetic pleasure in the causes and consequences of a central event conveyed to them only by participants' reports.

A similar absence is at the centre of the action in Shakespeare's
Much Ado About Nothing. The moment when Claudio and Don
Pedro witness a sign of Hero's infidelity is only anticipated and
recalled in the play, not shown. First Don John promises 'Go but
with me tonight, you shall see her chamber window entered'
(III.ii.102–3), and in the next scene Borachio brags how he
brought Margaret into the deception: 'She leans me out at her
mistress' chamber window, bids me a thousand times good night'
(III.iii.140–2). Between III.ii and III.iii the deception takes place
without being shown to the audience. It certainly would have
been possible for Shakespeare's stage to represent Borachio
entering or leaving the bedchamber, so we should consider why
Shakespeare chose instead to use dialogue referring to these
actions. The point seems to be that these are actions which
would precede and follow the event – the putative sex between
Hero and Borachio – and which are taken for the event itself.
Whether entering or leaving Hero's bedchamber, Claudio and
Don Pedro are sure to infer from Borachio's presence that Hero
is sexually active. The audience are distanced from the sexual act
by a double frame: first the corollaries which precede and follow
the implied act, and second the *ekphrastic* narrative promise and
recollection of those corollaries. Branagh chose to show the audience the deception scene in his film of *Much Ado About Nothing*,
and he broke III.ii after Don John says ' I know not that [Claudio
means to marry] when he knows what I know' to cut to an
interior shot of excited kissing between Borachio and Margaret,
although from behind, Imelda Staunton playing Margaret might
easily be mistaken for Kate Beckinsale playing Hero. The next
shot shows Don John, Claudio and Don Pedro entering the
garden, and is followed by one showing Borachio and Margaret
having sex on the balcony of Hero's bedchamber. Putting perhaps too fine a point on it – and surely risking alienation of his
unwitting assistant in this deception – Borachio moans 'Hero,
Hero' in his sexual ecstasy. Returning to the dialogue of III.ii
more or less where we left it, Don John states what appears
obvious: 'The lady is disloyal.'

Branagh's realization of the absent deception scene replaced
Shakespeare's double framing device with the putative act itself,
since Don John brings Claudio and Don Pedro into the orchard
at precisely the moment when no inference is needed to

condemn Hero. As with Othello's misreading of the evidence against Desdemona, the inability of Don Pedro and Claudio to distinguish circumstantial evidence from matters bearing on the fact is an index of their gullibility. Branagh's interpolated scene diminishes this gullibility and increases Don John's skill at presenting a convincing deception. Horace Howard Furness pointed out that in Shakespeare's narrative, Don Pedro later says that Borachio has 'Confessed the vile encounters they have had / A thousand times in secret' (IV.i.94–5), and that this lie should 'mitigat[e] our condemnation of Claudio's conduct'.[24] In the theatre the proposed deception sounds implausible and Shakespeare's doubled 'befores' and 'afters', which pointedly draw attention to the absent 'during', highlight the essential difference between circumstantial evidence and proof. Furness, like Branagh, excused Claudio and Don Pedro a little too readily. Perhaps to counterbalance this simplification of the play, Branagh introduced ambiguity by showing only the back of Borachio's sexual partner, allowing the audience to wonder, at least momentarily, whether Hero is guilty of the accusation.

Shakespeare clearly did not intend to deceive the audience about Hero's fidelity in *Much Ado About Nothing*, but there are other moments in Shakespeare's work when we are justified in thinking that deception is intended. Usually the audience enjoy a privileged position from which the misunderstandings of the characters can be measured against a notional narrative truth, but in *The Comedy of Errors* the audience learn the identity of the Abbess only when it is revealed to the on-stage characters at V.i.346. At the other end of Shakespeare's career, Paulina's revelation that Hermione is alive at the end of *The Winter's Tale* is a similar surprise for the audience. Shakespeare rarely misled his audience, but Philip C. McGuire made a powerful case for thinking that the supposed ascent of the Dover cliff by Gloucester and Edgar in *King Lear* is another example.[25] On the flat Elizabethan stage, descriptions of the ground being walked upon are all an audience has to go on, as with Northumberland's 'These high wild hills and rough uneven ways / Draws out our miles and makes them wearisome' (*Richard II*, II.iii.4–5). An audience trained to accept such descriptions at face value are likely to wonder who to believe when faced with this exchange:

> *Gloucester*:   When shall I come to th' top of that same hill?
> *Edgar*:   You do climb up it now. Look how we labour.
> *Gloucester*:   Methinks the ground is even. *Edgar*: Horrible
>   steep.
>
> *(The Tragedy of King Lear,* IV.v.1–3)

McGuire described the likely reaction of the first audience to this as 'a combination of uncertainty and suspense',[26] for not only is Edgar's intention unclear – will he help his father to die? – but also the audience cannot tell where the action is set. Strong encouragement to believe that father and son are to be imagined standing at the top of a cliff comes in Edgar's remarkable *ekphrastic* speech describing the perspective foreshortening of the birds, people and boats he claims to see below (IV.v.11–24), which, McGuire argued, shows the impact upon Shakespeare's thinking of the newly introduced perspective scenery of the court masque.[27]

A film director sensitive to Shakespeare's use of balanced ambiguity might well want to achieve the same effect. In his film of *King Lear*, Peter Brook[28] used a shot of Gloucester's and Edgar's legs and feet apparently labouring as Gloucester asked 'When shall I come to th' top of that same hill?', and Edgar replied, 'You do climb up it now. Look how we labour.' A shot from behind pulls out to reveal that they are in fact walking on the level beach, as Gloucester becomes suspicious: 'Methinks the ground is even. *Edgar*: Horrible steep.' The possibility of Gloucester seeing through the deception is forestalled by Edgar choosing to carry his father on his back, and Brook used only low-angle torso-and-head shots from this moment until Gloucester's 'fall'. Edgar's decision to carry Gloucester, to remove his direct sensory access, coincides with the director's removal of the audience's access to reference data in the framing, and presumably Brook thought that the establishing 'flat-beach' shot would have faded in the memory so that Edgar's 'trick' might work on the film audience. Even those who see through the trick may sense how it feels to be Gloucester, for Brook's sudden transition from low-angle upper-body shots before Gloucester's 'fall' to extreme high-angle long-distance shots after the 'fall' gives an impression of watching Gloucester fall from a great height, even as it reveals that he did not.

Earlier in his film of *King Lear* Brook interpolated a scene concerning the nature of damning evidence which, like Branagh's balcony sex-scene in *Much Ado About Nothing*, raises the possibility that the cinema audience may experience a deception for themselves while watching others being taken in by it. Edmond's plan to alienate Gloucester from Edgar begins with a promise, rather like Don John's, that incontrovertible evidence can be presented:

> *Edmond*: If your honour judge it meet, I will place you where you shall hear us confer of this, and by an auricular assurance have your satisfaction, and that without any further delay than this very evening.
>
> (*The Tragedy of King Lear*, I.ii.91–4)

It is easy to hear in 'auricular assurance' an echo of Othello's 'Give me the ocular proof' (III.iii.365), with which it shares this theme of damning evidence. With Gloucester hooked, Edmond makes effectively the same promise to Edgar: 'I will fitly bring you to hear my lord speak' (I.ii.157–8). Neither of these eavesdroppings takes place in the play, but Brook interpolated an opportunity for Gloucester to overhear Edgar damning himself by reading the letter written by Edmond. The letter ends: 'If our father would sleep till I waked him, you should enjoy half his revenue for ever and live the beloved of your brother, Edgar' (I.ii.53–6), and Brook might be criticized for improbably making Edmond take an unnecessary risk concerning Edgar's enunciation. For if Edgar paraphrased the signing off as 'live the beloved of your brother, *signed* Edgar', the entire scheme would unravel. However, we should note that Iago took a risk as great as this concerning Cassio's explanation of the handkerchief, and Brook's invented scene is true to the spirit of Edmond's daring wickedness.

I noted that Shakespeare's deceptions of his audience are rare and that Edgar's 'Dover cliff' trick is merely an arguable example. The entire first scene of *The Tempest*, however, is clearly a deception, since the audience have no reason to suppose that the storm is an illusion created by Ariel. As Peter Holland pointed out, theatre and film directors who show Prospero and/ or Ariel in a manipulative capacity in the first scene are spoiling

Shakespeare's intentional misleading of his audience.[29] The first comment on the apparent storm comes from Miranda, who suspects her father of creating it: 'If by your art, my dearest father, you have / Put the wild waters in this roar, allay them' (I.ii.1–2). It transpires that Ariel, on Prospero's instructions, created not a storm, but the likeness of one:

> *Ariel*:   I boarded the King's ship. Now on the beak,
> Now in the waste, the deck, in every cabin,
> I flamed amazement. Sometime I'd divide,
> And burn in many places; on the top-mast,
> The yards, and bowsprit, would I flame distinctly;
> Then meet and join. Jove's lightning, the precursors
> O' th' dreadful thunderclaps, more momentary
> And sight-outrunning were not. The fire and cracks
> Of sulphurous roaring the most mighty Neptune
> Seem to besiege, and make his bold waves tremble,
> Yea, his dread trident shake.
>
> (*The Tempest*, I.ii.197–207)

Ariel compares each aspect of his simulated storm with the real thing: his fake lightning was as brief as real lightning, his sounds and sights appeared to besiege the sea-god himself, and by these tricks he 'flamed amazement' in the boat's occupants. The point of the storm was to induce 'a fever of the mad' (I.ii.210) in Prospero's enemies, not to actually harm them. Ariel's description is *ekphrastic*, but Shakespeare used it not to enhance his deception of the audience, as was the case with Edgar's description of the view from the cliff, but to expose the deception. In Derek Jarman's film of *The Tempest* Prospero is seen sleeping and fitfully dreaming while the storm takes place, and there is a strong sense that the storm is a manifestation of the power of his imagination, or a force released from his id.[30] This reading of the scene manages both to spoil the deception and to turn the arch-manipulator of others' perceptions into a passive receiver of images, for when dreaming we are subjected to those personal mental processes which are least under our control. In Peter Greenaway's adaptation, *Prospero's Books*,[31] the protracted storm lasts into I.ii and troubles Miranda's sleep, and in *Forbidden Planet* the dark side of Morbius's (Prospero's) creative power is manifested in a Caliban-like figure who ('his thing of darkness I acknowledge mine') is repeatedly referred to as a monster from his creator's id.[32] The storm scene is unnecessary in *Forbidden Planet* since the astronauts are under orders to visit the isolated home of Morbius and his daughter, but it survives in an oddly attenuated form: an awkward moment of muted collective panic when the navigator mismanages the deceleration from lightspeed. Intellectual hubris forms the major theme of the film and, in an allusion to the mythical Greek Icarus, the navigator's error brings the spaceship too close to the sun. In *Forbidden Planet*, as in Jarman's film, the arch-creator is subject to forces of which he is unaware. At the other end of the poststructuralist spectrum Greenaway's treatment of the storm, indeed of the entire text, invests Prospero with complete authorial-narratorial control as he visibly directs the action and ventriloquizes all the parts. Greenaway's extensive imagery of books and papers, and his presentation of *The Tempest* as a story being narrated in its moment of composition, emphasize a primordial textuality which scholars and practitioners of theatre and film are apt to forget: plays and films first take shape as scripts and story-boards.

After a series of mind-games including the vanishing banquet and Ariel's impersonation of a harpy, Prospero's victory is complete when 'The King, / His brother, and yours, abide all three distracted' (V.i.11–12) in the lime grove, and there are good reasons to see parallels between Prospero and Shakespeare as manipulators of the imagination. But Prospero needs strong prompting to appreciate a verbal description of a powerfully moving visual effect:

Ariel: Him that you termed, sir, the good old lord Gonzalo:
His tears run down his beard like winter's drops
From eaves of reeds. Your charm so strongly works 'em
That if you now beheld them your affections
Would become tender. *Prospero*: Dost thou think so, spirit?
Ariel: Mine would, sir, were I human. *Prospero*: And mine shall.
(*The Tempest*, V.i.15–20)

Stung by the implied rebuke from Ariel, Prospero decides to free his prisoners, since a human should 'be kindlier moved than thou art' (V.i.24). But the rebuke stands, since Prospero the bookish creator of visual effects is a dull consumer of them.

Shakespeare used powerful descriptions of visual effects which he might easily have presented on the stage and he exploited opportunities for 'painting with words'. More than once the point of using *ekphrastic* narration is to draw attention to the complex balance of manipulative powers in drama. Just as the choruses in *Henry V* should alert us to the power of disclaiming power, moments when Shakespeare demands that the audience imagine a scene rather than see it remind us that mental images are as constructed and manipulable as stage pictures. Repeatedly, Shakespeare used the stage's non-commitment to a single visual representation to put competing verbal representations into conflict. Cinema, too, can present absence and can problematize the conventions by which its operates, but it is striking how seldom this is attempted outside film comedy, and it is arguable that early modern theatre's visual ambiguity cannot properly be transferred to other media. Branagh's ambiguous visual images in his film of *Hamlet* are dependent on his use of a full text of the play, which makes them necessarily supplements rather than substitutes for speech, and in this important respect his film is not a cinematic adaptation at all but rather a filmed stage-play. Brook's use of camera angle to deny the audience access to background reference data in his filming of the 'Dover cliff' scene of *King Lear* introduced an element of the original staging, but it was preceded by a wide-angle shot establishing the narrative reality of Edgar's deception, which Brook presumably thought necessary to prevent spectator confusion. This is a not entirely successful attempt to transfer to cinema a device which fully works only on a bare stage. On the other hand, Branagh's provision of visual information not provided by the play (the close-ups of the pictures of Claudius and Hamlet Senior, and the sight of Borachio having sex) diminishes the functional ambiguity provided by Shakespeare's verbal representations of visual representations. The margin of directorial freedom between these two faults is small, but staying within these limits might provide a useful artistic constraint when Shakespeare is being adapted to a medium which now has seemingly unlimited technical resources.

12. Shakespeare and the Future

KIERNAN RYAN

The charge most commonly levelled at modern critical accounts of Shakespeare is that they are anachronistic. On the face of it, the charge seems entirely justified. Critics keen to claim Shakespeare's plays and poetry for the cause of psychoanalysis, feminism, queer theory or postcolonial critique may well offer all kinds of plausible insights into the texts they address, but in the end, how much credence can one really attach to interpretations that would have left the Bard himself baffled?

It is now a critical commonplace, for example, to perceive in the transvestite confusions of Shakespearean comedy an awareness of the modern feminist distinction between sex and gender: the knowledge that masculinity and femininity are not merely expressions of biological difference, but culturally crafted roles that are neither natural nor fixed, but open to dispute and disposed to mutate. Yet few would be so foolish as to contend that *As You Like It* and *Twelfth Night* were deliberately written to sabotage patriarchy and slake the raging thirst of Elizabethan playgoers for female emancipation. On the contrary, quite apart from the fact that Shakespeare and his audience would have found terms like 'patriarchy', 'gender' and 'feminism' unintelligible, it seems a pretty safe bet that the modern sexual politics to which those terms are hitched would have struck them as alien and absurd.

Or take the contention that *King Lear* constitutes a searing attack on the principle of monarchy and the unequal distribution of power and wealth upon which that principle depends. Pitched out on to the heath at the mercy of the elements, with his wits about to turn, the once-omnipotent sovereign – so this reading runs – is forced to feel for the first time what the 'poor, naked wretches' (III.iv.28) of his kingdom feel, and to realize that royal robes and beggars' rags cloak the same 'poor, bare, forked animal' (III.iv.101–2).[1] Through Lear's traumatic transformation, in other words, the play demolishes the concept of innate social difference that supports hierarchy itself, climaxing in a snarl of contempt for all who arrogate to themselves the right to rule others: 'there thou mightst behold the great image of authority. A dog's obeyed in office' (IV.v.153–5). In place of division and domination, moreover, the tragedy appears to recommend a compassionate egalitarianism diametrically opposed to the values that preside so destructively over the universe of *King Lear*: 'So distribution should undo excess, / And each man have enough' (IV.i.64–5). Yet one need only recall that Shakespeare's company at the time was the King's Men, who thrived beneath the shelter of their monarch's personal patronage, and that *King Lear* is known to have been performed at court before King James himself on St Stephen's night in 1606, to bring this radical reading of the play stumbling to a halt. How could Shakespeare even dream of entertaining the sovereign on whom he depended for his livelihood with a tragedy designed to divest the Crown of its mystique and undermine the foundations of its power?

Equally suspect, from the same historical point of view, are the by now routine treatments of *The Tempest* as a precocious post-colonial text and the ubiquitous assumption that *The Merchant of Venice* and *Othello* are centrally preoccupied with questions of race that have become all too insistent in our own time. That the relationship between Prospero and Caliban betrays striking parallels with the relationship of colonizer to colonized, both then and since, and that Caliban is allowed to address piercing rebukes to the master who has usurped him as sole sovereign of the isle, cannot be gainsaid: 'This island's mine,' protests Caliban, 'by Sycorax my mother, / Which thou tak'st from me' (*The Tempest*, I.ii.333–4). But these are surely shaky grounds on which to build a view of Shakespeare as bolstering or spiking the ambitions of empire in his final masterpiece. By the same token, no one who knows *The Merchant of Venice* needs reminding of the impact the character of Shylock has had on the cultural memory of the West, not least through his unanswerable plea for Jews to be treated as the equal of Christians by virtue of their shared vulnerability and mortality: 'If you prick us, do we not bleed? . . . If you poison us, do we not die?' (III.i.59–61). It is quite another matter, however, to approach the play as if it had been written in the wake of the Holocaust and judge it in the light of an understanding four centuries beyond its author's reach. Nor is it any easier to discern a credible historical warrant for regarding *Othello* as Shakespeare's attempt to tackle the predicament of blacks in a white community and the toxic issue of miscegenation, when these matters were not at that time the national political battlefields they have subsequently become.

To read or perform *King Lear, The Merchant of Venice, Othello* or any of Shakespeare's plays as if their author were our contemporary is to foist upon these plays interpretations whose blatant anachronism disqualifies them at the outset, because they ascribe to Shakespeare ideas and attitudes that belong to our world, not to his. That is the crime that critics and theatre companies around the globe stand accused of in the court of common sense. But, although the case for the prosecution appears to be cut and dried, the charge simply refuses to stick, and the defendants are soon back to their old trick of discovering in a dramatist dead for centuries a writer more vital than any playwright of the present. And the reason why the charge refuses to stick is that the case for the prosecution, however self-evident it may seem, is based on a fundamental misconception of both literature and history.

For one thing, we do not live in a world that is completely different from the world in which Shakespeare lived and about which he wrote. Most historians now prefer to refer to Shakespeare's time as the 'early modern' era rather than the Renaissance, in order to emphasize its continuity with the 'late modern' or 'postmodern' epoch, to which Western cultural commentators maintain that we belong. From this standpoint, it is no longer so surprising to find Shakespeare grappling with problems of gender, race, power and social injustice that were only in their infancy in Elizabethan England, but whose full-grown form could already be envisaged at that time. It is scarcely an accident that audiences are not queuing up across the continents to watch the latest stage or screen version of the anonymous morality play *Everyman* or the mystery cycle penned by the nameless Wakefield Master. Important though these masterpieces of medieval drama undoubtedly are, the gulf that divides the Catholic, feudal universe that cradled them from our own epoch is far wider than that which separates Shakespeare's culture from modernity, and bridgeable only by a formidable leap of the historical imagination. Whereas to hear *Hamlet* or *Macbeth* open his tormented heart to us, or to watch the blighted loves of Romeo and Juliet or Antony and Cleopatra unfold, is like travelling to a foreign country and finding ourselves immediately at home.

It should go without saying, of course, that no approach to Shakespeare will carry much conviction unless it is anchored in a knowledge of the forces that originally shaped the language and form of his drama. Without such a genetic perspective, without the information quarried by generations of linguistic and cultural historians, the basic meaning of whole swathes of Shakespeare's works would remain opaque, their topical allusions would be lost on us, and the theatrical conventions that govern their impact would confound where they had once served to communicate.

It is equally apparent, however, that the significance of Shakespeare's writings – the sense that audiences, readers and critics subsequently make of them – cannot be confined to what we suppose they must have meant to Shakespeare's contemporaries, or even to Shakespeare himself. To review, for example, the critical reception of *Macbeth* since the seventeenth century, or to track its performance history on stage and screen, is to become aware of how much the play's import has changed, as successive ages have discovered its purchase on their own situation. There are now compelling arguments for regarding *Macbeth* as the tragedy of a man chained to a destructive model of masculinity and the pitiless creed of self-promotion captured in the lines: 'For mine own good / All causes shall give way' (III.iv.134–5). A modern concern with gender, fuelled by feminist critiques of patriarchy, has conspired with a modern distrust of unbridled individualism to turn *Macbeth* into a play for today, whose own author would be hard put to recognize it as his creation.

This conception of *Macbeth* remains persuasive and valid nonetheless, but not because those persuaded by it are raring to ride roughshod over the constraints of history and the evidence of the text. All manner of interpretations have been inflicted on Shakespeare, from the abysmally banal to the frankly deranged, but widespread and sustained assent has generally been secured only by those that correspond to visible features of the works themselves. The reading of *Macbeth* as a tragedy of masculinity and an indictment of individualism commands credence because it is demonstrably rooted in the words and deeds scripted by Shakespeare. That such a reading may never have crossed Shakespeare's mind as he wrote the play does not diminish *Macbeth*'s capacity to enshrine insights into Shakespeare's world – and the worlds that would succeed it – that could not find expression at that time in any other way. The play testifies to the power of Shakespeare's poetic imagination to grasp dramatically matters whose full significance could only become apparent centuries after he wrote. *Macbeth* always possessed this modern understanding of masculinity and individualism, *but it possessed it in a different form*. It possessed it and expressed it implicitly, in the concrete, theatrical terms of a dramatized predicament, rather than through explicit, abstract contention. So when critics and productions activate this understanding of *Macbeth*, it would be truer to say that, far from imposing upon the play an illegitimate, retroactive perception, they are actually unlocking implications that it has always harboured, implications historically inscribed in its poetic language and theatrical techniques.

In fact, the accusation of anachronism directed at recent interpretations, performances and adaptations of Shakespeare could be turned on its head. It might be more accurate to argue that what these new views of the plays demonstrate – provided that they are consistently grounded in the evidence of the texts – is not the anachronism of their own assumptions, but the anachronism of Shakespeare's imagination, which propelled his plays ahead of their time to speak with such authority to ours. To appreciate the power of the plays to adumbrate the present, however, is also to concede the limits that our standpoint in the present places on our perception of them. If a latter-day concern with colonialism, power, class, race and gender prompts us to see the same themes foreshadowed in Shakespeare's drama, it inevitably blinds us in the process to all the other interpretive possibilities stored in the texts, waiting to be unpacked by critics, directors and actors of the future, with other matters on their minds. There will always be more to Shakespeare's plays and poems than meets the eye at a given moment. His works may presage the obsessions of the present age, but that does not mean that the most acute critics of our day have had the last word. The imaginative reach of Shakespeare's plays exceeds our critical grasp, but by how much, and in what ways, only readers and spectators yet to be born will be able to tell.

Another way of putting this would be to say that Shakespeare's drama bears out better than the work of any other author the truth of Shelley's belief that the poet 'not only beholds intensely the present as it is, and discovers those laws according to which present things ought to be ordered, but he beholds the future in the present'.[2] There is no need to cite Shelley, however, to confirm the importance of the prophetic impulse to a poet and dramatist whose works constantly proclaim their endeavour to trace in the texture of 'present things' the imprint of things to come. Indeed, almost everywhere one looks in Shakespeare's writings, one finds evidence of their eagerness to slip the shackles of the moment in which they emerged and reach out to futures that lie not merely beyond Shakespeare's horizon, but beyond the scope of our conception as well. Today's Shakespeare criticism offers few sights more ironic or depressing than that of old and new historicists straining to immure *Hamlet* or *Much Ado* in the Elizabethan matrix from which it has expressly striven to extract itself. The past-bound approach of antiquarian scholarship, however modishly it may disguise itself, cannot begin to cope with plays that refuse to make complete sense in terms of their time, because they are also addressed to prospective audiences, whom their author will never know.

The first place to turn, however, for proof of the proleptic cast of Shakespeare's imagination, is not to the plays but to the *Sonnets*. For here, in a sequence celebrated for its obsession with braving the ravages of time, we encounter poem after poem projecting itself into the future, anticipating some eventual scenario or boldly predicting what shall come to pass, as in the opening lines of Sonnet 55: 'Not marble nor the gilded monuments / Of princes shall outlive this powerful rhyme' (1–2); or the closing lines of Sonnet 107: 'And thou in this shalt find thy monument / When tyrants' crests and tombs of brass are spent' (13–14). Shakespeare's conviction that his poetry will live on the lips of citizens of centuries to come receives its most haunting expression in Sonnet 81:

> Or I shall live your epitaph to make,
> Or you survive when I in earth am rotten.
> From hence your memory death cannot take,

Although in me each part will be forgotten.
Your name from hence immortal life shall have,
Though I, once gone, to all the world must die.
The earth can yield me but a common grave
When you entombèd in men's eyes shall lie.
Your monument shall be my gentle verse,
Which eyes not yet created shall o'er-read,
And tongues to be your being shall rehearse
When all the breathers of this world are dead.
    You still shall live – such virtue hath my pen –
    Where breath most breathes, even in the mouths of men.

To read these lines now is to testify to their uncanny prescience,
to fulfil Shakespeare's prophecy of their fate by ourselves becoming those 'eyes not yet created', those 'tongues to be' that he
foretold. As we read the *Sonnets*, it is hard to escape the eerie
realization that Shakespeare *knew* that we would be reading them
now, in a world and time beyond even his imagination.

In Sonnet 106, moreover, we find Shakespeare adopting
the role of the reader of the poetry of long ago – adopting the
equivalent of our role, in other words, as we read him now – in
order to stress not only the prophetic power of past literature,
but also the vital part to be played by later readers in discerning
the precocious modernity of its bequest:

When in the chronicle of wasted time
I see descriptions of the fairest wights,
And beauty making beautiful old rhyme
In praise of ladies dead and lovely knights;
Then in the blazon of sweet beauty's best,
Of hand, of foot, of lip, of eye, of brow,
I see their antique pen would have expressed
Even such a beauty as you master now.
So all their praises are but prophecies
Of this our time, all you prefiguring,
And for they looked but with divining eyes
They had not skill enough your worth to sing;
    For we which now behold those present days
    Have eyes to wonder, but lack tongues to praise.

What Coleridge shrewdly identified as Shakespeare's 'fondness for presentiment'[3] is not simply a fascination for 'divining' the shape of things to come, for the phenomenon of prediction as such. It is, more precisely, a gift for catching glimpses of the present and the potential in the past, and a recognition of the prefigurative power of his own anachronistic art.

That Shakespeare the dramatist is as possessed as Shakespeare the poet by 'the prophetic soul / Of the wide world dreaming on things to come' (Sonnet 107, 1–2) is apparent throughout his theatrical career. Clairvoyant characters crop up in several of the plays to cast the pre-emptive shadow of futurity across the ensuing action, or to foretell the destiny that looms beyond the final *Exeunt* of the dramatis personae. The soothsayer in the opening scene of *Julius Caesar* famously warns Caesar with 'a tongue shriller than all the music' to 'Beware the ides of March' and is rashly dismissed as 'a dreamer' (I.i.18, 20, 26). His equally perspicacious counterpart in *Antony and Cleopatra* claims: 'In nature's infinite book of secrecy / A little I can read' (I.i.8–9), and proceeds to tell Charmian her fortune, whose cruel irony becomes apparent only at the close of the play: 'You shall outlive the lady whom you serve' (I.i.27). Clarence foresees his own imminent doom in a dream, which fills what turns out to be his last 'miserable night' on earth with 'dismal terror': 'Methought what pain it was to drown, / What dreadful noise of waters in my ears, / What sights of ugly death within my eyes' (*Richard III*, I.iv.2, 7, 21–3). And *Henry VIII* (or *All is True*) concludes with Cranmer's prediction of the glorious fate awaiting the royal infant Elizabeth and her successor to the throne of England over half a century later:

> Peace, plenty, love, truth, terror,
> That were the servants to this chosen infant,
> Shall then be his, and, like a vine, grow to him.
> Wherever the bright sun of heaven shall shine,
> His honour and the greatness of his name
> Shall be, and make new nations. He shall flourish,
> And like a mountain cedar reach his branches
> To all the plains about him. Our children's children
> Shall see this, and bless heaven.
>   (V.iv.47–55)

The proleptic point being that this prediction was addressed, of course, to those 'children's children' of Cranmer's generation at the play's first performance in 1613. A Jacobean play about the historical past presages a future which is actually the recent past and immediate present of its original audience, who in turn have now dwindled into the distant past, as we perceive it today.

The likelihood that not a few members of that original audience, who had actually grown up under Elizabeth and were currently the subjects of King James, would have greeted Cranmer's prophecy with a wry smile or a bitter grimace as they struggled to recall the 'peace' and 'plenty' and repress their memories of 'terror', affords a salutary reminder of the retrospective ironies that lie in wait for forays into the future. Of these ironies Shakespeare is acutely aware, and his plays repeatedly strive to cultivate in his audience a readiness to conceive of reality in the future perfect tense, to remember that the fate of every present is to become what *will have been* the case. *Henry VIII* is not the only history play that demonstrates the vulnerability of chronicles of national fact to the startling transformations of perspective that arrive on the heels of hindsight. The epilogue furnished by the Chorus at the end of *Henry V* scuppers its triumphant tale of its royal protagonist by reminding its Elizabethan audience, and every audience that would succeed it, of what happened to Henry's heroic legacy:

> Henry the Sixth, in infant bands crowned king
>   Of France and England, did this king succeed,
> Whose state so many had the managing
>   That they lost France and made his England bleed,
> Which oft our stage hath shown;
>
> (Epilogue, 9–13)

And, with that, the future of the world of *Henry V* recedes in a flash into antiquity.

Shakespeare never treats the past as finished, as over and done with, because he knows that it is the nursery of times to come, which will change the significance of the stories the past tells about itself. In *Henry IV Part II*, Warwick makes a confident

speech about the possibility of inferring the future from a careful
scrutiny of the past:

> There is a history in all men's lives
> Figuring the natures of the times deceased,
> The which observed, a man may prophesy,
> With a near aim, of the main chance of things
> As yet not come to life, who in their seeds
> And weak beginnings lie intreasurèd.
> Such things become the hatch and brood of time;
> (III.i.75–81)

But 'the hatch and brood of time' have an awkward habit of
turning into creatures quite different from what 'the times
deceased' had seemed to promise.

None of the plays makes the slipperiness of the future clearer
than *Macbeth*, which is Shakespeare's most profound and complex meditation on prolepsis, on the urge to apprehend the
future before it has transpired. Macbeth is persuaded by his
own dark desires and the seductive prognostications of the
witches that he has been 'transported . . . beyond / This ignorant
present' and now can feel 'The future in the instant' (I.v.54–6),
and in a sense, or to a certain extent, he has and he can. As the
tragedy unwinds, however, it rapidly dawns on him that he has
been the eager dupe of 'th' equivocation of the fiend, / That lies
like truth' (V.v.41–2). The 'imperfect speakers' (I.iii.68) of the
heath can indeed foresee 'the coming on of time' (I.v.8–9) and
impart it to Macbeth, but the veracity of their prophecies is only
subsequently apparent, and their full catastrophic significance
remains closed to him till after the event.

The reliance of prophecies on retrospection to unfold their full
import is intriguingly problematized at the close of *Cymbeline*.
After the avalanche of revelations and reconciliations subsides,
Lucius summons forth his soothsayer, Philharmonus, to 'declare
the meaning' (V.vi.436) of the cryptic prophecy inscribed on the
tablet that was placed on Posthumus's breast in a dream by the
ghosts of his parents and siblings. An exorbitant amount of space
and time is devoted to Philharmonus's painstaking elucidation of
the tablet, which concludes thus:

The lofty cedar, royal Cymbeline,
Personates thee, and thy lopped branches point
Thy two sons forth, who, by Belarius stol'n,
For many years thought dead, are now revived,
To the majestic cedar joined, whose issue
Promises Britain peace and plenty.

(V.vi.454–9)

But en route to the gratifying punchline of the prophecy, the soothsayer's reasoning reveals itself as strained, almost desperate, at key points, most notably when he struggles to decipher the prediction that 'a lion's whelp shall... be embraced by a piece of tender air' (V.vi.437–9). The 'lion's whelp' he convincingly construes as signifying Posthumus Leonatus, but his credibility begins to crumble when he tries to turn 'tender air' into Innogen:

> (*To Cymbeline*) The piece of tender air thy virtuous daughter,
> Which we call '*mollis aer*'; and '*mollis aer*'
> We term it '*mulier*', (*to Posthumus*) which '*mulier*' divine
> Is this most constant wife, who even now,
> Answering the letter of the oracle,
> Unknown to you, unsought, were clipped about
> With this most tender air.

(V.vi.447–53)

Even Cymbeline cannot stifle his scepticism: 'This hath some seeming' (V.vi.453) is the most enthusiastic response he can muster to the soothsayer's attempt to place a 'fit and apt construction' (V.vi.445) on the prophecy.

This curious incident is instructive, because it provides a paradigm of what is at stake in the modern critical interpretation of Shakespeare's plays. The coded forecast on the tablet requires the hermeneutic art of the soothsayer to unearth its buried meaning, and up to a point the interpreter, armed with the advantage of hindsight, does a plausible job of squaring the semantic potential of the text with the ensuing events that it purports to foreshadow. But only up to a point, because the fit between the forecast and the facts can be seen to be imperfect, and the limits of the interpretation are exposed. However satisfactory the construction placed upon some parts of the text may be, other parts remain intractable and refuse to be converted into the terms of current understanding. The tablet secretes meanings that are still to be mined, and thus it harbours the possibility of evolving a significance more complex than, or quite different from, that which Philharmonus has laboured to extract from it. In much the same way, the poetically encoded texts bequeathed to posterity by Shakespeare offer themselves to be construed today as memories of the future, as prefigurative parables not only of the present time, but also of times to come. Yet, no matter how complete or conclusive our interpretations appear, and however faithfully they comply with the constraints of the texts, they will always be subject to revision and replacement by more competent and compelling versions of Shakespeare's vision. The soothsayer scene in *Cymbeline* is a salutary reminder that the plays themselves, just like cryptic prophecies, will never stop saying one thing and meaning another.

To grasp a Shakespeare play as fully as possible at any point in time is to recognize that its gaze is bent upon a vanishing point at which no reader or spectator can hope to arrive. Like the hat that the circus clown kicks out of reach every time he steps forward to pick it up, final comprehension of the play is perpetually postponed by each act of interpretation. Built into Shakespeare's plays, as into his poems, is the expectation that whatever eyes are viewing them at a given moment, other 'eyes not yet created' (Sonnet 81) will one day view them in another light. The most memorable expression of this awareness is placed in the mouth of Cassius, as the conspirators smear their hands with Caesar's blood:

> How many ages hence
> Shall this our lofty scene be acted over,
> In states unborn and accents yet unknown!
> (*Julius Caesar*, III.i.112–14)

What is so extraordinary is the effect of infinite regression created by these lines, whose vertiginous perspective is calculated to ensnare every subsequent cast and audience, obliging them to apprehend the historicity of the performance in hand and hence the impermanence of their own era.

The same point is made even more powerfully by the personi-
fication of Time, the Chorus of *The Winter's Tale*, who steps out
through the illusion of the play world at the start of Act IV to
address the spectators directly:

> Impute it not a crime
> To me or my swift passage that I slide
> O'er sixteen years and leave the growth untried
> Of that wide gap, since it is in my power
> To o'erthrow law, and in one self-born hour
> To plant and o'erwhelm custom. Let me pass
> The same I am ere ancient'st order was
> Or what is now received. I witness to
> The times that brought them in; so shall I do
> To th' freshest things now reigning, and make stale
> The glistering of this present as my tale
> Now seems to it.
>
> (IV.i.4–15)

This stunning speech lays bare the mind-bending perspective
from which Shakespeare invites us to perceive not only *The
Winter's Tale*, but his other plays as well. It requires the audience
to accept that 'what is now received' as reality is simply 'custom',
the arbitrary contrivance of a particular culture, which is as
vulnerable to the transforming hand of time as 'ancient'st
order', the earliest form of human society that can be recalled.
To the audience of Shakespeare's time and the audience of our
time alike, nothing could be more immediate and unpredictably
alive than 'th' freshest things now reigning', the performance of
the actor speaking these words and each spectator's response to
them. Yet the day can already be foreseen when 'the glistering of
this present' will have faded into a memory as 'stale' as the yarn
spun by *The Winter's Tale*. Shakespeare's plays anticipate the
impending displacement and disappearance of their world, and
they solicit the reciprocal recognition that our world, likewise,
conceals the evolving past of a prospective present. Their aim is
to project us forward in time to a point where we can look back
on Shakespeare's age and our own as the prehistory of an epoch
whose advent humanity still awaits.

An alertness to the fact that Shakespeare's drama belongs as much to the future beyond the horizon of our time as it does to its own era is vital. It is vital because it fosters dissatisfaction with both the attempt to consign the plays to the past and the urge to delete the centuries that divide them from us and reduce them to reflections of modernity. There is no doubt that Shakespeare's scripts are stubbornly rooted in the now remote milieu that nourished them. And it is also true that, notwithstanding their anchorage in a bygone age, those scripts possess the vatic power to foresee our own epoch, four hundred years after their author's demise. But no account of Shakespeare's drama can begin to do it justice by sacrificing the constraints of the past to the dictates of the present, or by dismissing the modern meaning of the plays as historically unfounded. For the whole point of Shakespeare's drama is to stage an unpredictable dialogue between his world and our world about what we might one day become.

13. Why We Talk Shakespeare

MICHAEL J. COLLINS

During Bill Clinton's first term of office, before the world had ever heard of Monica Lewinsky, Hillary Clinton tried unsuccessfully to define a formal role for herself in her husband's administration. Although she had successfully practised law in Arkansas while Clinton was governor, many Americans were incensed that she chose to support her husband not through the adoring reticence of her predecessors, but by contributing actively and publicly to his Presidency. With 'her image as a tough career woman... used to dominating whatever situation she is in by force of mind',[1] commentators and (usually right-wing) political opponents were fond of comparing her to Lady Macbeth. Ruthless, ambitious, the shaping force behind her husband's policies as well as his success, Hillary, they proposed, like Lady Macbeth, had unsexed herself (abandoning her daughter in pursuit of her career) and driven her husband, more 'full of the milk of human kindness' (I.v.17),[2] to seek and achieve 'the golden round' (I.v.28) of the Presidency. While the comparison did nothing for Hillary Clinton's reputation (and only further complicated her role in American public life), it seemed implicitly to enhance Shakespeare's, for his apparent anticipation, some four hundred years earlier, of the relationship between Bill and Hillary Clinton seemed further evidence of his status as our greatest writer.

If (as the subsequent scandal over Monica Lewinsky seems to make clear) the comparison of Hillary Clinton to Lady Macbeth really said very little about the complex relationship of the President and his wife, it finally said even less about why we enjoy Shakespeare's plays and value them more than the work of any other writer in English. Although the many books with titles like *Shakespeare on Management*, *Shakespeare on Politics* and *Shakespeare on Love* claim otherwise, the plays actually tell us almost nothing that we do not already know or might not learn more directly from other sources. Even Harold Bloom's more profound claim for the plays (in his best-selling *Shakespeare: The Invention of the Human*) seems, for all the erudition that supports it, equally mistaken. For Bloom, 'Shakespeare's plays are the wheel of all our lives, and teach us whether we are fools of time, or of love, or of fortune, or of parents, or of ourselves.'[3] But Shakespeare's plays never do (and, as any human construct, never could) answer such enduring and mysterious questions.

As I often remind my students, anything we might learn from *Romeo and Juliet*, for example, we have (as the recent film by Baz Luhrmann made eminently clear) already learned in the lunch room when we were students in secondary school or in the staff room when we became teachers. (As Frank McCourt, the author of *Angela's Ashes* and *'Tis*, once explained in a talk on teaching, he grew tired of reading papers in which his students imagined ending their disappointed love affairs by drowning themselves at Rockaway Beach in Brooklyn.) It needs no playwright, come some four hundred years ago from Stratford, to tell us about love, violence, drugs and suicide among adolescents: the newspapers and the talk shows provide whatever we need to know. And yet, although it tells us nothing we do not already know or might not learn elsewhere, *Romeo and Juliet* is generally regarded a great play, enduringly popular and highly valued throughout much of the world.

At the same time, we implicitly diminish the value of Shakespeare's plays when (like Hillary Clinton's critics) we celebrate them because they in some way remind us of the world in which we live, because the stories they tell seem to reflect some public event or private experience. If it were the story Shakespeare tells in *Romeo and Juliet* that made the play valuable, then we might as well (as students are sometimes asked to do) read *West Side Story* or a news report of the latest tragic love affair between a Serb and an Albanian in Kosovo or a Catholic and a Protestant in Northern Ireland, for both the musical and the report are set in worlds more immediately recognizable and written in idioms more easily accessible.

Some years ago, a *Peanuts* cartoon showed Peppermint Patty, the perennial D– student, giving an oral report to her class. 'This is my report on *The Brothers Karamazov*,' she begins, 'of which there were three. It reminded me of a similar story, *The Three*

Little Kittens, because there were three of them also.' Before she can continue, however, the teacher, whose words do not hear, interrupts the report, and Peppermint Patty, in the last frame, replies: 'I'm surprised the similarity never occurred to you.' Although she will probably get another D– for her report, Peppermint Patty may nonetheless go on to enjoy a successful career as a literary critic, not simply because she has a sophisticated understanding of the negotiations among texts, a new historical sense of intertextuality, but also because she has done what critics always do – noticed similarities, parallels, echoes, analogies, image patterns within and between texts. Indeed, the most successful literary critics, for better or worse, are often those who notice things that no one, sometimes for good textual or theatrical reasons, has ever noticed before.

The kind of conclusions Peppermint Patty is prevented by her teacher from drawing often turn up in the introductions to popular editions of Shakespeare's plays. With *Twelfth Night*, for example, editors, inevitably engaged by Feste, ordinarily explain his function and meaning in relation to some of the larger themes and motifs of the play. For Herschel Baker, 'only the Clown, it seems, is clear-eyed and wise enough to stand somewhat above the antics of the others and to comment on their follies.... In a world where everyone is slightly mad, his motley is a badge of knowledge.'[4] Anne Barton proposes that

> it is the task of Feste in his final song to... build a bridge from that remote, enchanted place where the two romantic couples remain forever to the very different world outside the theatre which is our own.... Precisely because of his anonymity and aloofness in the play now ended, he can be trusted to speak for all mankind, and not simply for himself.[5]

Stephen Greenblatt finds that while 'Feste is irresponsible, vulnerable, and dependent,... he also understands... that it is foolish to bewail forever a loss that cannot be recovered. ... His counsel is for "present mirth" and "present laughter." '[6] Charles T. Prouty suggests that

> the conventions and pretenses [of comedy and love] are not mocked in the satiric spirit, for here all is gaiety, and the

lyricism which animates the play is found not only in the songs
but in the characters themselves. ... So...both Orsino and
Olivia reveal that they belong to the world of fancy..., a land
of 'cakes and ale' far removed from the mundane. Feste sums
it all in...[the] concluding stanza [of his final song].[7]

Each of the four editors is an experienced, distinguished,
highly respected critic, and each of their readings reflects the
ideas, the issues *Twelfth Night* seems to be about. At the same time,
however, the readings all seem somehow beside the point, in
some way to ignore, rationalize, reduce, falsify our experience
of the play, to say things that are entirely plausible, but not quite
consonant with what we have encountered in it. As Stephen
Booth puts it, 'the recurring topics of the play make it feel
pregnant with profound significance that critics acknowledge by
their respect for *Twelfth Night* but never do–and, I think, never
could–deliver to us'.[8]

Luckily for Peppermint Patty, however, she is stopped from
taking the next step, the step the introductions inevitably take:
she never gets to tell what the similarities mean (and thus, by
implicitly challenging her teacher's reading, risk another D–).
Anyone who talks about Shakespeare (student, teacher, critic of
theatre or literature, an audience during the interval or at dinner
after the show) soon becomes adept at noticing the seemingly
endless similarities in the plays – parallels, echoes, analogies of
language, image, character and plot – and thus at finding a vast
array of meaning and significance in them. While Shakespeare's
plays readily provide us apparently limitless opportunities to talk
about ourselves, our world, our beliefs, our values, our lives,
many other things – the dialogues of Plato, news reports, a
history of the First World War – do the same. If we value Shakespeare's plays more highly than the work of any other writer in
English, it must be for something other than the stories they tell,
the things they teach, or the varied meanings we discover in them
or make from them.

Although the marvellous film *Shakespeare in Love* turned the
playwright into a quintessentially romantic figure, a brooding
poet who could not write what he had not first lived, Shakespeare
did not invent the stories his plays tell. In almost every case
(*Love's Labour's Lost* and probably *The Tempest* are the exceptions),

we know the source or sources of Shakespeare's plays. But since Shakespeare always transformed his sources into something more 'rich and strange' (*The Tempest*, I.ii.404), we clearly value the plays not for their stories, but for Shakespeare's ability to tell their stories effectively, for the experience his way of telling the stories offers us as we read the plays or see them performed.

As the response of children almost always makes clear, hearing the story of the Three Little Pigs is an extraordinarily satisfying experience. While some would find its value in the moral lesson it teaches (only hard work keeps the metaphorical wolf at bay), what we really value in the story, the quality that makes it both satisfying and enduring, is the way it is told to us, our experience of it. The wordplay, the rhymes ('let me come in', 'chinny chin chin', 'blow your house in'), the repetitions and variations (straw, sticks, bricks, houses that do and do not fall in, pigs that start out together, separate, and end up together) all combine to make our experience of the story deeply satisfying. And while we might, once we have tired of telling them the story over and over again, discuss with children the competing values of work and play implicit in it (just as we discuss them after hearing Hal's soliloquy in *Henry IV Part I*, I.ii), we finally value *The Three Little Pigs* (as we do Hal's soliloquy) for the way its words act upon us, for our experience of it.

What *The Three Little Pigs* does simply, Shakespeare's plays do with mind-boggling complexity. In *Hamlet*, for example, words, images, characters, plots, motifs reflect and refract one another so as to leave us with the eminently satisfying sense that we have encountered a profoundly intricate, richly patterned structure of vibrant words that seems simultaneously to capture both the complexity and the meanings of the human experience it articulates. If the intricacy ultimately precludes our ever precisely defining the meanings, we nonetheless find the experience of the play significant and satisfying.

As the customary occupation in seminar rooms and lecture halls attests, our talk about Shakespeare's plays consumes at least as much time as our experience of them. And since it does, it is important to recognize the profound difference between the two activities, between our reading or watching the play and our subsequent talk about it. In *As You Like It*, for example, Touchstone, recently arrived in Arden, finds in Corin 'another simple sin': 'to offer to get your living by the copulation of cattle' (III.ii.77, 79). Later in the scene, Rosalind, describing the varied roles she once played to cure a lover, proposes that 'boys and women are for the most part cattle of this colour' (409). Finally, in the last scene, Touchstone, entering with Audrey, says, 'I press in here, sir, amongst the rest of the country copulatives' (V.iv.56–7).

While a sensitive (or perhaps ingenious) reader of texts might find relevant meaning in the repetitions of 'copulation of cattle', 'cattle of that color' and 'country copulatives', an audience, hearing the second or third variation, would have neither the time nor the inclination to do so. Yet, in hearing the repetition, they would at the same time feel the patterning of the play and the satisfying response such patterning had here evoked. This subtle repetitive pattern reflects the myriad patterns of *As You Like It* as a whole and functions in little as they do.

Only a few lines later, an audience encounters Touchstone's routine on the seven degrees of the lie. Here again, while a term paper (if not a scholarly article) might easily be written on it, it seems to have been included in the play (even if does allow the actor playing Rosalind time for a costume change) simply for its own eminently satisfying sake. Back in lecture hall, out in the lobby, if we have enjoyed the play or the production and hope perhaps to recall or recapture the experience of it, we might find it enjoyable to spend some time discussing how Touchstone's routine connects to the various ideas, themes, images whirling about in the play: the discussion might even allow us to think and talk usefully about (as we say these days) conflict resolution. As we read the play or watch it performed, however, the connection of Touchstone's routine to such other elements of *As You Like It* is at once instantly felt and absolutely irrelevant.

The same thing might be said about the scene (IV.i) between Desdemona and Emilia in *Othello*. As the two women speak and Desdemona sings her song, their lines not only catch up and, as in a piece of music, work variations on melodies we have heard before, but seem also to comment on what we have previously encountered. If the exact import of that comment remains ultimately elusive, beyond precise and compelling articulation, the lines nonetheless act upon their audience or their readers in a deeply moving way. Similarly, although its tone is very different, a comparable kind of patterning is at work in *A Midsummer Night's Dream*, a play that, as the varied critical responses readily suggest, seems, like Bottom's dream, to have no bottom. The image of Bottom and Titania, probably the most theatrically engaging element in the play, necessarily acts a particularly crucial role in any understanding of the play: it suggests multiple and often contradictory meanings that grow plausibly out of its relation to the play's complex, interlocking patterns.

A catalogue of plausible meanings for Bottom and Titania would include at least the following: the humble and virtuous acceptance of love the others lovers lack; love as simultaneously absurd and ennobling; the bestial, the lustful dimension of love; the humiliation and manipulation of a woman (Titania) by a man (Oberon) or of the lower class (Bottom) by the ruling class (the King and Queen of the fairies); the play's generous, comic vision of humankind; the reconciliation of differences to achieve the comic goals of private and social harmony; the love of God for men and women. While such a bald list ignores the sensitivity and nuance of the critical readings that have proposed such varied meanings, it does seem to me to suggest (1) that subsequent discussion of the play has missed something essential to our experience of it, to the immediate impacts it makes upon us; (2) that comparable readings of *The Three Little Pigs* would find its value in the lessons about work and play it putatively teaches; and (3) that what we really value in the play are not the meanings we find in it or make from it, but our experience of it, our encounter with a richly patterned structure of words that, through their structure, come to engaging and apparently significant life on the stage or in our reading. As with our response to Touchstone's routine on the degrees of the lie, the connection of Bottom and Titania to the rest of the play is at once immediately felt and utterly irrelevant.

The openness of the plays to a variety of readings is, however, what both actors and directors particularly value them for. While we tend at times to forget it, the plays are actually scripts, written to be performed, not simply open to interpretation, but demanding it, offering actors (and readers who consider the theatrical possibilities of the scripts) the opportunity of endlessly remaking the plays. On the stage (or on film), we never see the same Hamlet twice, not simply because Laurence Olivier, Richard

Burton, Derek Jacobi, Mark Rylance and Kenneth Branagh are all different people, but because, as they work with Shakespeare's open script, they must inevitably make choices, not simply about how they will say the lines or act on the stage, but also about who Hamlet is at each moment of the play, about the thoughts and feelings that drive and shape his words and actions. If the play's innumerable references, explicit and implicit, to Hamlet open up countless possibilities for an actor, through wit and imagination, to bring Shakespeare's words to life on a stage, the need to make choices ensures that not all the possibilities can ever be enacted in a single production.

The actor who plays Macbeth, for example, must at some point decide (to put it as simply as possible) whether to play his character as a tragic hero or a criminal. When Derek Jacobi played Macbeth (for the Royal Shakespeare Company in 1993–94), he seemed a gentle, even genial figure, clearly more a decent man than a warrior or a murderer. He entered laughing with Banquo, fell to his knees in remorse after murdering Duncan, poured wine for the murderers, danced on to the stage for the banquet scene with a long line of guests, and never seemed entirely capable of the evil deeds he and his agents were carrying out. He spoke his lines with considerable attention to their poetic possibilities, particularly the two great soliloquies of the last act. Derek Jacobi thus played Macbeth as a fundamentally good man drawn tragically, despite his goodness, to evil.

In contrast to Jacobi's, Rufus Sewell's Macbeth (at the Queen's Theatre in 1999) seemed clearly a warrior. He entered in a costume of black leather and, unlike Jacobi, put little emphasis on the poetic possibilities of the language or the reflective possibilities of the character, speaking his lines throughout the evening in a restrained, repressed, sometimes snarling tone which occasionally gave way to anger, the only emotion he seemed ever to feel. Even in his soliloquies and asides, spoken downstage, directly to the audience, he sounded staccato and detached. He played part of the last act in a black box, downstage centre, pacing back and forth within it. As a result of Rufus Sewell's understanding of his character and a generally static staging (with ordinarily little movement or fluidity to the scenes), the production turned *Macbeth* into something of a morality play, with a criminal Macbeth contrasted first with Duncan (who was kneeling at prayer when he first appeared in I.ii) and then with Macduff. While Shakespeare's Macbeth seems finally both a murderous tyrant and a tragic hero, no actor could play both: Derek Jacobi chose the second and Rufus Sewell the first.

As I have tried to suggest, then, we value Shakespeare's plays not for the things they tell us, the wisdom they impart, the meanings we find in them or make from them, but for our experience of them, an experience that seems, as we live through it, profoundly satisfying and meaningful, although its meaning, once we have time to reflect on it, persistently eludes us. Indeed, we value Shakespeare's plays because they remain intractably elusive, because they do not offer easy answers to vexing questions, because they do not make simple a world that is complex, indefinite, ambiguous, even because, at times, instead of offering easy explanations, they leave readers and audiences perplexed by their experience of the play.

In the ending of his comedies, for example, Shakespeare, unlike Hollywood, characteristically mutes his happy endings and recalls the world of ordinary reality. Jaques withdraws from the wedding celebration in *As You Like It* to join the newly converted Duke Frederick. The marriage of Toby and Maria in *Twelfth Night* or, more disturbingly, of Angelo and Mariana in *Measure for Measure* may dilute the joy an audience should conventionally feel. In *The Merchant of Venice*, the shadow of Shylock inevitably chastens such comedy as the final scene contains and sometimes, in performance, makes it embarrassing or even painful to encounter. *The Tempest* gives Antonio no lines when Prospero forgives him and thus dilutes the feeling of triumph the final scene may evoke. Our experience of Shakespeare's comic endings are profoundly different from our experience of Hollywood's: our feelings of joy and elation are alloyed with darker, more troubling feelings.

Such alloyed responses, however, are often lost in performance, for directors usually want to bring the play to either a comic or an ironic close. When Sir Peter Hall directed Dustin Hoffman in *The Merchant of Venice* in 1989, for example, he played for a comic ending. As the actors began to clear the stage, they did so in pairs, first Lorenzo and Jessica, then Gratiano and Nerissa, and finally Bassanio and Portia, all running diagonally across the stage to exit up right. At the last moment, however, as Bassanio and Portia were about to exit, they stopped, turned back towards Antonio, who had remained diagonally downstage from them, and held out their hands towards him. Antonio ran upstage and all three, an image of harmony and reconciliation, exited together.

The scene made a very different impact on its audience in Bill Alexander's production for the Royal Shakespeare Company in 1987. As the couples exited for the last time, Jessica dropped the gold cross she had ostentatiously worn since her elopement with Lorenzo. Antonio, who had stood alone and disdainful at centre stage as the couples moved off, bent down to pick it up. Jessica moved back and knelt to his right, just behind him. Looking straight ahead, out at the audience, Antonio held the cross just above her extended hand as the stage went black. As they had throughout the production, a Christian again abused a Jew, a man again abused a woman.

Puzzling, enigmatic, textually and theatrically insistent, the Fool in *King Lear* also leaves a reader or an audience perplexed. Although his words at times seem apt and meaningful, at others they seem either nonsensical or related to their dramatic context in ways we can not fathom. As Alec McCowen, who played the Fool in Peter Brook's production, has pointed out (in a talk at Georgetown University), it is impossible to know at every moment what the Fool's words mean. But the Fool is troubling in another way, for the play never tells us what becomes of him after he speaks his last words, 'And I'll go to bed at noon' (III.v.84).

On the stage, the question to some degree is answered. He (or sometimes she) has been found dead when Kent says 'Come help to bear thy master / Thou must not stay behind' (III.v.98–9); has been left (in Nicholas Hytner's production for the Royal Shakespeare Company in 1990) folded in a chair on a revolving stage, her arms waving spastically; has exited for the last time with Lear, Kent and Gloucester; has hanged himself on the stage (in Jude Kelly's production in London in 1995); has turned sharply around and walked deliberately off the stage after his last words (in David Hare's production for the Royal National Theatre in 1986); or has exited at II.i.v, rejoined Lear and Cordelia in IV.vii, been separated from them again when they are taken to prison in V.iii, and finally been dragged dead on to the stage just before

Lear's final speech (at the Shakespeare Theatre in Washington in 1999). But the play itself leaves the Fool's fate a mystery that grows ever more mysterious through the opening words of Lear's final speech ('And my poor fool is hanged'), and then through the possibility that on Shakespeare's stage the actor who played Cordelia doubled as the Fool. While critics propose complex and (sometimes ingenious) meanings for his lines and directors invent actions to account for his disappearance from the play after III.v, the perplexity we feel in our encounter with the Fool inevitably has an impact on our experience of the play and in part shapes our response to it.

The perplexity at the Fool reflects our more encompassing perplexity at the end of the play. As Lear looks at the body of Cordelia, the one daughter who has loved him, he speaks his final words:

> Do you see this? Look on her. Look, her lips,
> Look there, look there.
>
> (V.iii.312–13)

What does Lear see, what does he ask us to look at, in the last moments of his life? What is the tone of his words here? For some, Lear's words suggest that he sees some transcendent vision, as Robert Stephens, playing Lear in Adrian Noble's production for the Royal Shakespeare Company in 1993, implied when he crawled upright towards the apron of the stage, pulling Cordelia behind him, looking diagonally up and out over the audience, pointing to something unseen in the far corner of the theatre. For others, they suggest that Lear sees only the absurd insult of Cordelia's body lying as dead as earth on the ground.

As the critical history of *King Lear* makes immediately clear, the play characteristically evokes contradictory understandings of itself and of the world it reflects. For G. Wilson Knight, *King Lear* tells us that human suffering has meaning:

> Sometimes we know that all human pain holds beauty, that no tear falls but it dews some flower we cannot see. Perhaps humour, too, is inwoven in the universal pain, and the enigmatic silence holds not only an unutterable sympathy, but also

the ripples of an impossible laughter whose flight is not for the wing of human understanding.[9]

For J. Stampfer, *King Lear* tells us that human suffering makes no sense:

> And with Lear's death, each audience...shares and releases the most private and constricting fear to which mankind is subject, the fear that penance is impossible.., because its partner has no charity, resilience, or harmony–the fear, in other words, that we inhabit an imbecile universe. It is by this vision of reality that Lear lays down his life for his folly.[10]

While they seem to offer mutually exclusive readings of *King Lear*, both these conclusions grow out of essays that are intelligent, sensitive and alert to the complexities of the text.

As these two familiar and representative readings of the play suggest, *King Lear* leaves us, then, where our own lives leave us, poised between the fundamental possibilities of the human condition, between meaning and absurdity, between light and dark, between, as the critic Barbara Everett, quoting Pascal, puts it, between ' "all and nothing" ',[11] speaking the only words it can. Do not despair: Lear may see Cordelia living. Do not presume: Lear may see Cordelia dead. And here, in its final refusal to answer the fundamental question it has raised through the way it has told its story, the question of whether we live in a sane or a lunatic universe, in its refusal to rejoice or despair, lies another reason to value not simply *King Lear*, but all of Shakespeare's plays, for they do magnificently what all literature seeks to do: to create a richly patterned, resonant, engaging structure of words that evokes, for reader and audience alike, an experience that, while true to the complexity of the world it reflects, seems at once greatly significant and profoundly satisfying.

Appendix: Bibliography of Shakespeare and Electronic Sources

JOSEPHINE WEBB

Rather than merely supply a listing of what is accessible at the time of writing in 2000, this bibliography will also attempt to provide an overview of the kinds of material that are available, and their relative importance. One of the (justified) concerns of librarians about electronic information is that users are often less selective with electronic resources than they are with print, and differentiate less between the various publishing formats and kinds of information content.

Scholars and librarians have used the term 'virtual library' since the early 1990s to describe the Internet, but information and communications technologies offer the researcher rather more than a vision of an electronic library, stacked with catalogues and electronic texts. Anyone observing the expansion in use of electronic information in the 1990s should see that the increasing popularity of digital resources derives not just from their easy availability. Indeed, information and communications technologies have immense scope to change the nature and focus of scholarship and teaching in the arts and humanities.

This potential resides in a number of areas, which this Appendix will highlight in later sections. The first opportunity is the increased ease in identifying and finding material, both in terms of published works, traced in bibliographies and catalogues, and in identifying unpublished or semi-published material in catalogues or electronic archives. Even in the mid-1990s, tracing the bibliographical details of particular editions might take several hours of searching through printed bibliographies or catalogues, or some hours negotiating hostile library catalogue interfaces. Now, all of this can be done in a matter of minutes, from any computer with access to a network. Increased processing power and more attractive, easier-to-use interfaces also mean that searching is more enjoyable, and more interactive. A catalogue might include, for example, image, text and media clips, with links to resources in each of these areas, thus offering a more multimedia experience.

The second area of potential is in access to electronic texts. Sometimes an electronic text is purchased on CD-ROM; at other times, the text may be freely available on the Internet, or a subscription paid to access the website. Electronic texts are exciting. In the first place, it is possible to

213

access material which may have been available only in a handful of
libraries before, and to download, save and print it, usually free of
copyright restrictions (though this may depend on the licence agreement in specialist sites). You may be able to find different versions of the
same texts – and compare sections of text more directly than when
hunting around for printed copies. But most importantly, electronic
texts facilitate textual analysis to a level that might previously have
taken very many hours of meticulous and dull research. Text-search
programs enable the researcher to analyse language across the text of
a single piece of work or the whole *oeuvre*.

The third opportunity in the virtual library rests in the enhanced
access to criticism and review. It is possible to trace secondary criticism
and research findings around the world from any computer with Internet access. Scholars may create their own websites, with copies of
their own papers, freely available to all who visit. Even CD-ROM databases can make accessible a great body of criticism and review, previously
difficult to retrieve in publications like the *Annual Bibliography of English
Language and Literature*. And finally, the very nature of Information and
Computing Technology (ICT) means that everyone becomes an actor in
the process of finding, using, sharing and imparting information. The
Web is democratic; by using it, you become part of it. Discussion lists
exist to foster communication: everyone can publish either through
e-mail or on a web page somewhere.

It is easy to paint too idealistic a picture. Using ICT is not necessarily
as easy or straightforward as the Internet apostles might suggest. Just
because something is available may not mean it is either good, useful or
appropriate. Nor may it be easy to find exactly what you are looking for.
And because we live in a capitalist economy, many of the best resources
are only available to fee-paying visitors: scholarship costs money and
intellectual property has a financial value, so not everything is available
to everyone all of the time.

In general, there is less material easily available on the Web than you
might expect, and what is available is somewhat disappointing. Gabriel
Egan[1] made a rather extreme statement that 'Nothing currently available
on the web would justify the cost of buying the computer', but at times the
range of what is available can be dispiriting. We must realize, however,
that despite the relative paucity of material (and some critical complaints
about what is available anyway), because the technology is interactive and
easy to access, it is more likely to be used than inaccessible scholarly texts.

Rebecca Bushnell[2] discusses some of the potential teaching applica-
tions of these sites, and the sources listed below provide links to excellent
examples. This Appendix lists some of the main electronic resources on
Shakespeare. It is far from comprehensive, but rather offers paths to
finding what you need. It is particularly important to remember the
paths rather than the destinations, since Internet addresses seem to
change constantly.

FINDING TOOLS

Internet search programs and portals

The Internet includes many different kinds of resources: the Web, Usenet and e-mail. No single source provides links to everything. There are varying estimates about how much on the Web is linked to something else, but you might assume that any search program you use links to less than 50 per cent of what might be relevant to your current search.
Additionally, each search engine works in a slightly different way. Certainly all of them look for your keywords, but the design of the retrieval program will vary, and this influences the results. Expert searchers find what they want by using more than one program regularly, by being confident about the functionality of the programs they use, and keeping up to date. Metasearch engines are particularly popular with these sorts of people. Essentially, a metasearch program searches several databases at the same time, stripping out duplicates and ranking the findings according to relevance.
Well-known search engines are usually well maintained and develop all the time. There are many sites which list them, but the best starting point is:

Search engine watch   www.searchenginewatch.com
Amongst the many resources on this website is an analytical review of the major search engines, with links to them all. This is an excellent site, which can be used to identify new programs and other ways of searching.
Favourite search engines include:

Google   http://www.google.com
A fast and comprehensive search engine. Goole ranks sites by the number of links to them, so the popular sites appear higher.

Northern Light   http://www.northernlight.com/
This is a huge index of the Web, with links to other special collections. The latter include journal and magazine articles. It is a favourite search engine among professional researchers and librarians because it clusters documents by topic.

Gateways

Gateways are a different way of finding material on the Web. Whereas a search engine finds links to material identified through various kinds of computer programs, subject gateways or directories are compiled

by humans. They are catalogues of the Web and other Internet resources. They tend to be smaller and more selective, but are also well-
structured and focused catalogues of links to more academic or reputa-
ble resources.

BUBL   http://www.bubl.ac.uk
The name is an acronym of the Bulletin Board for Libraries, and is a
selective and fairly effective gateway to material in all subjects.

HUMBUL   http://www.humbul.ac.uk
Based in Oxford, HUMBUL is a humanities bulletin board. It offers
options to search and browse links to sites, all of which have been
selected for their scholarly value. HUMBUL is the best starting point
to find texts and archives.

Yahoo!   http://www.yahoo.co.uk
Yahoo is the most popular route to finding material on the Web. As a
subject directory, you can enter a search term and findings are listed in
broad subject headings. This means that it can be easier to find material
by subject, since it is all classified, and what you find has already been
selected for its relevance.

Specialist gateways

Scholars around the world have also created their own specialist gateways to resources. These are also called metasites, since they are sites
which are about all the other relevant sites. For reasons of brevity, we will
list only the most significant ones.

Literary Resources – Renaissance
http://andromeda.rutgers.edu/~jlynch/Lit/ren.html
Maintained by Jack Lynch at Rutgers University, this is a critical listing of
Renaissance websites, and includes brief, critical comments.

Mr William Shakespeare and the Internet
http://daphne.palomar.edu/shakespeare/
Run by Terry Gray, this is a specialist gateway that includes links to
almost everything else. Described by Jack Lynch as 'The best of the lot:
extensive and scholarly.'

The Voice of the Shuttle   http://vos.ucsb.edu/
Highly respected metasite for humanities research. Always worth book-
marking to visit again.

Library catalogues and other general sources

No library catalogue or bibliography can be entirely comprehensive. Just as with search engines, it is important to look in more than one place.

COPAC   http://www.copac.ac.uk/copac
This is the combined catalogue of British and Irish research libraries, including Oxford, Cambridge, John Rylands and Trinity College Dublin. COPAC combines simple search facilities, with good output options and excellent coverage of material.

OPAC97   http://opac97.bl.uk/
The catalogue of the British Library's Reference and Document Supply collections.

Amazon   http://www.amazon.co.uk
One of many online booksellers. These have a quite different purpose from library catalogues. Whereas the latter enable the searcher to find what has been published, online bookshops facilitate the identification of what may be purchased. Book descriptions may also include reviews and synopses.

Specialist bibliographies

World Shakespeare Bibliography 1990–
The Arden Shakespeare in association with The Folger Shakespeare Library. When complete, the bibliography aims to provide a single, comprehensive source of secondary information on Shakespeare, published since 1990. This includes books, articles and dissertations which have at least a chapter relating directly to Shakespeare; accounts of stage productions, films and adaptations; book and theatre reviews; popular journalism; details of any recordings and obituaries of scholars and performers.

The bibliography is a scholarly, refereed source with admirable ambitions; to quote from its publicity, it will be possible to search for 'all studies of a character type, or theme, or image, or trope, for all examinations of a particular scene'.

Other secondary sources include the *MLA International Bibliography* database, the *Arts and Humanities Citation Index* and *ABELL*. All of these are available in different formats and from a variety of hosts. They are important for any serious research, but more detailed descriptions have not been included since they are both more general than the precise scope of this listing, and information about them is widely available.

ELECTRONIC TEXTS, DIGITAL ARCHIVES AND OTHER RESOURCES

Since many editions of Shakespeare are out of copyright, anyone can make them available in the form of digital texts. Sometimes one may find nothing more than an electronic version of the text, unstructured and only searchable in the most general sense. Other sites are more interesting. To a large extent, you get what you pay for; so most completely free sites are just not as good – by any measure used – as the fee-based ones.

Ardenonline http://www.ardenshakespeare.com/ardenonline

This aims to be the definitive website on the works of Shakespeare and contains the complete contents of the ten Arden third series plays published to date, including introductions, text and commentary notes, along with the text of the second series and a wealth of supplementary material. This includes a new introduction to Shakespeare in performance, an illustrations bank, a reviews bank, topic-based indexes and a chronological chart of performance with hypertext links to illustrations and reviews.

The site is intended to serve as a utility for teaching, as well as research. It differs from LION (see below) by emphasizing Shakespeare in performance, rather than textual analysis. It is a development of the Arden Shakespeare CD-ROM which has been available since 1997.

Early English Books Online (EEBO) http://wwwlib.umi.com/eebo/

The electronic equivalent of Bell and Howell's collection of microfilmed early English texts. This is a collection containing over 96,000 titles listed in Pollard and Redgrave's Short-Title Catalogue (1475–1640) and Wing's Short-Title Catalogue (1641–1700) and their revised edition. This is still at project stage, but early results are impressive.

Furness Shakespeare Library
http://www.library.upenn.edu /etext/collections/furness/index.html

Based on the holdings of the Furness Memorial (Shakespeare) Library at the University of Pennsylvania, this is a digitized collection of resources, freely available on the Web.

Internet Shakespeare Editions http://castle.uvic.ca/shakespeare/

Anne Lancashire[3] describes the purpose of this project in detail. In essence it hopes to create electronic texts of Shakespeare's plays and related works, meeting the highest standards of scholarship while making all of its material freely available on the Web. Very little is available so far, but what there is has been praised by Gabriel Egan and John Lynch.

LION http://lion.chadwyck.co.uk/

A fully searchable library of more than 260,000 works of English and American poetry, drama, and prose, plus biographies, bibliographies and key secondary sources. LION is a resource centre providing very well-structured access to electronic versions of texts and links to other significant, relevant websites around the world. It has a specialist database of editions and adaptations of Shakespeare. However, LION has been criticized for its reliance on particular editions, and for the absence of any facsimiles.

Shakespeare's Globe http://www.reading.ac.uk/globe/

A brief online guide to the reconstructed playhouse in London and an online archive about the Globe from 1599 to 1999.

Sites on Shakespeare and the Renaissance
http://web.uvic.ca/shakespeare/Annex/ShakSites1.html

Pages of links to criticism, performance, fun stuff, texts and other metasites. Easy and clear to read and follow.

Oxford Text Archive http://ota.ox.ac.uk/

This was one of the earliest text archives, but its focus is more on collecting together rare texts than making Shakespeare's works available.

CRITICISM AND REVIEW

The majority of journal literature and monographs relevant to Shakespeare continues to exist in printed form. There are very few alternatives to books, save for course handbooks and other documentation available online – the sources listed above can direct you to the best of those. Periodical titles may also be available electronically, from publisher websites, or specialist services, like the Gale Group's *Expanded Academic* database, which includes about 900 full-text journals, plus another 1,000 in abstract form – and there are many similar services. Sometimes electronic access to a specific journal is only available alongside a print subscription.

There are significantly fewer pure electronic journals – probably only *Early Modern Literary Studies* and *Renaissance Forum* are of serious importance and both of these carry material on Shakespeare.

The principal secondary sources listed in the sections above direct the researcher to the best current sites.

DISCUSSION LISTS AND OTHER INTERACTIVE SOURCES

There is only one moderated discussion list on Shakespeare: *SHAK-SPER*. This is described as an international electronic conference for Shakespearean researchers, instructors and students, which has some 1,250 members. Like many lists, its size and the changing nature of the Web means that the debates are not always terribly interesting. To subscribe, e-mail: SHAKSPER@ws.BowieState.edu

ArdenNet http://www.ardenshakespeare.com/main/welcome.html

This is an attempt to create an electronic community or bulletin board around the Arden Shakespeare. There are some useful pieces, but it is not very busy. Most of the correspondence in the e-mail archives has been about a less than flattering comment made about SHAKSPER. The site also has links to other Internet sites. It is worth a visit, but beware of publisher puffs!

There is a Usenet list, humanities.lit.authors.shakespeare, which receives very mixed reviews. In general, it is perhaps safe to say it is more useful for those with a need for general information, or who relish an argument, particularly on authorship.

CONCLUSION

It is surprisingly difficult to write a comprehensive bibliography on electronic resources on Shakespeare. Most of the main sites link to each other, so once you find this ring of interlinked sites, you can be directed to the related sites. On the other hand, the rather incestuous nature of the websites means that comments can be bland, and that by following one particular route of links, you find yourself stranded in the intellectual shallows of guides to writing term papers. As with most Internet resources for English literature, the Internet promises much, but it often fails to provide what you really need, either because you cannot afford to access it, or because it is work in progress. Nevertheless, the potential is enormous, and the range of what is available at your fingertips remains impressive.

Notes and References

INTRODUCTION *Deborah Cartmell and Michael Scott*

1. Introduction to *The Miller's Tale*, l.78 in *Chaucer's Poetry*, ed. E. T. Donaldson, 1958 (rpt. New York: Ronald Press Co., 1978).
2. In '*Henry V* and the Paradox of the Body Politic' Claire McEachern considers the employment of 'personableness' in critical responses to Henry V in relation to the Elizabethan vocabulary of corporate identity and the opposition between hegemony and mutuality, or power and personhood. *Shakespeare Quarterly* 45, 1 (1994): 33–56.
3. See p.38, this volume.
4. P. 81, this volume.
5. See James Agee's review of the film in *Film Theory and Criticism*, ed. G. Mast and M. Cohen (Oxford: Oxford University Press, 1974), p. 334.
6. Quoted by Martin Kettle in the *Guardian*, 22 January 1994, p. 23.
7. *Observer*, 30 January 1994, p. 18.
8. Geoffrey O'Brien, 'The Last Shakespearean', *The New York Review* 46, 3 (18 February 1999): 27.

1   TALKING SHAKESPEARE *Michael Scott*

1. *The Independent on Sunday*, 3 January 1993.
2. Quoted by Peter Hall in the Introduction, *The Wars of the Roses*, adapted from *Shakespeare's Henry VI Parts I, II, III and Richard III* by John Barton in collaboration with Peter Hall (London: BBC, 1970), p. x. See Michael Scott, 'Truth, History and Stage Representation: The Henry VI Plays at Stratford-upon-Avon', in *Shakespeare and History*, ed. Holger Klein and Rowland Wymer, *Shakespeare Yearbook* 6 (Lewiston, Queenston, Lampeter, 1995), pp. 75–90.
3. See Terence Hawkes, *Meaning by Shakespeare* (London: Routledge, 1992).
4. James C. Bulman, 'Introduction', in *Shakespeare, Theory and Performance*, ed. James C. Bulman (London and New York: Routledge, 1996), pp. 3–4.
5. Michael Attenborough's production at the Royal Shakespeare Theatre in 1999, with the black actor Ray Fearon as the Moor, was the first production on the main stage at Stratford-upon-Avon since 1985, although the black actor/singer Willard White played the role at the studio theatre, The Other Place, in 1989, in a production by Trevor Nunn.
6. See Michael Scott, *Shakespeare and the Modern Dramatist* (Basingstoke and London: Macmillan, 1989), pp. 44–59 for a discussion of Arnold

Wesker's *The Merchant* and Charles Marowitz, *Variations on The Merchant of Venice*. Wesker's play was later retitled *Shylock*.

7. All quotations from Shakespeare's works are from *The Complete Works*, ed. Stanley Wells, Gary Taylor, John Jowett and William Montgomery (Oxford: Clarendon Press, 1988).

8. Edward Bond, *Bingo: Scenes of Money and Death* (London: Methuen, 1974), p. 27.

9. Michel Foucault, *The Archaeology of Knowledge*, trans. A. M. Sheridan Smith (London: Tavistock, 1972), p. 103.

10. Stephen Greenblatt, *Renaissance Self-Fashioning From More to Shakespeare* (Chicago and London: University of Chicago Press, 1980), p. 5.

11. George Bull, 'Introduction' to Baldesar Castiglione, *The Book of the Courtier* (rev. ed. Harmondsworth: Penguin, 1976), p.14. I discuss the relationship of Castiglione's work on Shakespeare's *Hamlet* in Michael Scott, '*Hamlet*, Castiglione and the Renaissance Courtier', *Italian History and Culture* 4 (1998): 29–38.

12. Charles Marowitz, *An Othello*, in *Open Space Plays* (Harmondsworth: Penguin, 1974), pp. 292–3.

13. John Webster, *The Duchess of Malfi*, ed. Elizabeth M. Brennan, New Mermaids (2nd ed. London: Ernest Benn, 1983).

2   HOW DOES *HAMLET* END? *Nigel Wood*

1. The phrase may be governed to a degree by the preceding contrast of 'heavy' Seneca and 'light' Plautus (II.ii.396–7), i.e. calculated tragedy and more extempore comedy, but, even if so, the sentiment is unaltered.

2. *Is There a Text in This Class?: The Authority of Interpretive Communities* (Cambridge, MA.: Harvard University Press, 1980), p. 1.

3. *William Shakespeare: The Complete Works*, general editors: Stanley Wells and Gary Taylor; editors: Stanley Wells, Gary Taylor, John Jowett and William Montgomery (Oxford: Oxford University Press, 1986), pp. xxxiv–xxxv.

4. *Ibid.*, p. xxxiv.

5. *Hamlet*, ed. Philip Edwards (Cambridge: Cambridge University Press, 1985), pp. 8–9. I admit that Edwards's formulation is more forceful than that provided by either Harold Jenkins (London and New York: Routledge [Arden Shakespeare], 1982) or G. R. Hibbard (Oxford: Oxford University Press, 1987), but the net result is virtually the same.

6. He is even at pains to grant the demonstrably corrupt Q1 text some vestiges of authenticity: 'Q1 is, as it stands, a sorry thing, and, from the editor's point of view, an extremely unreliable one.... Its main value, however, lies in this: that through the fog, growing thicker as the play goes on and recollection becomes fainter, one catches glimpses of an acting version of the tragedy current in the early seventeenth century'

(p. 89). See also his main reason for not regretting the loss of Q2 text in F: that it is part of a 'logical and coherent' process of revision for the stage (p. 109). Jenkins's preference for Q2 does not derive from a disagreement about ontology but rather about the value we should give to viable dramatic action: 'In seeking to present the play as Shakespeare wrote it rather than as it was shortened for performance I do no more than follow tradition [i.e. that of Rowe in 1709 onwards]' (p. 75).

7. *Re-Editing Shakespeare For The Modern Reader* (Oxford: Oxford University Press, 1984), pp. 62–3.

8. See the text in *Brecht on Theatre: The Development of an Aesthetic*, ed. and trans. John Willett (2nd ed. London: Methuen, 1974), pp. 107–15.

9. *Appropriating Shakespeare: Contemporary Critical Quarrels* (New Haven: Yale University Press, 1993), p. 151.

10. *Why Does Tragedy Give Pleasure?* (Oxford: Oxford University Press, 1996), p. 78.

11. *Shakespeare's Plays in Performance* (London: Edward Arnold, 1993; orig. ed. 1966), p. 151.

12. *Staging in Shakespeare's Theatres* (Oxford: Oxford University Press, 2000), pp. 122; 160–2.

13. *Coriolanus* (Oxford: Oxford University Press, 1991), p. 115.

14. *Narrative and Dramatic Sources of Shakespeare*, ed. Geoffrey Bullough (London and New York: Routledge & Kegan Paul and Columbia University Press, 1973), V:292.

15. *Selections from Johnson on Shakespeare*, ed. Betrand H. Bronson with Jean O'Meara (New Haven: Yale University Press, 1986), p. 317; *Selected Prose of T. S. Eliot*, ed. Frank Kermode (London: Faber & Faber, 1973) p. 48.

16. 'The Case Against Hamlet', *The Times Literary Supplement* 4838 (22 December 1995): 6–8.

17. Note to line 397, 'Commentary', p. 361.

18. Leah S. Marcus, *Unediting the Renaissance: Shakespeare, Marlowe, Milton* (London and New York: Routledge, 1996), pp. 132–76. See also Grace Ioppolo's revival of a *Revising Shakespeare* (Cambridge, MA and London: Harvard University Press, 1991), especially pp. 133–46.

19. Oxford edn, 1987, p. 356.

20. Ibid., p. 362.

21. Ibid., pp. 47–8.

22. *Shakespearean Negotiations: The Circulation of Social Energy in Renaissance England* (Oxford: Oxford University Press, 1988), p. 3. The Wimsatt reference can be found in 'The Structure of the "Concrete Universal" in Literature', in *Criticism: The Foundations of Modern Literary Judgement*, ed. Mark Schorer, Josephine Miles and Gordon McKenzie (rev. ed. New York: Barnes & Noble, 1958), p. 403.

23. *Recovering Shakespeare's Theatrical Vocabulary* (Cambridge: Cambridge University Press, 1995), especially pp. 39–63.

3. SHAKESPEARE AND THE ELIZABETHAN STAGE: TOURING PRACTICE IN SHAKESPEARE'S DAY *Peter Davison*

1. John Wasson, 'Elizabethan and Jacobean Touring Companies', *Theatre Notebook* XLII (1988): 52; hereafter 'Wasson'.

2. Tate Wilkinson, *The Wandering Patentee: A History of the Yorkshire Theatres, from 1770 to the Present Time*, 4 vols (York, printed for the author, 1795), IV: 45, 44; facsimile edition, 4 vols in 2 (Ilkley: Scolar Press, 1973).

3. Private records of John and Daisy Tresahar (Helen Thimm), 6 vols, in the author's possession.

4. 'Itinerant, Roguish Entertainers in Elizabethan and Early Stuart Norwich', *Theatre Notebook* LII (1998): 125.

5. Andrew Gurr, in *Playgoing in Shakespeare's London* (2nd ed. Cambridge: Cambridge University Press, 1996), remarks that 'Identifying what has been called the "rival" repertories that belonged to the duopoly of companies offering London playing through these years is made difficult by the varying character of the evidence' for the Chamberlain's Men and for that for Henslowe's Rose Theatre (p. 152). I shall stress this 'varying character of the evidence' later.

6. *Politics, Plague, and Shakespeare's Theater: The Later Stuart Years* (Ithaca: Cornell University Press, 1991), pp. 211–22, in which he gives the evidences for performances between 1580 and 1613 between Ash Wednesday and Easter Sunday. Hereafter 'Barroll'.

7. Barroll, pp. 222–6.

8. Barroll, p. 173.

9. Marlborough, General Accounts, 1572–1772, Wiltshire Records, Trowbridge, G22/1/205/2.

10. Barroll shows they received £30 'for the pains and expenses' of travelling from Mortlake (Barroll, pp. 112 and 114); in addition, they received an unprecedentedly large gift from the Masters and Burgesses of the Borough of £6 5s (Wiltshire Records, G25/1/91).

11. The assignment to years cannot always be precisely judged because of variations in the way town records were compiled. Thus 1603 may take in parts of 1602–03 and 1603–04.

12. For populations for all but Marlborough, see Peter Clark and Paul Slack, *English Towns in Transition 1500–1700* (Oxford: Oxford University Press, 1976), p. 83. Marlborough's accounts for 1597 showed expenditure of £59 3s 11d; Bristol expended just over £514.

13. London wages were regulated by royal proclamation; see Ann Jennalie Cook, *The Privileged Playgoers of Shakespeare's London, 1576–1642* (Princeton: Princeton University Press, 1981). For Wiltshire, see B. Howard Cunnington, *Records of the County of Wilts* (Devizes, 1932).

14. R. A. Foakes, in his New Cambridge edition of *A Midsummer Night's Dream* (Cambridge: Cambridge University Press, 1984), says 'Shakespeare needed no other source than imagination working on life' to create these characters (p. 9).

15. *From Text to Performance in the Elizabethan Theatre: Preparing the Play for the Stage* (Cambridge: Cambridge University Press, 1992), p. 58, and ch. 3 *passim*, pp. 58–74. Hereafter 'Bradley'.

16. Wasson, p. 55.

17. G. E. Bentley, *The Profession of Player in Shakespeare's Time*, 1590–1642 (Princeton, NJ: Princeton University Press, 1984), pp. 184–6.

18. E. K. Chambers, *The Elizabethan Stage* (Oxford: Clarendon Press, 1923), I: 12 and IV: 311–12; quoted by Bradley, pp. 69–70.

19. *Henslowe's Diary...with Supplementary Material*, ed. R. A. Foakes and R. T. Rickert (Cambridge: Cambridge University Press, 1961), p. 280. Hereafter 'Foakes and Rickert'.

20. Quoted by Michael Justin Davies in *The Landscape of William Shakespeare* (Exeter: Webb & Bower, 1987), p. 55.

21. *Authentic Memoirs of the Green-Room*, Anonymous (London: J. Roach, 1806), II: 56, 57.

22. For a detailed account of these companies, see G. W. Boddy, 'Players of Interludes in North Yorkshire in the Early Seventeenth Century', *North Yorkshire County Record Office Journal* 3 (1976): 95–130.

23. For various depositions, see J. T. Murray, *English Dramatic Companies, 1558–1642* (London: Constable, 1910), II: 163–7; hereafter 'Murray'. See also Bradley, p. 62.

24. As quoted by David George in 'Jacobean Actors and the Great Hall at Gawthorpe, Lancashire', *Theatre Notebook* XXXVII (1983): 111; hereafter 'George'.

25. Murray, II, 165.

26. *Tarltons Iests* (London: J. Budge, 1613), D1r. Tarlton also tells of travelling by ship from Southampton to London and encountering a storm (D3v). It is at least possible that actors made journeys along the south coast by sea.

27. Foakes and Rickert, p. 280. This is referred to in the same letter, that of 28 September 1593, which refers to Pembroke's Men selling their apparel: see n. 19.

28. Marlborough accounts for 1606 show that 18d was spent on hiring two horses to go to Littlecote, ten miles away (G22/1/205/2). The Bath accounts for 1619 show that to hire a horse for two days cost two shillings, Records of Early English Drama, *Somerset including Bath*, ed. James Stokes and, for Bath, Robert J. Alexander (Toronto: University of Toronto Press, 1996), I: 18.

29. Foakes and Rickert, pp. 238, 268.

30. See above and n. 19.

31. Chambers gives some account of supporting staff engaged: II: 80–1. Supporting staff nowadays overwhelm in numbers the actors engaged.

32. For fuller details see my edition of *The First Quarto of King Richard III* (Cambridge: Cambridge University Press, 1996), pp. 37–48 (hereafter 'Davison'); and 'Commerce and Patronage: The Lord Chamber-

lain's Men's Tour of 1597', Scaena Conference, Cambridge, 13 August 1997; amplified in *Shakespeare Performed*, ed. Grace Ioppolo (Newark: University of Delaware Press, 2000), pp. 56–71.

33. That they were different visits is certain because in 1596 they were properly described in the Faversham records as Lord Hunsdon's Men (the title-page of *Romeo and Juliet*, 1597, states that that play was performed by 'L. of Hunsdon his Seruants'); Hunsdon became Lord Chamberlain on 17 March 1597 and the company took their patron's new title and this is recorded in the Faversham accounts for 1597.

34. Foakes and Rickert, p. 60.

35. Lady Elizabeth was James I's daughter and became Queen of Bohemia; she is often called 'the Winter Queen'.

36. Foakes and Rickert, pp. 56–7; Davison, pp. 42–4.

37. Bradley, pp. 17–20, 71, 229; for the Admiral's Company in 1597, see p. 234.

38. 'The Cost of Touring', *Renaissance and Medieval Drama in England* 6 (1993): 59; quoted by Alan Somerset in his very useful ' "How Chances it they Travel": Provincial Touring, Playing Places, and the King's Men', *Shakespeare Survey* 47 (1994): 51. Somerset calculates that one of the places visited, the Leicester Guildhall (which still stands and which he illustrates on p. 58), could accommodate an audience of 300–355 (p. 59).

39. Bradley, p. 59 and ch. 3 *passim* pp. 58–74. The Welsh National Opera regularly reduces the size of its company when touring small towns; the Royal Ballet splits into two for its annual winter tours of small towns.

40. See especially Davison, Tables 2 and 3, pp. 17, 19.

41. George, p. 113.

42. See Laurence Stone, 'Companies of Players Entertained by the Earl of Cumberland and Lord Clifford, 1607–39', Malone Society, *Collections V*, 1959 (Oxford: Oxford University Press, 1960); *The House and Farm Accounts of the Shuttleworths of Gawthorpe Hall in the County of Lancaster and Gawthorpe, September 1582–1621*, ed. John Harland (Chetham Society, 1856–58), IV (as vol XLVI): 893–4; and see George, pp. 109–21, especially 112–15.

43. *Titus Andronicus*, ed. Jonathan Bate (London: Routledge, 1995), p. 43. A drawing of a scene from *Titus Andronicus* of about 1595 is now among the papers in the library of the Marquess of Bath at Longleat House, Wiltshire. It cannot be related to any performance at Longleat House, but Longleat (completed 1580; about 25 miles from Wilton and 35 miles from Marlborough) would be a possible venue for visiting players in Shakespeare's day. For the drawing and a commentary, see R. A. Foakes, *Illustrations of the English Stage* 1580–1642 (London: Scolar Press, 1985), pp. 48–51.

44. *Aubrey's Brief Lives*, ed. Oliver Lawson Dick (Harmondsworth: Peregrine Books, 1962), p. 309.

4. STUDYING SHAKESPEARE AND HIS CONTEMPORARIES *Emma Smith*

1. Jan Kott, *Shakespeare our Contemporary* (2nd ed., Oxford: Oxford University Press, 1967), p. 300. John Elsom has edited a collection of essays taking up Kott's premise: see *Is Shakespeare Still Our Contemporary?* (London: Routledge, 1989). On the history of the ways Shakespeare has been adapted and interpreted as the contemporary of different ages, see Gary Taylor, *Reinventing Shakespeare: a Cultural History from the Restoration to the Present* (London: Hogarth Press, 1990).

2. Robert Greene, *Greens Groats-worth of witte, bought with a million of Repentance* (1592), sig. F1vo.

3. Francis Meres *Palladis Tamia. Wits Treasury* (London: 1598), pp. 283–4.

4. Andrew Gurr, *Playgoing in Shakespeare's London* (Cambridge: Cambridge University Press, 1987), p. 226; p. 216.

5. On the question of early modern dramatic authorship see Jeffrey Masten, *Textual Intercourse: Collaboration, Authorship and Sexualities in Renaissance Drama* (Cambridge: Cambridge University Press, 1997) and Emma Smith, 'Author v. Character in Early Modern Dramatic Authorship: The Example of Thomas Kyd *and The Spanish Tragedy*', *Medieval and Renaissance Drama in England* 11 (1998): 129–42.

6. Other possible pairings might include: *Hamlet* and Marston's *Antonio's Revenge*; *Henry IV Part I* and the anonymous *Sir John Oldcastle; The Tempest* and Marlowe's *Dr Faustus; The Merchant of Venice* and Marlowe's *The Jew of Malta*.

7. All quotations from Shakespeare refer to *William Shakespeare: The Complete Works*, ed. Stanley Wells and Gary Taylor (Oxford: Clarendon Press, 1986).

8. This line is taken from Q1, *The Tragedie of King Richard the Second* (1597). In Q2 (1608), the line reads 'the part I had in Woodstocks blood'.

9. One of the practical obstacles to the project of relocating Shakespeare among his contemporaries is the relative difficulty of obtaining non-Shakespearean texts. *Woodstock* exists in a modernized and annotated text, edited by A. P. Rossiter (London: Chatto & Windus, 1946), and quotations in this chapter are taken from this edition. Alternatively, an electronic version of the play, entitled *Thomas of Woodstock*, can be obtained, free of charge for private and educational purposes, on the Internet. The Oxford Text Archive at http://firth.natcorp.ox.ac.uk/ota/public/index.shtml gives full and clear details of how to obtain the text.

10. Margot Heinemann, 'Political Drama', *in The Cambridge Companion to Renaissance Drama*, ed. A. R. Braunmuller and Michael Hattaway (Cambridge: Cambridge University Press, 1990), p. 184.

11. Ibid., p. 185. This 'orthodox doctrine' has its clearest expression in the Elizabethan homily 'Against Disobedience and Wilfull Rebellion', printed as Appendix 3 to Andrew Gurr's New Cambridge edition of *Richard II* (Cambridge: Cambridge University Press, 1984), pp. 215–20.

12. Richard Helgerson has discussed the radical implications of a similar manoeuvre in a different context in chapter 3 of his *Forms of Nationhood: the Elizabethan Writing of England* (Chicago and London: University of Chicago Press, 1992).

13. Geoffrey Bullough, *Narrative and Dramatic Sources of Shakespeare*, III (London and New York: Routledge & Kegan Paul, 1966), p. 359.

14. For other comparisons between *Woodstock* and *Richard II*, see Giorgio Melchiori, 'The Corridors of History: Shakespeare the Remaker', in *British Academy Shakespeare Lectures* 1980–89, ed. E. A. J. Honigmann (London: Oxford University Press for the British Academy, 1993); Donna B. Hamilton, 'The State of Law in Richard II', *Shakespeare Quarterly* 34 (1983): 5–17.

15. Ann Thompson (ed.), *The Taming of the Shrew* (Cambridge: Cambridge University Press, 1984), p. 18.

16. *The Woman's Prize, or the Tamer Tam'd* is printed in volume 4 of *The Dramatic Works in the Beaumont and Fletcher Canon*, ed. Fredson Bowers (Cambridge: Cambridge University Press, 1979). An electronic text is available on the Internet via the Oxford Text Archive at http://firth.natcorp.ox.ac.uk/ota/public/index.shtml

17. Carol Rutter, *Clamorous Voices: Shakespeare's Women Today* (London: The Women's Press, 1988), pp. 22–4. Charles Marowitz, *Recycling Shakespeare* (Basingstoke and London: Macmillan, 1991), p. 23.

18. B. L. Joseph, '*The Spanish Tragedy* and *Hamlet*: Two Exercises in English Seneca', *in Classical Drama and Its Influence: Essays Presented to H. D. F. Kitto* (London: Methuen, 1965), p. 133; Emma Smith (ed.), *Thomas Kyd: The Spanish Tragedie* (Harmondsworth: Penguin, 1998), p. xxix.

19. *William Shakespeare: The Complete Works*, ed. Wells and Taylor, p. 735.

20. A. C. Bradley, *Shakespearean Tragedy: Lectures on 'Hamlet', 'Othello', 'King Lear', 'Macbeth'* (2nd ed. Macmillan: London, 1932), p. 89.

21. References to *The Spanish Tragedy* are taken from Philip Edward's Revels edition (Manchester: Manchester University Press, 1959).

22. James Shapiro, '"Tragedies Naturally Performed": Kyd's Representation of Violence', in *Staging the Renaissance: Reinterpretations of Elizabethan and Jacobean Drama*, ed. David Scott Kastan and Peter Stallybrass (London and New York: Routledge, 1991), p. 103.

23. Harold Bloom, *The Anxiety of Influence* (New York: Oxford University Press, 1973).

24. Terry Eagleton, *Literary Theory: An Introduction* (Oxford: Basil Blackwell, 1983), p. 183.

25. On the continuing popularity of *The Spanish Tragedy*, see 'Hieronimo's Afterlives', in Smith (ed.), *Thomas Kyd*, pp. 133–59.

5. SHAKESPEARE AND HISTORY *Dermot Cavanagh*

1. Douglas Bruster, 'New Light on the Old Historicism: Shakespeare and the Forms of Historicist Criticism', *Literature and History*, 3rd series, 5 (1996): 1–18, 6.

2. Claire Colebrook, *New Literary Histories: New Historicism and Contemporary Criticism* (Manchester: Manchester University Press, 1997), p. 22.

3. Bruster, 'New Light on the Old Historicism', 3.

4. Jean E. Howard, 'The New Historicism in Renaissance Studies', *English Literary Renaissance* 16 (1986): 13–43, 25.

5. Stephen Greenblatt, 'Resonance and Wonder', in *Learning to Curse: Essays in Early Modern Culture* (New York and London: Routledge, 1990), pp. 161–83, 166–7.

6. D. R. Woolf, *The Idea of History in Early Stuart England: Erudition, Ideology and 'The Light of Truth' from the Acession of James I to the Civil War* (Toronto: Toronto University Press, 1990), p. xiii.

7. Jean E. Howard, *The Stage and Social Struggle in Early Modern England* (London and New York: Routledge, 1994), p. 7.

8. Margot Heinemann, 'Political Drama', in *The Cambridge Companion to English Renaissance Drama*, ed. A. R. Braunmuller and M. Hattaway (Cambridge: Cambridge University Press, 1990), pp. 161–205, 177.

9. David Scott Kastan, 'Proud Majesty Made a Subject: Shakespeare and the Spectacle of Rule', *Shakespeare Quarterly* 37 (1986): 459–75, 461.

10. Ibid.: 469.

11. Jonathan Dollimore and Alan Sinfield, 'History and Ideology: The Instance of Henry V', in *Alternative Shakespeares*, ed. John Drakakis (London and New York: Methuen, 1985), pp. 206–27, 225.

12. Janet Clare, 'Historicism and the Question of Censorship in the Renaissance', *English Literary Renaissance* 27 (1997): 155–76, 160. Clare's essay is a critique of Foucault's understanding of how 'power is dispersed throughout a culture and operates in the same way as sin in medieval allegory, subtle and alluring' (159).

13. James Holstun, 'Ranting at the New Historicism', *English Literary Renaissance* 19 (1989): 189–225, 197.

14. In *Forms of Nationhood: The Elizabethan Writing of England* (Chicago and London: Chicago University Press, 1992), pp. 193–245.

15. Ibid., p. 214.

16. Ibid., p. 235.

17. Andrew Gurr, *Playgoing in Shakespeare's London* (Cambridge: Cambridge University Press, 1987), p. 150.

18. *Shakespearean Iconoclasm* (Berkeley, Los Angeles and London: University of California Press, 1985), p. 28.

19. Ibid., pp. 118–19.

20. All citations will refer to the Arden edition of *King Richard II*, ed. Peter Ure (London: Methuen, 1961).

21. David Norbrook, 'The Emperor's New Body? Richard II, Ernst Kantorowicz, and the Politics of Shakespeare Criticism', *Textual Practice* 10 (1996): 329–57, 348–9.

22. Donald R. Kelley, 'Elizabethan Political Thought', in *The Varieties of British Political Thought, 1500–1800*, ed. J. G. A. Pocock (Cambridge: Cambridge University Press, 1993), pp. 47–79, 50–3.

23. Martha A. Kurtz, 'Rethinking Gender and Genre in the History Plays', *Studies in English Literature, 1500–1900* 36 (1996): 267–87.

24. T. W. Adorno, *Aesthetic Theory*, trans. C. Lenhardt (London: Routledge & Kegan Paul, 1984), p. 361.

25. Hanna H. Gray, 'Renaissance Humanism: The Pursuit of Eloquence', *Journal of the History of Ideas* 24 (1963): 497–514, 512.

26. *The Tudor Play of Mind: Rhetorical Inquiry and the Development of Elizabethan Drama* (Berkeley, Los Angeles and London: University of California Press, 1978).

27. *Machiavellian Rhetoric: From the Counter-Reformation to Milton* (Princeton, NJ: Princeton University Press, 1994), p. 5.

28. The only substantial attempt to deploy the work of the Frankfurt School in relation to Shakespeare has been that of Hugh Grady in *The Modernist Shakespeare: Critical Texts in a Material World* (Oxford: Oxford University Press, 1991) and *Shakespeare's Universal Wolf: Studies in Early Modern Reification* (Oxford: Clarendon Press, 1996).

29. Adorno, *Aesthetic Theory*, p. 272.

30. Catherine Gallagher, 'Marxism and New Historicism', in *The New Historicism*, ed. H. Aram Veeser (New York and London: Routledge, 1989), pp. 37–48, 44–5.

6.   'HOME, SWEET HOME': STRATFORD-UPON-AVON AND THE MAKING OF THE RSC AS A NATIONAL INSTITUTION   Colin Chambers

1. Peter Hall, quoted in David Addenbrooke, *The Royal Shakespeare Company: The Peter Hall Years* (London: William Kimber, 1974), p. 66.

2. Illustrated Programme of the World Theatre Season, Aldwych Theatre, March 1964.

3. Foreword to Judith Cook, *At the Sign of the Swan* (London: Harrap), p. 9.

4. John Goodwin (ed.), *Peter Hall's Diaries: The Story of a Dramatic Battle* (London: Hamish Hamilton, 1983), p. 209.

5. Chairman's Report, *RSC Annual Report: 121st Report of the Council 1996/97*.

6. Illustrated Programme of the World Theatre Season.

7. Quoted in Stephen Fay, *Power Play: The Life and Times of Peter Hall* (London: Hodder & Stoughton, 1996), p. 187.

8. Goodwin (ed.), *Peter Hall's Diaries*, p. 222.

9. *The Times*, 5 December 1972.

10. Addenbrooke, *The Royal Shakespeare Company*, p. 66.

11. Actor Hugh Quarshie, who played Antony in Hall's 1995 Stratford production of *Julius Caesar*, used this description, quoted in Peter Holland, *English Shakespeares* (Cambridge: Cambridge University Press, 1997), pp. 4–5. In an interview with the author of this chapter (20 March 1998, unpublished), Hall volunteered this label himself.

12. Addenbrooke, *The Royal Shakespeare Company*, p. 227; and Sally Beauman, *The Royal Shakespeare Company: A History of Ten Decades* (Oxford: Oxford University Press, 1982), p. 267.

13. Peter Hall, *Making an Exhibition of Myself* (London: Sinclair-Stevens, 1993), pp. 76–7.

14. Nahum Tate (1652–1715), playwright and poet whose adaptations included *King Lear* with a happy ending; Thomas Bowdler (1754–1825) published an expurgated 'Family Shakespeare', hence to 'bowdlerize'; David Garrick (1717–79), Henry Irving (1838–1905), Donald Wolfit (1902–68) and Laurence Olivier (1907–89), leading Shakespearean actors.

15. Quoted in *The Independent*, 2 February 1993.

7. *TWELFTH NIGHT*: 'ONE FACE, ONE VOICE, ONE HABIT, AND TWO PERSONS!' *Janice Wardle*

1. The RSC refer in their Mission Statement to 'keeping alive the rich tradition of Shakespeare as well as performing classics of world drama and work by today's leading playwrights... Our aim, in this age increasingly dominated by the visual image, is to expound and extend the power of language and poetry. It is an ambitious goal but, we believe, an important one.'

2. Quoted in Judith Cook, 'King John Barton', *Plays and Players* 21 (June 1974): 27.

3. John Barton, as quoted in Vincent Guy, 'Director in Interview: John Barton talks to Vincent Guy', *Plays and Players* 17 (November 1969): 49.

4. Stanley Wells, *Royal Shakespeare: Four Major Productions at Stratford-upon-Avon* (Manchester: Manchester University Press, 1977), pp. 48–9.

5. Guy, 'Director in Interview', p. 49.

6. Ibid.

7. Gareth Lloyd Evans, 'Judi Dench talks to Gareth Lloyd Evans', *Shakespeare Survey* 27 (1974): 141.

8. Wells, *Royal Shakespeare*, p. 62.

9. M. M. Mahood, 'Shakespeare's Middle Comedies: A Generation of Criticism', *Shakespeare Survey* 32 (1979): 6.

10. *The Riverside Shakespeare*, ed. G. Blakemore Evans (Boston: Houghton Mifflin, 1974).

11. Anne Barton, *Twelfth Night*, RSC programme, 1969.

12. Northrop Frye, *Anatomy of Criticism: Four Essays* (Princeton, NJ: Princeton University Press, 1957); C. L. Barber, *Shakespeare's Festive*

Comedy: A Study of Dramatic Form and its Relation to Social Custom (Princeton, NJ: Princeton University Press, 1959).
13. Ibid., p. 181.
14. Ibid., p. 184.
15. Barton, *Twelfth Night*.
16. Ibid.
17. Anne Barton (née Righter), *Shakespeare and the Idea of the Play* (London: Chatto & Windus, 1962).
18. Frye, *Anatomy of Criticism*, p. 183.
19. Barton, *Twelfth Night*.
20. Barber, *Shakespeare's Festive Comedy*, p. 4.
21. Barton, *Twelfth Night*.
22. For example, in the case of the Comedies, A. C. Bradley, 'Feste the Jester', in *A Book of Homage to Shakespeare*, ed. I. Gollancz (London: Oxford University Press, 1916) reprinted in A. C. Bradley, *A Miscellany* (London: Macmillan, 1929); H. B. Charlton, *Shakespearian Comedy* (London: Methuen, 1938); B. Evans, *Shakespeare's Comedies* (Oxford: Clarendon Press, 1960); John Palmer, *Comic Characters in Shakespeare* (London: Macmillan, 1946); John Dover Wilson, *Shakespeare's Happy Comedies* (London: Faber & Faber, 1962).
23. John Barton, *Playing Shakespeare* (London: Methuen, 1984), p. 8.
24. Ibid., p. 9.
25. John Barton, as quoted in Gareth Lloyd Evans, 'Directing Problem Plays: John Barton talks to Gareth Lloyd Evans', *Shakespeare Survey* 25 (1972): 65.
26. Barton, *Playing Shakespeare*, p. 15.
27. J. W. Lambert, *Sunday Times*, 24 August 1969.
28. Promptbook description. The promptbooks for the 1969 and 1971 productions have been lost. I consulted the one used at the Aldwych theatre in 1970.
29. Stanley Wells, 'The Academic and the Theatre', in *The Triple Bond: Plays Mainly Shakespearean in Performance*, ed. Joseph G. Price (Pennsylvania and London: Pennsylvania University Press, 1975), p. 16.
30. Wells, *Royal Shakespeare*, p. 49.
31. Frye, *Anatomy of Criticism*, p. 182.
32. Wells, *Royal Shakespeare*, p. 50.
33. Barton, *Twelfth Night*: 'the sea captain who first tells Viola about Illyria might justly have said to her what the Cheshire Cat says to Alice: "They're all mad here".' Interestingly, critics have often made the connection between Lewis Carroll and *Twelfth Night*. For example, in *Shakespeare's Festive World* (Cambridge: Cambridge University Press, 1991) François Laroque comments: 'This nonsense logic, which Lewis Carroll was later to develop in the scenes of *Through the Looking Glass* ... boils down to pointing out that, however different things look on the surface, it's all the same underneath. Festivity takes us into the realm of illusion, a land where contraries seem to keep good company' (p. 228).

34. Richard David, 'Of an Age and For All Time: Shakespeare at Stratford', *Shakespeare Survey* 25 (1972): 167.

35. *Twelfth Night*, ed M. M. Mahood (Harmondsworth: Penguin, 1968).

36. Wells, *Royal Shakespeare*, p. 51. See also Laroque, *Shakespeare's Festive World*, in which his description of Sir Toby and Sir Andrew is that 'the veteran champions of festivity have become the pensioners of pleasure' (p. 256).

37. Anne Barton, *Twelfth Night*.

38. Ronald Bryden, *Observer*, 24 August 1969.

39. J. Kingston, *Punch*, 19 August 1970.

40. Frank Marcus, *Sunday Telegraph*, 24 August 1969 noted that 'Donald Sinden, as Malvolio, struggles valiantly but uselessly against the production. He is an expert comedian, and at times seems to enter into shamefaced conspiracy with the audience in order to rescue some threatened laughs.'

41. Benedict Nightingale, *New Statesman*, 21 August 1969.

42. Wells, *Royal Shakespeare*, p. 50.

43. Ibid., p. 62.

44. Stanislavsky, *My Life in Art*, quoted in the 'Introduction' to *Chekhov: Plays*, trans. and ed. Elisaveta Fet (Harmondsworth: Penguin, 1959), p. 8. This translation differs from the J. J. Robbins translation of *My Life in Art* (Boston: Little, Brown, 1924), in which this section forms part of Chapter XXXIII, 'Symbolism and Impressionism'.

45. Chekhov in a letter to Maria Lilana, Stanislavsky's wife and one of the leading actresses of the Moscow Art Theatre, 15 September 1903. Quoted in David Magarshack, *The Real Chekhov: An Introduction to Chekhov's Last Plays* (London, Allen & Unwin, 1972), p. 189.

46. Stanislavsky, quoted in ibid., p. 10.

47. Stanislavsky, *My Life in Art*, p. 240: 'in my great desire to help the actors I tried to create a mood around them, in the hope that it would grip them and call forth creative vision.... I invented all sorts of mises en scène, the singing of birds, the barking of dogs, and in this enthusiasm for sounds on the stage I went so far that I caused a protest on the part of Chekhov.' In a letter to Olga Knipper on 29 March 1904, Chekhov complained: 'One thing I can say. Stanislavsky has ruined my play. Oh well, I don't suppose anything can be done about it' (Magarshack, *The Real Chekhov*, p. 192).

48. Alexander Leggatt notes that 'this kind of tension is basic to Shakespearian comedy: it is at bottom a tension between stylized and realistic art. The lovers, having engaged our feelings as human beings, are now fixed in a harmony we can only believe in by trusting the power of fantasy' (*Shakespeare's Comedy of Love*, London, Methuen, 1974, p. 253).

49. This is taken to greater extremes in Nunn's adaptation because he is afforded the filmic luxury of 'flashback' in the sense that he creates the scene of the shipwreck before the play begins. The film opens with a

234   *Notes and References*

reconstruction of this fateful journey from Messaline, where Viola and Sebastian, both dressed as women, are entertaining the passengers with a comic song. The song draws out the sexual ambiguity of Sebastian's assuming another gender role. Critics also commented on the melancholic 'Chekhovian' context. 'The settings and costumes place it firmly within the orbit of "heritage" cinema but with more than a hint of Chekhov about it. As in Chekhov's short stories, landscape is used to mirror the characters' emotions. Clive Tickner's photography with its emphasis on dark, autumnal hues, underlines the sense of wistful melancholy which runs through the play' (Geoffrey McNab, *Sight and Sound* 6, 11 (November 1996), p. 60.

50. James Treadwell, *Spectator*, 6 December 1997.

51. Robert Hanks, *Independent on Sunday*, 30 November 1997.

52. *Guardian*, 27 November 1997.

53. *Daily Telegraph*, 27 November 1997.

54. Benedict Nightingale, *The Times*, 27 November 1997.

55. Michael Billington, *Guardian*, 27 November 1997.

56. Peter Kemp, *Times Literary Supplement*, 12 December 1997.

57. RSC, *Twelfth Night* Programme, 1997.

58. For example, the character analysis for Viola quoted the critics Joseph H. Summers, C. L. Barber and Harold Jenkins, and Viola was identified as 'Type 2: The Helper – the caring, nurturing type. Loving, caring adaptable, insightful, tuned into feelings'.

59. *Guardian*, 27 November 1997.

60. *Times Literary Supplement*, 12 December 1997.

61. *The Heath Introduction to Drama*, ed. J. Y. Miller (Lexington, KY, D. C. Heath, 1996), p. 17.

62. This appears in the promptbook but had disappeared from the performance by August 1998.

63. Peter Thomson's comment from 1973 still holds true: 'The exploitation of performances as evidence of the superiority of his own conceptions over the theatre's is the meanest use the academic makes of his role as audience' ('Shakespeare Straight and Crooked: A Review of the 1973 Season at Stratford', *Shakespeare Survey* 27 (1973): 143–54).

64. Wells, *Royal Shakespeare*, p. 80.

65. Both productions used the New Cambridge edition of the text. Barton emended or cut 148 lines, and Noble 7 lines.

8.   SHAKESPEARE AND THE HOMOEROTIC   *Miles Thompson and Imelda Whelehan*

1. Peter J. Smith, *Social Shakespeare: Aspects of Renaissance Dramaturgy and Contemporary Society* (London: Macmillan, 1995), p. 9.

2. See Roger Baker, *Drag: A History of Female Impersonation on the Stage* (London: Triton Books, 1968), pp. 54–7.

3. See ibid., p. 69.

4. Ibid., p. 90.

5. John Rainolds, *Th' Overthrow Of Stage-Players* (1599; rpt. Oxford 1629), cited in Denise Walen, ' "Lust Exciting Apparel" and the Homosexual Appeal of the Boy Actor: The Early Modern Stage Polemic', *Theatre History Studies* (June 1995): 92.

6. Jean E. Howard, *The Stage and Social Struggle in Early Modern England* (London: Routledge, 1994), p. 96.

7. Ibid., pp. 94–8.

8. Valerie Traub, *Desire and Anxiety: Circulations of Sexuality in Shakespearian Drama* (London: Routledge, 1992), p. 146.

9. Ibid.

10. Bassnett, Susan, *Elizabeth I: A Feminist Perspective* (London and New York: Berg, 1988), p. 5.

11. Kate Chedgzoy, *Shakespeare's Queer Children: Sexual Politics and Contemporary Culture* (Manchester: Manchester University Press, 1995), p. 147.

12. See Alan Bray, *Homosexuality in Renaissance England* (New York: Columbia University Press, 1995), p. 19.

13. Michel Foucault, *The History of Sexuality – Volume One: A Introduction*, trans. R. Hurley (London: Allen Lane, 1979), p. 43.

14. Traub, *Desire and Anxiety*, p. 12.

15. Howard, *The Stage and Social Struggle*, p. 111.

16. Ibid., p. 23.

17. Alan Sinfield, *The Wilde Century: Effeminacy, Oscar Wilde and the Queer Movement* (London: Cassell, 1994), p. 27.

18. Ibid., p. 27.

19. Phyllis Rackin, 'Foreign Country: The Place of Women and Sexuality in Shakespeare's Historical World', in *Enclosure Acts: Sexuality, Property, and Culture in Early Modern England*, ed. Richard Burt and John Michael Archer (Ithaca: Cornell University Press, 1994), p. 69.

20. William Prynne, *Historio-Matrix the Player's Scourge, or Actors Tragedie* (London 1633), cited in Denise Walen, ' "Lust Exciting Apparel" ': pp. 88–9.

21. *Phillip Stubbes's Anatomy of the Abuses in England in Shakespere's Youth, A.D.1583*, ed. Frederick Furnivall (London: Trübner, for the New Shakspere Society, 1877–82, Kraus Reprint 1965, pp. 144–5).

22. Ibid., pp. 144–5.

23. Laura Levine, *Men in Women's Clothing: Anti-theatricality and Effeminization 1579–1642* (Cambridge: Cambridge University Press, 1994), p. 6.

24. Baker, *Drag*, p. 79.

25. Ibid.

26. Ibid.

27. Ibid., p. 52.

Notes and References

28. Ibid., p. 81.
29. Smith, *Social Shakespeare*, p. 184. Smith gestures towards the amount of texts which have recently been published on the subject. These include Alan Bray, *Homosexuality in Renaissance England* (2nd ed., 1998), Gregory Bredbeck, *Sodomy and Interpretation: Marlowe To Milton* (1991), Bruce R. Smith, *Homosexual Desire in Shakespeare's England: A Cultural Poetics* (1991) and Jonathan Goldberg, *Sodometries: Renaissance Texts, Modern Sexualities* (1992).
30. Traub, *Desire and Anxiety*, p. 94.
31. Smith, *Social Shakespeare*, p. 205.
32. See, for example, *Political Shakespeare: New Essays in Cultural Materialism*, ed. Jonathan Dollimore and Alan Sinfield (Manchester: Manchester University Press, 1985).
33. 'Shakespeare, Cultural Materialism and the New Historicism', in *Political Shakespeare*, ed. Dollimore and Sinfield, p. 15.
34. Lisa Jardine, 'Boy Actors, Female Roles and Elizabethan Eroticism', in *Staging the Renaissance: Reinterpretations of Elizabethan and Jacobean Drama*, ed. David Scott Kastan and Peter Stallybrass (London: Routledge, 1991), p. 57.
35. Stephen Greenblatt, *Shakespearean Negotiations* (Oxford: Clarendon Press, 1988), p. 68.
36. Ibid., p. 91.
37. Ibid., p. 92.
38. Howard, *The Stage and Social Struggle*, p. 115.
39. From John Northbrooke's *A Treatise wherein Dicing, Dauncing and Vaine Plays or Enterluds . . . are reproved* (1577), cited in Howard, *The Stage and Social Struggle*, p. 25.
40. *Parliamentary Debates (Hansard)*, Monday 25 January 1999 (Norwich: HMSO, 1999), p. 89.
41. Simon Shepherd, 'Shakespeare's Private Drawer: Shakespeare and Homosexuality', in *The Shakespeare Myth*, ed. Graham Holderness (Manchester: Manchester University Press, 1988), p. 96.
42. Chedgzoy, *Shakespeare's Queer Children, p. 167.*
43. See *Guardian*, 22, 27 January 1994.
44. See *Variety*, 1 February 1999, p. 63.

9. SHAKESPEARE AND RACE: *OTHELLO* I.iii *Deborah Cartmell*

The term 'race' is used throughout as in popular contemporary usage, notwithstanding, as Margo Hendricks and Patricia Parker have stressed, ' "race" as that term developed across several European languages was a highly unstable term in the early modern period, a period that saw the proliferation of rival European voyages of "discovery" as contacts with what from a Eurocentric perspective were "new" and different worlds, the drive toward imperial conquest and the subjugation of indigenous peoples, and the development of (and increasingly "racial" defense) of slavery'. ('Introduction', in *Women, 'Race', and Writing in the Early Modern Period*, ed. Margo Hendricks and Patricia Parker, London and New York: Routledge, 1994, pp. 1–2).

1. All quotations from Shakespeare's plays are taken from *The Complete Works*, ed. Stanley Wells, Gary Taylor, John Jowett and William Montgomery (Oxford: Clarendon Press, 1988). I have also made extensive use of my own edition of the first half of I.iii of play/film soundtracks in *Moving Shakespeare: Interpreting Shakespeare on Film* (London and Basingstoke: Macmillan, 2000).

2. 'Performing Race in Early Modern England', *Shakespeare Quarterly* 49, 2 (1998): 168–86, p. 175. See also Stephen Greenblatt, 'Learning to Curse', in *Learning to Curse: Essays in Early Modern Culture* (New York and London: Routledge, 1990), pp. 16–39.

3. This is the first definition cited in the *Oxford English Dictionary*. The second refers to culture: 'absence of culture; uncivilized ignorance and rudeness'.

4. Philip Sidney, for example, attacks Edmund Spenser's 'old rustic language' as leading to widespread 'barbarism' (*An Apology for Poetry*, ed. Geoffrey Shepherd, Manchester: Manchester University Press, 1973, p. 133). In the *OED* 'barbarism' is defined: 'the use of words or expressions not in accordance with the classical standard of a language, especially such as are of foreign origin'.

5. '"And Wash the Ethiop White": Femininity and the Monstrous in *Othello*', in *Shakespeare Reproduced*, ed. Jean E. Howard and Marion O'Connor (London: Methuen, 1987), p. 150.

6. See Kim F. Hall, 'A World of Difference: Travel Narratives and the Inscription of Culture', in *Things of Darkness: Economies of Race and Gender in Early Modern England* (Ithaca: Cornell University Press, 1995), pp. 25–61.

7. Jyotsna Singh, 'Othello's Identity, Postcolonial Theory, and Contemporary African Rewritings of *Othello*', in *Women, 'Race', and Writing in the Early Modern Period*, ed. Hendricks and Parker, pp. 287–99.

8. Hall, 'A World of Difference', p. 60.

9. Greenblatt, 'Learning to Curse', p. 22.

10. Ibid., p. 22.

11. Traditionally, to blame Desdemona at all is considered a taboo. Graham Bradshaw, for example, in taking to task Stephen Greenblatt's influential reading of the play in *Renaissance Self-Fashioning: From More to Shakespeare* (Chicago and London, 1980), asks the rhetorical question: 'But are we then to conclude that Shakespeare's audiences would have thought that Desdemona's forthright declaration in the Senate of what Greenblatt himself describes as "frankly, though by no means exclusively sexual" passion was "Damnable"? And if not, why not?' *Misrepresentations: Shakespeare and the Materialists* (Ithaca: Cornell University Press, 1993), p. 198. For Bradshaw, Ophelia is unproblematic throughout: 'of course Desdemona is externally and internally fair' (213).

12. *Othello's Countrymen: The African in English Renaissance Drama* (London: Oxford University Press, 1965), p. 95.

13. Ibid., p. 97.

14. In her analysis of the use of personal pronouns and private verbs in *Pericles*, Nelly Keinanen has argued that although Shakespeare's women 'do say "I"', they seem infrequently to become the subjects of their own sentences, and hence in effect, the subjects of their own discourse', '"The Great Ones Eat Up the Little Ones": Vanishing Women in *Pericles*', paper presented at the European Society for the Study of English, 1997, Debrecen, p. 1. Miraculously, Desdemona succeeds not just in becoming the subject of her own discourse, but the subject of her husband's discourse as well.

15. See Evelyn Gajowski, 'The Female Perspective in *Othello*', in *Othello: New Perspectives* (Rutherford, Madison: Fairleigh Dickinson University Press, 1991), pp. 97–114.

16. Quoted in Ania Loomba, *Gender, Race, Renaissance Drama* (Manchester: Manchester University Press, 1989, pp. 40–1.

17. Jones, *Othello's Countrymen*, p. 109.

18. Quoted in the Arden edition *Othello*, ed. M. R. Ridley (1959; rpt. London: Methuen, 1982), p. li.

19. Ibid.

20. 'Remembering Fanon', foreword to F. Fanon, *Black Skin, White Masks* (London: Pluto Press, 1986), p. xxvi.

21. 'Introduction: Friday on the Potomac', in *Race-ing Justice, En-gendering Power: Essays on Anita Hill, Clarence Thomas and the Construction of Social Reality*, ed. Toni Morrison (London: Chatto & Windus, 1993), p. xiv.

22. '"Othello Was a White Man": Properties of Race on Shakespeare's Stage', *Alternative Shakespeares*, vol. 2, ed. Terence Hawkes (London and New York: Routledge, 1996), pp. 192–215.

23. English-speaking television/video productions include: *Othello*, 1955, directed by Tony Richardson, starring Gordon Heath and Paul Rogers; *Othello*, 1965, directed by Stuart Burge, starring Laurence Olivier and Frank Finlay; *Othello*, 1981 (BBC Video), directed by Elijah Moshinsky, starring Anthony Hopkins and Bob Hoskins; *Othello*, 1988 (South Africa – C4), directed by Janet Suzman, starring John Kani and Richard Haddon Haines; *Othello*, 1989 (Pickwick Video Ltd) for Educational Film Service, directed by Trevor Nunn, starring Willard White and Ian McKellen (Film of a Royal Shakespeare Company production). Notably, two use a black actor in the title part, Janet Suzman's (1988) and Trevor Nunn's (1989).

24. *How to Read a Film* (New York and Oxford: Oxford University Press, 1981), p. 225.

25. Barbara Hodgdon, 'Race-ing *Othello*, Re-EnGendering White-Out', in *The Shakespeare Trade: Performances and Appropriations* (Philadelphia: University of Pennsylvania Press, 1998), pp. 39–73, p. 70.

26. Parker's shooting script contains further flashbacks illustrating the story of Othello's life from youth to manhood, including a young Othello

fending off a group of attackers with a bone. (It's probable that they were
removed as they overstated Othello's position as 'alien', or 'other.)

10. THE UNKINDEST CUTS: FLASHCUT EXCESS IN KENNETH BRANAGH'S
Hamlet Bernice W. *Kliman*

My endnotes document my obligations, but I would like to thank Russell
Jackson, the film's text adviser, for very helpful information – published,
conveyed by e-mail, and in person; and Sam Crowl, for his work on the
film and on the stage production directed by Adrian Noble that stands
behind the film.

1. Samuel Crowl refers to a two-hour, 35mm version of the four-hour
70mm version film that is 'likely to end up in general release and in high
school and college libraries': see *'Hamlet* "Most Royal"', *Shakespeare
Bulletin* 12, 4 (Fall 1994): 5–8. So far the shorter version has not been
released in the USA or Canada but has been seen on Spanish television.
According to pre-release interviews, Branagh had no artistic stake in the
shorter version; Castle Rock Entertainment stipulated it for non-English
markets and for airline screenings.

An earlier version of this chapter was presented at the first International Shakespeare on Screen Conference: The Centenary Conference
at Benalmádena, 21–24 September 1999: my thanks to Sarah Hatchuel
for generously sharing her impressive archives of Branagh interviews, to
other conference participants for their helpful suggestions, and above all
to José Ramón Díaz Fernández, conference organizer, for his encouragement and enthusiasm. My work on *Hamlet* is supported by a grant from
the National Endowment for the Humanities.

2. According to a letter from his assistant, Branagh had no script for
the shorter version. It was shortened at the editing table (letter from
Tamar Thomas, Assistant to Mr Branagh, 4 August 1999).

3. Samuel Crowl, *'Hamlet'*, *Shakespeare Bulletin* 15, 1 (Winter 1997):
34.

4. Russell Jackson, e-mail, 28 July 1999. Jackson screened the omitted
segment at the Málaga conference.

5. Irene Dash, quoted in Nina daVinci Nichols, 'Branagh's *Hamlet*
Redux', *Shakespeare Bulletin* 15, 3 (Summer, 1997): 38–41, p. 39.

6. Michael Kahn, reported in John F. Andrews, 'Kenneth Branagh's
Hamlet', *Shakespeare Newsletter* 46, 3 (Fall 1996): 53. See also John W.
Mahon, 'Editor's View' (appended to Andrews's essay), who thinks the
insets 'work' (66). Andrews (62) and Thomas Pendleton ('And the
Thoughts of the Other Editor', *Shakespeare Newsletter* 46, 3 (Fall 1996):
60) disagree. Samuel Crowl approves at least of one set that I would
extract, and remarks, approvingly, that Branagh 'resists giving us pictures that other films have made standard' (*'Hamlet'*: 34). Some of these
standard insets appear in the shooting script, and thus Branagh con-

templated using them at some point. Unfortunately, since Branagh has not sent me a copy of his shooting script, all references to a script (unless otherwise noted) refer to the published version.

7. Emrys Jones, *Scenic Form in Shakespeare* (1971, Oxford: Oxford University Press; rpt. New York: Clarendon Press, 1985, p. 28).

8. Branagh, strangely enough, lists cast but not crew in his published screenplay. The experience of cinematographer Alex Thomson (b. London 1929) includes a job as an uncredited cameraman for *Dr Zhivago* (1965), to which some have compared scenes in Branagh's *Hamlet*. He has been cinematographer for many films in a long career, but none of distinction, as far as I know. See Kenneth Branagh, Hamlet *by William Shakespeare: Screenplay and Introduction by Kenneth Branagh* (New York: Norton, 1996).

9. Russell Jackson confirmed my impression. He told me that the Ghost, meant to be invisible in the first scene, was added because 'something was not working'. I surmise that the problem was not the absence of the Ghost but the shots directed to where it *should* have been, showing viewers the Ghost's absence rather than allowing them to infer its presence.

10. Russell Jackson, 'Kenneth Branagh's Film of *Hamlet*: The Textual Choices', *Shakespeare Bulletin* 15, 2 (Spring 1997). The first quotation is on p. 38; the second on p. 37.

11. Andrews, 'Kenneth Branagh's *Hamlet*': 62. Other quotations during this interview reported by Andrews show that Branagh had the audience in mind with his flashcuts: justifying the lovemaking scenes, he 'said that if he were a thirteen-year-old who'd been dragged to a bloody four-hour *Hamlet*, he'd be very grateful for an occasional nude scene'.

12. See Anthony B. Dawson, *Shakespeare in Performance: 'Hamlet'* (Manchester and New York: Manchester University Press, 1995), p. 17. A reading of Dawson's fine description of the stage production (11–22; 238–41), written before Branagh produced the film, reveals how many details in the film derive from the stage production: the Edwardian setting and costumes; the winter landscape; the over-full 'complete' text; the railway that conveys Rosencrantz and Guildenstern in the film (Fortinbras and the players are conveyed by railway on stage). Like the stage production, the film seems to aim for ' "reality-effects" as well as "alienation- effects" '.

13. Andrews, 'Kenneth Branagh's *Hamlet*', makes this point also: 62.

14. Nichols, 'Branagh's *Hamlet* Redux': 39, points out that the flashback in the first act makes ' "The Mousetrap" scene [feel] quite superfluous and its dumbshow almost as tedious to us as it is to the Danish court'. She compiles a good number of critics' views about the film, in addition to her own analysis.

15. See Graham Bradshaw, 'The "Encrusted *Hamlet*": Mousetrap in Text and Performance', in *Approaches to Teaching* Hamlet, ed. Bernice W. Kliman (New York: MLA, forthcoming). Maurice Charney faults Branagh for trying, in the eighteenth-century manner, to tie up every loose end, to answer all questions. Quoted in ibid., p. 39.

16. In England, the title of the film was *In the Bleak Midwinter*. Dinitia Smith reports that Branagh can get into fits of giggling that he cannot stop. 'Much Ado about Branagh: The New Orson Welles', *New York* (24 May 1993): 36–45, at 38.

17. Russell Jackson, 'Diary', in Kenneth Branagh, Hamlet, p. 177.

18. Branagh, in the interview reported in *Shakespeare Newsletter* 46, 3 (Fall 1996): 62, adds a more convincing explanation: 'the intensity implied by a sexual relationship with the Prince would make Ophelia's "descent into madness" seem more plausible later in the action'. See also n. 11. Russell Jackson pointed out (privately) that any one explanation for choices is liable to be incomplete; each explanation is a selection made from an array of reasons.

19. The Norton edition (1997), using the Oxford text, has the Folio line here; G. R. Hibbard, the editor of the freestanding Oxford *Hamlet* (1987), uses the Quarto line. All references to *Hamlet* in this chapter are from the *Riverside Shakespeare*.

20. Her cry is another transposition, and I wonder if it too was absent in the shooting script. In the play, in the Folio only, unnamed gentlemen, probably Rosencrantz and Guildenstern, call out to Hamlet at the beginning of IV.ii. In the film, Ophelia cries out at the end of the scene, a bridge to the next scene.

21. Given the aims of the King and Laertes, a smaller audience would seem a more appropriate choice.

22. For a positive view, see Walton, who admires the way Branagh contrasts the two sons through these flashcuts; Fortinbras 'resolutely advances through any obstacle while Hamlet cannot manage to kill Claudius despite having "cause, and will, and strength, and means / To do't" (IV.iv.46–7)' (37). However, it is difficult for me to admire Fortinbras.

23. Jones, *Scenic Form*, p. 79.

24. Jackson, e-mail, 28 July 1999.

25. ' "You Kilt My Foddah": or Arnold, Prince of Denmark', *Shakespeare Quarterly* 50, 2 (Summer 1999): 127–51, p. 128.

11. SHOWING VERSUS TELLING: SHAKESPEARE'S *EKPHRASEIS*, VISUAL ABSENCES, AND THE CINEMA *Gabriel Egan*

1. All references to Shakespeare are from William Shakespeare, *The Complete Works*, ed. Stanley Wells, Gary Taylor, John Jowett and William Montgomery (Oxford: Oxford University Press, 1986).

2. In Laurence Olivier's film version, a flashback to the pirate attack was shown while Horatio read Hamlet's letter describing it, but all reference to Hamlet's fatal substitution of Rosencrantz and Guildenstern's letter to the English king was cut (Laurence Olivier, *Hamlet*, Motion Picture. Two Cities/Pilgrim, 1948). Grigori Kosintsev and Franco Zeffirelli made Hamlet's departure and the switching of the letter a

seamlessly realistic continuum with no flashback or narration, but removed the pirates entirely and offered no explanation for Hamlet's return to Denmark (Grigori Kosintsev, *Hamlet*, Motion Picture. Soyuz-film, 1964; Franco Zeffirelli, *Hamlet*, Motion Picture. Warner/Le Studio Canal+/Carolco/Icon/Marquis/Nelson, 1990). Kenneth Branagh used the play's narration technique for the letter switching and the pirate attack, but as we shall see, he depicted other events which are only referred to in dialogue (Kenneth Branagh, *Hamlet*, Motion Picture. Turner/Castle Rock/Columbia/Fishmonger, 1996).

3. Although it need not constrain modern producers, Caliban and Ariel – once the latter became like a 'nymph o' th' sea' (I.iii.303) – were originally played in aquatic costumes. See Michael Baird Saenger, 'The Costumes of Caliban and Ariel *qua* Sea-nymph', *Notes and Queries* 240 (1995): 334–6 and Gabriel Egan, 'Ariel's Costume in the Original Staging of *The Tempest*', *Theatre Notebook* 51 (1997): 62–72.

4. Gabriel Egan, 'Reconstructions of the Globe: A Retrospective', *Shakespeare Survey* 52 (1999): 1–16.

5. Antony Hammond, '|"It Must be Your Imagination Then": the Prologue and the Plural Text in *Henry V* and Elsewhere', in *'Fanned and Winnowed Opinions': Shakespearean Essays Presented to Harold Jenkins*, ed. John W. Mahon and Thomas A. Pendleton (London: Methuen, 1987).

6. E. K. Chambers, *The Elizabethan Stage*, 4 vols. (Oxford: Clarendon Press, 1923), vol. 3, p. 40.

7. Tim Fitzpatrick, 'Shakespeare's Exploitation of a Two-door Stage: *Macbeth*', *Theatre Research International* 20 (1995): 207–30.

8. John Fletcher and William Shakespeare, *The Two Noble Kinsmen* (London: T. Cotes for J. Waterson, 1634), M1v-M2r.

9. Simon Hornblower and Antony Spawforth (eds), *The Oxford Classical Dictionary* (3rd edn Oxford: Clarendon Press, 1996).

10. Grant F. Scott, 'The Rhetoric of Dilation: Ekphrasis and Ideology', *Word and Image* 7, 1 (1991): 301.

11. Oliver Parker, *Othello*, Motion Picture. Castle Rock/Columbia/Dakota/Imminent/Sony, 1995.

12. William Shakespeare, Othello, *Dir. Alan Parker: Shooting Script* (Beverly Hills: Castle Rock, 1995), p. 12a.

13. William Shakespeare, *Hamlet*, ed. G. R. Hibbard, The Oxford Shakespeare (Oxford: Clarendon Press, 1987), pp. 280–1.

14. Authorial revision commonly entails the cutting of some things and the addition of others, and important differences between early editions of *Hamlet* most likely reflect such planned changes. In this situation conflation effaces authorially sanctioned cuts and brings together material which the dramatist would have thought mutually exclusive or pleonastic. For the evidence concerning *Hamlet* see Stanley Wells et al., *William Shakespeare: A Textual Companion* (Oxford: Oxford University Press, 1987), pp. 396–402.

15. This image is preceded by one of Hamlet Senior asleep in his orchard surrounded by midwinter snow. His behaviour might be

thought eccentric and Deborah Cartmell observed that 'it's hard not to imagine why he didn't die of hypothermia' (Deborah Cartmell, 'The Shakespeare on Screen Industry', in *Adaptations: From Text to Screen, Screen to Text*, ed. Deborah Cartmell and Imelda Whelehan, London: Routledge, 1999, p. 36.). However, Branagh apparently wanted the juxtaposition of these images of inversion: that which should be within (Hamlet Senior) is without and that which should be without (curling is normally played on snow) is within.

16. William Shakespeare, *The Tragicall Historie of Hamlet, Prince of Denmarke. Newly Imprinted and Enlarged to Almost as Much Againe as it Was, According to the True and Perfect Coppie* (London: [J. Roberts] for N. L[ing], 1604), B2v, C2r.

17. William Shakespeare, *The Norton Facsimile of The First Folio of Shakespeare*, ed. Charlton Hinman (New York: Norton, 1968), *Hamlet*, TLN 374.

18. Carol Chillington Rutter, 'Snatched Bodies: Ophelia in the Grave', *Shakespeare Quarterly* 49 (1998): 316.

19. Ibid., n. 32.

20. Kenneth Branagh, '*Hamlet*' *By William Shakespeare: Screenplay and Introduction* (London: Chatto & Windus, 1996), pp. 181, 195, 203.

21. Kenneth Branagh, *Much Ado About Nothing*, Motion Picture. BBC/Renaissance/Goldwyn, 1993.

22. Rutter, 'Snatched Bodies': 317.

23. David M. Bergeron, 'The Deposition Scene in *Richard II*', *Renaissance Papers* (1974): 37.

24. William Shakespeare, *Much Ado About Nothing*, ed. Horace Howard Furness, New Variorum, 12 (Philadelphia: Lippincott, 1899), III.iii.142n.

25. Philip McGuire, *Shakespeare: The Jacobean Plays*, English Dramatists (Basingstoke: Macmillan, 1994), pp. 87–90.

26. Ibid., p. 89.

27. Ibid., pp. 91–2.

28. Peter Brook, *King Lear*, Motion Picture. Filmways/Laterna/Athena/RSC, 1971.

29. Peter Holland, 'The Shapeliness of *The Tempest*', *Essays in Criticism* 45, 3 (1995): 224.

30. Derek Jarman, *The Tempest*, Motion Picture. Boyd's, 1979.

31. Peter Greenaway, *Prospero's Books*, Motion Picture. VPRO Television/Camera One/Le Studio Canal+/Channel Four Films/Elsevier/Vendex/Cinea/Allarts/ NHK/Palace Pictures/Penta Films, 1991.

32. Fred M. Wilcox, *Forbidden Planet*, Motion Picture. MGM, 1956.

12. SHAKESPEARE AND THE FUTURE *Kiernan Ryan*

1. All quotations from Shakespeare's works are from *The Complete Works*, ed. Stanley Wells, Gary Taylor, John Jowett and William Mon-

tgomery (Oxford: Clarendon Press, 1988). References to *King Lear* are to the Folio text, *The Tragedy of King Lear*, pp. 943–74.
2. *Shelley's Poetry and Prose*, ed. Donald H. Reiman and Sharon B. Powers (New York: W. W. Norton, 1977), pp. 482–3.
3. *The Romantics on Shakespeare*, ed. Jonathan Bate (Harmondsworth: Penguin, 1992), p. 323.

13. WHY WE TALK SHAKESPEARE *Michael J. Collins*

1. Margaret Carlson, 'All Eyes on Hillary', *Time*, 12 September 1992, pp. 30, 33.
2. All citations of Shakespeare's plays are taken from *The Complete Signet Classic Shakespeare*, ed. Sylvan Barnet (New York: Harcourt Brace Jovanovich, 1972). Some parts of this chapter have been adapted from my article 'Teaching *King Lear*', in *Teaching Shakespeare into the Twenty-First Century*, ed. Ronald E. Salomone and James E. Davis (Athens: Ohio University Press, 1998), pp. 166–71.
3. Harold Bloom, *Shakespeare: The Invention of the Human* (New York: Riverhead Books, 1999), p. 735.
4. *Twelfth Night*, ed. Herschel Baker (rev. ed. New York: Signet, 1998) pp. lxix–lxx.
5. Anne Barton, Introduction to *Twelfth Night*, *The Riverside Shakespeare*, ed. G. Blakemore Evans (2nd ed. Boston: Houghton Mifflin, 1997), p. 441.
6. *The Norton Shakespeare*, ed. Stephen Greenblatt (New York: W. W. Norton, 1997), pp. 1766–7.
7. *Twelfth Night*, ed. Charles T. Prouty (Harmondsworth: Penguin Books, 1958), p. 23.
8. Stephen Booth, *Precious Nonsense: The Gettysburg Address, Ben Jonson's Epitaphs on His Children, and 'Twelfth Night'* (Berkeley: University of California Press, 1998), p. 145.
9. G. Wilson Knight, '*King Lear* and the Comedy of the Grotesque', in *The Wheel of Fire* (London: Methuen, 1949), p. 123.
10. J. Stampfer, 'The Catharsis of *King Lear*', *Shakespeare Survey* (1960); rpt. in *Shakespeare's Tragedies: An Anthology of Modern Criticism*, ed. Lawrence Lerner (Harmondsworth: Penguin, 1963), p. 160.
11. Barbara Everett, 'The New *King Lear*', *Critical Quarterly* 2 (1960); rpt. in *'King Lear': A Collection of Critical Essays*, ed. Frank Kermode (London: Macmillan, 1992), p. 173.

APPENDIX: *Josephine Webb*

1. Gabriel Egan, *The Internet for Shakespeare scholars*. http://www.ardenshakespeare.com/main/ardennet/internet/web-rev.html, 1998.

2. Rebecca. Bushnell. *Teaching Shakespeare using the Internet.* http://www.ardenshakespeare.com/main/ardennet/teaching/feb1998/bushnell.html, 1998.

3. Anne Lancashire, 'What do users really want?' Early modern literary studies 3.3. / Special issue 2 (January): 3.1–22 htp://purl.oclc.org/emla/03–3/alanshak.html, 1998.

Notes on Contributors

Deborah Cartmell is a Principal Lecturer in the Department of English, De Montfort University, Leicester. She is co-editor of the Film/Fiction annual (Pluto) which includes *Pulping Fictions* (1996), *Trash Aesthetics* (1997), *Sisterhoods* (1998), *Alien Identities* (1999) and *Classics* (2000) and co-editor of *Adaptations* with Imelda Whelehan (Routledge, 1999). She is author of *Interpreting Shakespeare on Screen* (Macmillan, 2000) and is working on books on children's literature on screen and Edmund Spenser and the language of architecture.

Colin Chambers is a theatre historian and writer. He was a journalist and theatre critic before becoming Literary Manager of the Royal Shakespeare Company (1981–97). He is Senior Research Fellow in Performing Arts at De Montfort University, Leicester. Among his books are *Other Spaces: New Theatre and the RSC* (1980), *Playwrights' Progress: Patterns of Postwar British Drama* (co-written with Mike Prior, 1987), *The Story of Unity Theatre* (1989) and *Peggy: The Life of Margaret Ramsay, Play Agent* (1997), which in 1998 won the inaugural Theatre Book Prize awarded by the Society for Theatre Research. He is also the editor of *The Companion to Twentieth Century Theatre* (2000).

Dermot Cavanagh is Lecturer in English at the University of Northumbria at Newcastle upon Tyne. He is the editor, with Tim Kirk, of *Subversion and Scurrility: Popular Discourse in Europe from 1500 to the Present* (Ashgate, 2000) and is completing a book on the Tudor history play.

Michael J. Collins is Adjunct Professor of English and Dean of the School for Summer and Continuing Education at Georgetown University, Washington, DC.

Peter Davison, OBE, MA, Ph.D., D.Litt, Hon.D.Arts, is Research Professor of English at De Montfort University, Leicester. He has written and edited 15 books (mainly on Shakespeare and drama) as well as the Facsimile Edition of the Manuscript of *Nineteen*

Eighty-Four and the twenty volumes of Orwell's Complete Works (with Ian Aungus and Sheila Davison), a second edition of which is now in press. He is currently preparing, for Penguin Books, *Orwell's England*, *Orwell and the Two Nations*, *Orwell in Spain*, and *Orwell and Politics*. He is a Past President of the Bibliographical Society, whose journal he edited for 12 years. He was appointed an OBE in 1999 for services to literature.

Gabriel Egan is a lecturer at Shakespeare's Globe, London, and has published articles on playhouse design and original staging in *Shakespeare Survey*, *Review of English Studies*, and *Theatre Notebook* and contributed entries to *The Oxford Companion to Shakespeare* edited by Michael Dobson and Stanley Wells (Oxford University Press, 2002). He is currently working on a book on Shakespeare and Marx.

Bernice W. Kliman is author of *Hamlet: Film, Television and Audio Performance* (1988), *Macbeth in Performance* (1992, 1995), and numerous essays and reviews in journals such as *Shakespeare Bulletin* and *Shakespeare Newsletter*. She is editor and co-ordinator of the new variorum *Hamlet* project, editor of the *Enfolded Hamlet* (1996, online at global-language.com/enfolded.html), former co-editor of the *Shakespeare on Film Newsletter* (1976–92), and co-editor of The Three-Text *Hamlet* (1991).

Kiernan Ryan is Professor of English at Royal Holloway College, University of London, and a Fellow of New Hall, University of Cambridge. He is the author of *Shakespeare* (1989; 3rd ed., 2000), and the editor of *King Lear: Contemporary Critical Essays* (1993), *Shakespeare: The Last Plays* (1999) and *Shakespeare: Texts and Contexts* (2000).

Michael Scott is Professor of English and Theatre Studies and Principal and Chief Executive of the North Wales Institute of Higher Education, Wrexham. Until recently, he was Professor of English and Pro-Vice-Chancellor of De Montfort University, Leicester. His publications include *John Marston's Plays: Theme, Structure and Performance* (1978), *Renaissance Drama and a Modern Audience* (1982) and *Shakespeare and the Modern Dramatist* (1989). He is general editor of the Macmillan Text and Performance

Series and the Macmillan Critics Debate Series. He has recently published 'Ill Mannered Marston' in *The Drama of John Marston: Critical Re-Visions* (ed. T. F. Wharton, Cambridge University Press, 2000).

Emma Smith is a fellow of Hertford College, Oxford. She has edited Thomas Kyd's *The Spanish Tragedy* and an edition of *Henry V* for the Shakespeare in Production series. She is currently working on the idea of dramatic authorship in the early modern period, and on a cultural history of ghosts.

Miles Thompson is engaged in Ph.D. research around effeminacy, camp and cross-dressing. He is particularly interested in examples of historical cross-dressed performance, and the effect of the cross-dressed boy actor upon Elizabethan and Jacobean audiences.

Janice Wardle is Senior Lecturer in English at the University of Central Lancashire, where she teaches courses on Renaissance and American literature. She is currently working on a project on memory and gender in Renaissance drama.

Josephine Webb is an Academic Librarian for Business, Law and Humanities at De Montfort University, Leicester. She has published several papers on collection management in the UK and teaches research methods in humanities and social sciences, with a particular emphasis on the Internet and IT.

Imelda Whelehan is Principal Lecturer in English and Women's Studies at De Montfort University, Leicester. Her publications *include Modern Feminist Thought* (Edinburgh University Press, 1995), *Overloaded* (Women's Press, 2000) and *Adaptations* (with Deborah Cartmell, Routledge, 1999). She is also a co-editor of the Film/Fiction annual journal series which to date boasts five volumes. She is currently researching the history of the bra and co-writing a book on key concepts in gender studies.

Nigel Wood is Professor of English Literature at De Montfort University, Leicester. His Shakespeare work includes the editing of six volumes on Shakespeare plays in the 'Theory in Practice' series, and he has advised both the National Theatre and Royal Shakespeare Company on Shakespeare productions.

Index

Note: With the exception of Shakespeare and anonymous works, plays are listed by author. The index excludes material contained in bibliographies, endnotes and appendix.

Adorno, Theodor   80–1
Africanus, Leo   5, 139, 147
Alexander, Bill   210
All is True (Henry VIII)   57, 61, 194–5
Alleyn, Edward   46, 53
Altman, Joel   80
Antony and Cleopatra   22, 32–3, 125, 137, 190, 194
Artaud, Antonin   92
   Marat/Sade   94
Arts Council of Great Britain   89, 91, 93
As You Like It   22, 134, 187, 205–6, 209
Aubrey, John   52–3
Avon, Lord   90, 93

Baker, Herschel   203
Baker, Roger   125, 131
Barber, C. L.   108, 109, 116
Barrol, Leeds   41, 54
Barton, Anne   107–10, 112, 203
Barton, John   3, 95, 99
   Twelfth Night   106–17, 121–2
Bassnett, Susan   127
Baylis, Lilian   87, 91
BBC TV Shakespeare   88
Beckinsale, Kate   180
Bentley, G. E.   44, 54
Beckett, Samuel   92
Benjamin, Walter   81
Bergeron, David   179
Bergman, Ingmar   164
Berliner Ensemble   92
Bhabha, Homi   143
Billington, Michael   118, 120

Blessed, Brian   154, 156, 174–5
Bloom, Harold   6, 68–9, 202
Bogdanov, Michael   62
Bond, Edward   13, 17
Bowdler, Thomas   98
Boxer, Stephen   119
Bradley, A. C.   31, 65–6
Bradley, David   43, 50, 51
Bradshaw, Graham   157
Bradshaw, Richard   45, 46
Branagh, Kenneth   208
   Hamlet (1996)   5, 151–67, 174–8, 186
   A Midwinter's Tale (In the Bleak Midwinter) (1995) 159
   Much Ado About Nothing (1993) 178, 180–1, 186
Brecht, Bertholt   27
Bridges-Adams, William   87, 99
Brook, Peter   92, 94
   King Lear   99, 182–3, 186
   Romeo and Juliet   99
Brown, Ivor   131
Brown, John Russell   30
Bruster, Douglas   70
Bull, George   18
Bullough, Geoffrey   61
Bulman, James   9
Burbage, James   41
Burton, Richard   207–8

Caird, John   116
Callaghan, Dymphna   144
Cann, Jamie   135
Castiglione, Baldassare   18
Chamberlain, Lord   43, 93

Chamberlain, Richard 166
Chamberlain's Men (Lord) 25,
    47–52, 54
Chambers, E. K. 54, 171
Chaucer, Geoffrey 2, 23
Chedgzoy, Kate 128, 135
Chekhov, Anton 116
Christie, Julie 152
Clinton, Bill 201
Clinton, Hillary 201–2
Cloutier, Suzanne 145
Coleridge, Samuel Taylor 194
Comédie Française 91
Comedy of Errors, The 181
Cook, Ann Jennalie 54
Coriolanus 33, 129
Cromwell, Thomas 52
Crossman, Richard 9
Crowl, Samuel 152
Curtain Theatre 41
Cusack, Sinead 62
Cymbeline 94, 196–8

Dash, Irene 152
Davenant, William 37
Davis, Michael Justin 54
Dekker, Philip 41, 46
Dessen, Alan C. 38
Dench, Judi 107, 112, 115, 153
Distley 40
Dollimore, Jonathan 73, 132
Doyle, Patrick 164–6

Eden, Anthony 90
Edwards, Philip 25–6, 30, 31
Eliot, T. S. 34, 37
Elizabeth I 43, 46
English National Opera 91
Everett, Barbara 212
Everyman 189

Fernández, José Ramón
    Díaz 151
Fish, Stanley 24, 25, 37–8
Fishburne, Laurence 146
Fitzpatrick, Tim 171
Fletcher, John 173

*The Woman's Prize, or The Tamer
    Tam'd* 57, 61–5
Flower, Archie 87
Flower, Charles 86–7, 92
Flower, Fordham 90
Forbidden Planet, The (Wilcox,
    1956) 184–5
Ford, John, *'Tis Pity She's a
    Whore* 19
Foucault, Michel 13, 19, 74, 128
Fowler, Alastair 34
Frankfurt School 80–81
Frye, Northrop 108–9, 112, 116
Furness, Horace Howard 181

Garrick, David 98
Gascoigne, George 129
Gaskill, Bill 94
George, David 51
Gielgud, John 152, 165
Gilbert, John 164
Goodbody, Buzz 99
Gosson, Stephen 129
Gray, Hanna 79
Greenaway, Peter, *Prospero's Books*
    (1990) 184–5
Greenblatt, Stephen 17, 19, 38,
    139, 71–2, 133, 203
Greene, Robert 56, 57
Gurr, Andrew 31, 54, 75

Hall, Kim F. 139
Hall, Peter 4, 88, 90–100, 107,
    164
Hamlet 15–16, 17, 24–38, 57, 58,
    65–9, 94, 151–67, 169, 173,
    174–9, 186, 190, 192, 205,
    207
Hammond, Anthony 171
Hands, Terry 96, 98–9, 116
Hare, David 210
Harington, John 52
Hawkes, Terry 9
Hayward, John 97
Helgerson, Richard 74–5, 77
Henry IV (I) 12, 205
Henry IV (II) 52–3, 195

Henry IV (*I* and *II*)   94, 97
Henry V   1, 3, 5, 73, 97–8, 168,
    170–1, 186, 195
Henry VI (*I–III*)   97, 99
Henry VIII, See All is True   57, 61,
    194–5
Henslowe, Philip   41, 46, 50, 75
Hertford, Earl of   52
Hertford's Men   49
Hibbard, G. R.   26, 27, 30, 31,
    34, 36, 37, 174
Hobby, Elaine   136
Hobley, Frederick   44
Holland, Norman   154
Holm, Ian   5
Howard, Jean   126, 128–9
Hudson, Richard   45
Hugill, Barry   4
Hytner, Nicholas   210

Ichikawa, Mariko   31
Ingram, William   50
Irving, Henry   98

Jackson, Barry   87
Jackson, Russell   152, 155, 158,
    160, 165
Jacob, Irene   146
Jacobi, Derek   166, 175, 208
Jardine, Lisa   132–3, 136
Jarman, Derek, *The Tempest*
    184–5
Johnson, Samuel   9, 33
Jones, David   93
Jones, Eldred   140, 141–3
Jones, Emrys   153, 164
Jonson, Ben   17, 44, 55, 57
Julius Caesar   33, 75–6, 172, 194,
    198
Junger, Gil, *10 Things I Hate About
    You* (1999)   1

Kahn, Michael   152
Kahn, Victoria   80
Kastan, David Scott   73
Keeler, Christine   90
Kelley, Donald R.   77

Kelly, Jude   210
Kemp, Peter   120–1
King Lear   11–12, 14–15, 99,
    181–3, 186–9, 210–12
King's Men   188
Knight, G. Wilson   111, 211
Kott, Jan   55, 92
Kozintzev, Grigori   152, 154
Kurtz, Martha A.   78
Kyd, Thomas, *The Spanish
    Tragedy*   27, 48, 57, 65–9

Lady Elizabeth's Players   58
Lancashire, Ian   54
Lawson, Nigel   9
Leavis, F. R.   95
Lee, Sidney   131
Leggatt, Alexander   116
Levine, Laura   130–1
Lewinsky, Monica   201
Loomba, Ania   143
Love's Labour's Lost   204–5
Lyth, Ragnar   155, 161, 164

Macbeth   6, 32, 131, 171,
    190–1,196, 201, 208–9
Machiavelli, Niccolò   80
Macmillan, Harold   90
Madden, John, *Shakespeare in
    Love* (1998)   50, 136–7,
    204
Mahood, M. M.   107
Major, John   4
Mallin, Eric W.   165
Manningham, John   57
Marcus, Leah S.   35–6
Marlowe, Christopher   57
Marrowitz, Charles   19, 20, 63
Maude, Angus   93
McCourt, Frank   202
McCowen, Alec   210
McDaniel, Hattie   144
McGuire, Philip C.   181–2
McQueen, Butterfly   144–5
Merchant of Venice, The   10, 188–9,
    209–10
Meres, Francis   56

Middleton, Thomas, *The
    Changeling* 19
Midsummer Night's Dream, A 207
Midwinter's Tale (1995) 159
    see also Branagh, Kenneth
Miller, Jonathan 62
Monaco, James 144
Morrison, Toni 144
Moscow Art Theatre 92
Much Ado About Nothing 172, 178,
    180, 183, 186, 190
Munden 44–5
Murray, J. T. 54

Nashe, Thomas 47
National Theatre 87–8, 91–2,
    94–5
Newman, Karen 139
Noble, Adrian 94–5, 97, 100,
    157, 165, 211
    Plantagenets, The 99
    Twelfth Night 106, 117–22
Northbrooke, John 134
Nunn, Trevor 86, 93, 116–17
Nuttall, A. D. 30, 32

Old Vic 87–8, 91
Olivier, Laurence 153–4, 175,
    207
    Henry V 3, 98
Orton, Joe, *Entertaining
    Mr. Sloane* 93
Othello 12–13, 19–20, 21,
    138–47, 131, 181, 173–4,
    188–9, 206–7
Other Place, The 99

Paltrow, Gwyneth 136
Parker, Oliver, *Othello* (1995) 5,
    146–7, 173–4
Parker, R. B. 33
Peanuts 202–4
Pembroke, Countess of 52
Pembroke's Men 44, 47, 48
Plantagenets, The 99
Popham, Lord Chief Justice
    52–3

Profumo, John 90
Prospero's Books (Greenaway, 1990)
    184–5
Prouty, Charles T. 203–4
Prynne, William 129–30

Quayle, Anthony 87
Queen's Players 50

Rackin, Phyllis 129
Rainolds, John 126, 128–9
Rankins, William 129
Records of Early English Drama 53
Richard II 3, 11, 47, 57–61, 73,
    76–9, 96–7, 179, 181
Richard III 48, 51, 53, 94,171,
    194
Richardson, Tony 94, 155
Riche, Barnabe 129
Ridley, M. R. 143
Romeo and Juliet 10, 99, 129,
    136–7, 190, 202
Royal Opera House 91
Royal Shakespeare
    Company 85–100,
    106, 122
Rutter, Carol Chillington 176–7
Rylance, Mark 137, 208
Rylands, George 95
Rymer, Thomas 142

Saint-Denis, Michel 92
Scates, Malcolm 119
Scott, Grant F. 172
Sewell, Rufus 163, 208–9
Shankly, Bill 6
Shakespeare in Love (Madden,
    1998) 50, 136–7, 204
Shakespeare Memorial National
    Theatre 87
Shapiro, James 67
Shaw, Fiona 62
Shaw, Glen Byam 87
Shelley, Percy Bysshe 192
Shepherd, Simon 135–6
Sidney, Philip 171
Siemon, James R. 75–6

Simpson, Christopher 45
Sinfield, Alan 73, 129–30
Singh, Jyotsna 139
Sir Thomas More 96
Smith, Ian 138
Smith, Peter 123, 132
Sonnets 135
  81 192–3, 198
  106 193
  107 194
  129 21
Spencer, Charles 118
Spencer, T. J. B. 34
Stampfer, J. 212
Stanislavsky, Konstantin 92, 110, 116, 121
Stanley, William 52
Staunton, Imelda 180
Stephens, Robert 211
Stone, Lawrence 51
Stubbs, John 130
Swan Theatre 87

Taming of the Shrew, The 10, 57, 61–5, 95
Tarantino, Quentin 179
Tarlton, Richard 46
Tate, Nahum 9, 98
Taylor, Gary 25, 32, 35
Tempest, The 22, 143, 169, 183–6, 188, 204, 209
10 Things I Hate About You (Junger, 1999) 1
Théâtre National Populaire 91
Theatre Workshop 91
Theatregoround 91
Thomas, Philip V. 40

Thompson, Ann 61
Three Little Pigs 205, 207
Titus Andronicus 52
Traub, Valerie 127–8, 132
Tronch-Perez, Jesús 151
Twelfth Night 13, 105–22, 125, 133–4, 187, 203–4, 209
Two Gentlemen of Verona 143–4
Two Noble Kinsmen 61, 172–4

Vickers, Brian 29–30, 32
Voss, Philip 119

Wakefield Master 189
Ward, Anthony 117
Warner, Jack 171
Wars of the Roses 97–9
Wasson, John 43
Webster, John 57
  The Duchess of Malfi 20
Welles, Orson 5, 145–6
Wells, Stanley 25, 26, 32, 35, 107, 111, 115, 119, 121
Wesker, Arnold 10
West Side Story (Robbins/Wise, 1961) 202
Wilcox, Fred McLeod, *Forbidden Planet* (1956) 184–5
Wilkinson, Tate 40, 45, 54
Wimsatt, W. K. 38
Winslet, Kate 159, 166
Winter's Tale, The 181, 199
Wolfit, Donald 98
Woodstock 57, 58–61, 78

Zeffirelli, Franco 154
  Hamlet 37, 175, 178–9